52 Weeks Through the Bible

52 WEEKS THROUGH THE BIBLE

JAMES MERRITT

Cover by Dugan Design Group, Bloomington, MN

Published in association with the literary agency of Wolgemuth & Associates, Inc.

52 WEEKS THROUGH THE BIBLE
Copyright © 2016 James Merritt
Published by Harvest House Publishers
Eugene, Oregon 97402
www.harvesthousepublishers.com

Library of Congress Cataloging-in-Publication Data
Names: Merritt, James Gregory, 1952- author.
Title: 52 weeks through the Bible / James Merritt.
Other titles: Fifty two weeks through the Bible
Description: Eugene, Oregon : Harvest House Publishers, 2016. | Includes bibliographical references.
Identifiers: LCCN 2016023551 (print) | LCCN 2016026721 (ebook) | ISBN 9780736965583 (pbk.) | ISBN 9780736962469 (hardcover) | ISBN 9780736965590 (ebook)
Subjects: LCSH: Bible—Meditations. | Bible—Devotional literature. | Christian life—Meditations. | Devotional calendars.
Classification: LCC BV4811 .M425 2016 (print) | LCC BV4811 (ebook) | DDC 220.6/1—dc23
LC record available at https://lccn.loc.gov/2016023551

Printed in the United States of America

16 17 18 19 20 21 22 23 24 / BP-CD / 10 9 8 7 6 5 4 3 2 1

I dedicate this book to Cross Pointe Church—
for their love for God's Word,
and their desire for their pastor to preach it.

Contents

Introduction: Going by the Book

The year was 1970. The place was Stetson University in sleepy Deland, Florida. The malady was homesickness. I was a newly minted college freshman seven hours and 465 miles from a home I had never been away from. I grew up in Georgia's version of Mayberry from *The Andy Griffith Show*. My dad wasn't the sheriff, but I was Opie. And Opie *never* left Mayberry.

The mossy-backed gnarly oaks at this idyllic campus were a far cry from the Georgia pines I was used to. The humidity and heat were stifling, and except for the library, the main academic buildings lacked air-conditioning. I knew nobody and had not even seen the campus until the first day I arrived.

The first time I ever saw my gruff, rough dad cry was when he hugged his baby boy goodbye. This meant I was seventeen years old when I realized how much he loved me. I remember the knot in my stomach and the hot tears flowing down my cheeks as my dad, mom, brother, and aunt drove over the hill looking back and waving a final farewell. Mid-August and I wouldn't see them again until Thanksgiving.

I turned to walk into a dormitory that felt more like a prison and went into my room to unpack what few clothes I had. Then I sat down and looked at my roommate—a weirdo who I split from after one semester (that *really is* another story for another time)—and the dorm that would be my home for the next nine months and learned for the first time that no sickness is like homesickness. For the first time in my life, I also learned what it meant to cry yourself to sleep.

But God intervened that first semester and drove me to the Bible.

I have never been a social animal. I didn't date in high school and was always shy around females. I went to one fraternity rush, and after seeing the biggest beer keg ever and drunk frat boys all over the floor, I rushed out the door, never to enter a frat house again. My days began at four in the morning when I rose to work the breakfast shift in the cafeteria. From there, my life was classes until early afternoon, study for a couple of hours, and then dinner.

Lost and alone.

With nothing else to do, I picked up the hardback Living Bible New Testament my mother gave me and started reading it. At first, seeing how much I could read in one sitting became a challenge. I could go for up to three hours straight. I have always been a fast reader, and it wasn't long until I had completed the New Testament.

I repeated the process until I lost track of how many times I'd read it after I hit ten. But by then it was more than a game. The parables, the teachings, the lessons were encouraging me, growing me, and drawing me closer to God than I had ever been. I was amazed how I would learn something new, seeing things I had never seen before. Still, it seems odd that a college freshman would read a book two thousand years old nonstop for an entire semester.

My story is nothing compared to another young man who lived four hundred years before. William Hunter was fifteen years old when he was burned at the stake in 1555. Like me, he had an insatiable thirst for the Bible, but he had a hurdle I didn't. Possessing Bibles was illegal for commoners in England. The priests had a monopoly on this book and kept it under lock and key from nonclergy. Other than one Bible chained at the church altar, no other Bible was permitted in William's village.

So why was he burned at the stake? Because he was so determined to read this book for himself, he walked into the church, opened the chained Bible, and freed its truth into his heart and soul. William was caught, arrested, and imprisoned for nine months.

At his trial, he was given the chance to go free if he would recant his "deed of evil" and promise never again to attempt to read the Bible. The bishop of the church even offered him the princely sum of forty pounds and the funds to start his own business in exchange for never again reading the Bible. The brave teenager refused and accepted his fate. On March 27, 1555, William Hunter was burned at the stake for one crime: refusing to refuse to read the Bible.[1]

Two teenagers, centuries and countries apart. What book would compel one to spend night after night on a college campus reading it for hours on end? What book would compel the other to give his life just trying to read it at all?

To say that out of the billions of books that have ever been published that the Bible is "the greatest" smacks of Muhammad Ali like braggadocio. But scholars agree that the Bible is the world's best-selling and most widely distributed book. Conservative estimates put the total number of Bibles sold at more than five billion. (The second best-selling book, the Koran, has sold eight hundred million.)

It is also by far the most read book in history. The whole Bible has been translated into 349 languages, and an astounding 2,123 languages have at least one book of the Bible in that language.

The Bible is not only the best-selling book of all time, but also the best-selling book of the year. Which year? Pick one. It is the best-selling book of *every* year by at least double whatever the second best-selling book may be. Many people own Bibles—the average American household contains more than four Bibles—but the world keeps buying them. In any given year, about twenty-five million copies are purchased.[2]

The impact of the Bible is unprecedented. As former Yale professor William Lyon Phelps stated, "Our civilization is founded upon the Bible. More of our ideas, our wisdom, our philosophy, our art, our ideals, come from the Bible than from all other books combined."[3]

The makeup of the book is without peer. It is a book of books, which is what the name "Bible" means. The Bible contains sixty-six books in one volume written by about forty different authors living on several continents. They hailed from such diverse places as Palestine, Babylon, Greece, Rome, Asia Minor, and perhaps Arabia. These authors wrote in three different languages—Hebrew, Greek, and Aramaic—and the first author was separated in time from the second author by some sixteen centuries. Despite this disparity, there is a unity of theme, an invisible seamless thread, connecting these books together that seems, well, divine.

The belief that this book is the word of God is the major explanation of its immense popularity and exposure.[4]

Liberal Bible scholar Bart Ehrman begins the first day of each semester's class by asking students, "How many of you would agree with the proposition that the Bible is the inspired Word of God?" Hands shoot up across the auditorium. He then asks, "How many of you have one or more of the Harry Potter books?" Hands again fire upwards. A third question: "And how many of you have read the entire Bible?" Only a few hands raise. Ehrman then laughs and says, "Okay, look. I'm not saying that I think God wrote the Bible. You're telling me that *you* think God wrote the Bible. I can see why you might want to read a book by J.K. Rowling. But if God wrote a book...wouldn't you want to see what he has to say?"[5]

As much as I hate to admit it, I couldn't agree more with Ehrman's logic. Why don't more people who own a Bible and believe its divine origin read it? Owning the Bible is not the same as believing or even reading the Bible.

A recent survey showed 88 percent of Americans own a Bible, 80 percent think the Bible is sacred, 61 percent wish they read the Bible more, and the average household has 4.4 Bibles. Yet of the ones who do read it, the majority read their Bibles only four times a year or less. Only 26 percent of Americans said they read their Bible regularly.[6]

So if people are still buying the Bible, keeping the Bible, and looking at the Bible, why don't people make a habit of reading the Bible? And why do people find the Bible hard to understand?

First, chronological and cultural differences exist. Depending on what part of the Bible you are reading, a 3,400-year and a 1,900-year gap exists between when the Bible was written and today. The culture of Bible days was different from all twenty-first century cultures.

Beyond that, the Bible contains many different types of literature. In the Bible you have history, law, poetry, songs, prophecy, wisdom, and letters. Different genres must be interpreted and understood in different ways. No wonder that when more than five million students from around the United States were asked why they weren't reading the Bible, they said:

1. I don't know where to begin.
2. I don't see its relevance.
3. I don't know how to find things.[7]

But does this mean we should wave the white flag and make the Bible a dust catcher on a bookshelf or coffee table? Not at all, as I hope this book will show.

If the average American life spans 4,097 weeks, why not devote a meager 52 of them to exploring this world-changing book? You don't have to know where to begin; that has been selected for you. You don't have to distill the relevance on your own; the signs will be marked. And by the end, you'll know better where to find what you're looking for.

Ever since my lonely college days, I've spent 365 days each year scouring the Bible. It has been a stalwart companion in times of celebration and defeat, clarity and confusion, peace and tumult, prosperity and wanting. While you may not be stranded in an empty dorm room, you too can find power in the Bible's pages for whatever life stage you're in.

Be warned. The Bible is a fresh wind to fill your lungs, a hot coal to inflame your mind, and water to quench your parched spirit. Turn back now if you wish to remain the same.

How to Read This Book

You may have guessed that this book is designed to be consumed over the course of a year. If you choose, you can digest the book more quickly, but the yearlong span is intended to provide time for reflection and let the material sink in. When you pour rich maple syrup over a stack of pancakes, it takes a few moments for the amber liquid to soak deep into the flapjack. Similarly, exploring the depths of the Bible is often best done over time.

You'll find fifty-two chapters, one for every week of the year—and each chapter is divided into five short segments. You can read one segment per day beginning Monday or you can read them all in one sitting and then revisit them throughout the week.

At the beginning of each chapter you'll find Scripture passages to be read and explored every day. At the end you'll discover a prayer and a question for consideration. Journaling as you go may be helpful.

If you miss a week—you accidentally leave the book on your nightstand and leave for a family vacation or experience an unexpected death of a loved one—don't worry. You can pick back up the following week. My hope is not to add one more obligation to your already packed life, but rather to provide you with a resource that has the power to transform it.

Section One

Like No Other

Even the most jaded critic of the Bible cannot deny the impact of this magnificent book on our culture, our nation, our world, and history itself. Its truths and teachings led to two of the greatest social movements in history—the abolition of lawful slavery throughout the Western Hemisphere and most other countries and the American Civil Rights Movement.[8] What the Bible has done for the world, it can do for your life. Read and be changed.

1

Let's Take It from the Beginning

Scriptures for This Week

- John 18:20-21
- John 16:25-28
- Genesis 1:26-27
- Genesis 1:28-31
- John 1:16-18

There Is a *Why* to My *Who*

The people who ask questions are the ones who get answers.

I was a seventeen-year-old freshman mama's boy who was now five hundred miles from friends and family, and I was suffering from one of the worst maladies known to the human race—homesickness. The one anchor I knew I could find for the stormy seas I was sailing was a church. So, one Sunday I made my way into one, walked into a group for college kids, and sat down. I wasn't given answers that day. Instead three questions penetrated my heart:

Who am I?

Why am I here?

Where am I going?

In order to figure out my *who,* I needed to address my *why.*

Everything is designed. Every car has a manufacturer, every building has a builder, every structure has an architect, every arrangement has a plan, every plan has a designer, and every design has a purpose. The first component of the grand story of the Bible tells us the same thing. We were put here for a purpose. We are not here by evolutionary accident—we are here by divine appointment. No one knows *when* the human race began, but the first two chapters of Genesis leave no question as to *why.* It is all about a personal relationship with the God of creation. Scripture devotes more space to describing the creation of the first human than any other facet of creation. God wants all of us to know why we are here.

Relate Your Heart to God

Genesis 1:26 is a watershed moment in the creation narrative. "Let us make man in our image after our likeness." This is the first time personal pronouns are used in Scripture. A personal relationship is established between God and the first human being, a relationship that does not exist with any other aspect of creation. God introduces himself for the first time with plural personal pronouns. He doesn't say, "Let me create," but he says, "Let us create." Who is the "us"? Biblical scholars recognize this as a reference to the Trinity.

God has always existed in a relationship as Father, Son, and Spirit in one. Out of that, God created us—you and me and everyone you know—*in* a relationship and *for* a relationship. That is why when God created the first human, he said it is not good for this human to be alone. It is not good for *you* to be alone either. Therefore, God gives us himself. He is a God of relationships, and he wants us to be in a personal relationship with him.

When God created Adam it was the first time in all of creation that God gets his hands dirty. Up to this point, everything was verbally spoken into existence, but humanity was a hands-on operation. Humans are special, and are to be specially and specifically related to God. The number one reason you are on this earth is to relate your heart to God.

Reflect the Image of God

We are told four times that we are created in the image of God. Something makes humans different from every other created being. We have a unique identity. *You* have a unique identity. This is why God got his hands dirty. Unlike any other part of creation, we alone have been created in his image and in his likeness.

The word for *image* comes from a root that refers to a carving. We were carved into the shape of God to reflect him. That is not true of anything else in the universe. No other created being has a mind to know God, a heart to love God, or a will to obey God. We are different mentally, morally, and spiritually. Only humans can have a relationship with God and God only has a personal relationship with humans.

The heavens may declare the glory of God, the moon, the stars, and the planets may reveal the greatness of God, the mountains and the oceans may show us the beauty of God, but only humans reflect the image of God. Plants have a body, animals have a body and soul, but only humans have a body, a soul, and a spirit. That spirit is part of the difference. The spirit is our reflection of the image of God.

Rule Over the Creation of God

God did not put us on this earth to do nothing. From the first moment that the first man took his first breath, he was given work to do that was exciting and fulfilling. Genesis 2:15 tells us, "The LORD God took the man and put him in the Garden of Eden to work it and keep it." That is a general job description of the human race. We were given this creation to tend and to keep. We are to manage it and take care of it. How is that to be done?

First we are told, "Be fruitful and multiply." We have a job to develop the *social* world that we live in. Building families, churches, schools, cities, government, and making laws—all of that is a part of what God put us here to do.

Then we are told to "fill the earth and subdue it." This is how we learn about and develop the *natural* world. We were put here to investigate and discover, innovate and invent, to plant and build, design and compose. All are part of the cultural mandate that God gave us in the beginning as we create culture and build civilizations.

Remember, every design has a purpose, and God created man and woman with a perfect physical and genetic compatibility. When we reproduce, we live into part of our design, so part of our work is to procreate. And part of our work is to labor. That means that work is more than just something you do to put food on the table. Work is a divine calling for which we were all created. Work is the plan through which we give glory and honor to the God who entrusted us with his creation. When we work we fulfill our design.

Receive Grace from God

After God created the first man and the first woman, we read again in Genesis 1:28 that "God blessed them." The word *blessed* was more than God just waving his hand over them and saying, "I bless you." It means he put them in a state of being happy in the right way. At that moment, Adam and Eve were the most blessed couple who have ever lived. They were in a perfect environment in a perfect relationship to God.

What had Adam and Eve done at that point to deserve God's blessing? Absolutely nothing. They received it because of grace. From the first breath that Adam and Eve drew, they were recipients of and the beneficiaries of the grace of God.

There was perfection. They were perfectly related to the God of perfection. There was perfect peace, perfect happiness, perfect contentment.

When we look at the world we live in today with weeds, pests, viruses, murder, rape, war, hatred, and violence, we must ask, "What's wrong with this picture?" The answer to that is found in chapter two of the Bible's big story.

The beginning of God's big story tells us the hole in our soul can be filled only by the One who created us. Jesus the creator came to earth to live among his creation, die on a cross, and then be raised from the dead to fill that hole with grace, forgiveness, and love.

When you understand not only that you were created but why you were created, and when you realize that the Christ of creation wants to personally relate to you both now and forever, that is when your life begins.

Prayer for This Week: *Father, thank you for creating me with a purpose. Help me to reflect you in my work and in my relationships and to expand your grace to the world.*

Question for This Week: What does your heart connect most to? How can you get your hands dirty to create a closer connection to God?

2

Paradise Lost

Scriptures for This Week

- Psalm 37:23-24
- 2 Kings 17:1-14
- Genesis 3:1-13
- Deuteronomy 12:28
- 3 John 11

Watch Your Step

Vesna Vulović made history on January 26, 1972, and landed herself in the *Book of World Records*. It is not an honor she wanted or was seeking.

She was a flight attendant on a DC-9 that was flying over what is now the Czech Republic when a bomb exploded and decimated the plane. She fell 33,330 feet inside a piece of the fuselage and landed on the side of a mountain. Though she suffered a fractured skull, three broken vertebrae, two broken legs, and was in a coma for twenty-seven days, she made a complete recovery. She holds a record that might never be broken; she survived the longest fall in history.

There was another fall, even longer and harder, which not only caused the death of the first victims but of the entire human race to this day. The account is found in Genesis 3, one of the most important chapters in the entire Bible. If you don't understand this chapter, the rest of the Bible doesn't make any sense. The world likely doesn't make sense.

The advancements of our day have made life better, but is the world better? We aren't riding horses, traveling by ship, or untangling cassette tapes much anymore. Life is better. But we lock our doors, escort our children to school, monitor Internet access, and have incorporated "terrorist attack" into our vocabulary. We each have within us a desire to improve this world because we know deep down it is not what it was meant to be. Paradise was lost.

Don't Doubt God's Word

As the story begins, Adam and Eve had been living a life we know nothing about in a garden called Eden. They knew nothing of crime, murder, road rage, war, credit card debt, or sickness. Everything was coming up roses when the first question ever asked in the Bible takes place in Genesis 3:1, "Did God actually say that?"

The serpent, otherwise known as "the devil" or "Satan," crafted his question to make Eve question God: "Did God actually say, 'You shall not eat of any tree in the garden'?" The answer was no. God said eat from *every* tree except the tree of the knowledge of good and evil.

The devil is never looking out for your best interests. Anytime he tells you to do something, he is not trying to help you; he is trying to hurt you. He will try to get you to doubt the word of God and he will lie in the process.

The first step over the cliff of the fall was the step labeled "doubt." Anytime doubt about God's word is planted in the minds of a home, a marriage, a family, a society, or a nation a free fall from God takes place that always ends in a crash landing. So never put a question mark where God has put a period. You don't have to like what God says in his word, but don't ever doubt what God says in his word.

Don't Distrust God's Motives

Everything that Eve had been enjoying up to this point—day and night, the sun, the moon, the stars, the beautiful garden, the flowers, the singing of the birds, and even her beloved husband—had all come from God's good word and God's good heart. But then the serpent suggests that God is holding out on her.

Doubting the ignorant or misinformed accuracy of someone's word is different from distrusting their motive. This is what the serpent does here. It is a pivotal point in the Garden conversation and where the battle for the human race will be won or lost.

The serpent knows that in order to get Eve to do what she shouldn't do, he's got to get her to distrust God's goodness and God's motives. He was trying to convince Eve that God was keeping back something that she ought to have.

God's expectations are clear. From the beginning, God built into the universe a law that dictates for every action there is a reaction. Though the consequence for disobedience is death, the serpent is still crafty enough to get us to begin to doubt God's design and question God's motives.

Haven't you found yourself thinking the same thing? That spouse, that child, that job, that position, that house, that privilege—they are all within your rights to have. Right? Not necessarily. *God has given you all you need to become all that you need to be.* If God says don't go to a place or don't do an action, you can trust it is for your health, holiness, and happiness. Remember, God doesn't want what is good for you; God wants what is best for you. Now comes the moment of decision.

Don't Disobey God's Command

Now we witness the single greatest tragedy in the history of the human race. Just as we have learned how it all began, now we are going to see how it all came apart. The woman ate the fruit, and the first nuclear bomb of sin was detonated whose shock waves are still being felt today.

They got what they wanted, but they didn't want what they got. Adam and Even now know some things God never intended for them or any other human to know. Now they know *shame.*

Before they were naked without shame and now they are naked with shame. What do they do? They sew fig leaves of denial and deception to cover their failures, faults, and flaws.

We cover our shame in similar ways. We lie on our tax returns, cheat on exams, and steal from employers in order to cover up hidden income, lack of preparation, and debt we can't repay. This "fig leaf mentality" goes back to the Garden of Eden.

Now they also know *fear.* They hid themselves in the trees, away from the presence of the Lord as he walked along their usual path. He called to them, "Where are you?" and Adam said, "I am here, afraid and naked and ashamed."

And they know *guilt*. Just hours before, Adam had been naked and it didn't bother him or God. For the first time we see a human haunted by the ghost of guilt. Guilt is an emotion God never intended for the human race to know, but it is the inevitable baby born from sin and denial delivered by a healthy conscience. It all results from disobeying God's commands.

Don't Deny God's Goodness

Have you ever played hide-and-seek with God? Adam thought he could play games with God. When hide-and-seek didn't work, he tried the blame game. Genesis 3:12 tells us he said, "The woman whom you gave to be with me, she gave me fruit of the tree, and I ate."

First, he blames God. "Hey, I didn't ask for this woman. You gave her to me. If you hadn't, I wouldn't have this headache on my hands, so it's your fault." Then, realizing that isn't going to get him anywhere, he throws Eve under the bus. This is the first case of "victim mentality" in history.

When God turns to Eve, she plays the same game. "The serpent deceived me and I ate." Adam blames Eve, Eve blames the snake, and the snake doesn't have a leg to stand on.

But only God knows how to play the blame game correctly and he puts the blame where it belongs—on everybody. All suffer the consequences, whether it's eating dust, experiencing painful childbirth, or living a sweaty life of toil and trouble.

Of course the ultimate consequence for all involved, including us, was death. From that moment until now, everything has been infected and defected by sin. Roses now have thorns. Cities need policemen. Nations need guns and bullets, and the world needs cemeteries to bury the dead. *The world that we live in is a result of the world that we lost.*

With a broken heart and tears of sorrow, our God acts on our behalf. He didn't want us to live forever in our sinfulness, but the gate was shut. The only way forward is toward the cross of Jesus Christ. Thus begins God's pursuit of humanity to rebuild the relationship that was broken, to restore us to the garden that was forfeited, and to rescue us from the sin that is killing us. The story continues.

Prayer for This Week: *Father, work in my heart in those areas where I doubt you and question your motives. Keep my hands away from the bad fruit that tempts me.*

Question for This Week: What games do you play with God in order to hide your own shame, fear, and guilt?

3

To the Rescue

Scriptures for This Week

- Genesis 3:14-15
- Colossians 2:13-15
- Ephesians 2:1-10
- Hebrews 10:19-25
- 1 Peter 2:21-25

A World Gone Wrong

For decades, hundreds of newspapers carried Ann Landers's advice as she became the most popular columnist in America. Her byline "Dear Ann" became famous all over the world. Toward the end of Ann's career, David Brinkley asked her, "Of all the questions you have received over all of your years, what is the most frequent question you have been asked?" Her answer was, "What's wrong with me?"[9]

Don't you find yourself asking that question? "What is wrong with everybody?" Adam and Eve were created connected to God, but their disobedience disconnected them from God. However, God promised that he would reconnect with the human race, and he would do it through the very humans who had made things wrong (Genesis 3:15).

God came in the flesh to our rescue, being conceived by the Holy Spirit in the womb of the virgin Mary. Because the first Adam fell, a second Adam had to come to our rescue; only a sinless human could undo what a sinful human had done. This seed had to be a human just like Adam because only a human can win the battle that Adam lost. But he had to be a sinless human, and therefore he had to be divine because only God is sinless.

But why Jesus?

Adam and Eve took two things with them from Eden: sin and guilt.

From that moment, the greatest single need of the human race has been forgiveness. Our sin and guilt have disconnected us from God, and we need God to forgive our sin, remove our guilt, and reconnect to us.

One tree caused our problem—the "tree of the knowledge of good and evil." However, another tree, in the shape of a cross, has solved it. How that happened is the third part of the story, found in the second chapter of Colossians, a book written by a Jewish convert to Christianity named Paul. He explains how Christ on the cross rescues us from sin and guilt.

The Walking Dead

Paul says, "And you, who were dead in your trespasses and the uncircumcision of your flesh..." (Colossians 2:13). Obviously Paul's readers were physically alive, so what was he saying? He was referring to spiritual death—the death of the soul. God warned Adam he would die the day he ate of the forbidden fruit (Genesis 2:17). Adam died the moment he sinned—not on the outside but on the inside.

Ultimately, he did die in his body, but immediately he died in his spirit. Death in the Bible refers not only to the separation of the spirit from the body but to the separation of the spirit from God.

Think of it this way. God is light and God is life. From the beginning God was with Adam and in Adam. But when sin moved in, God moved out—and so did his life and light. From that moment every baby leaves the womb in spiritual darkness and spiritually dead. We are all born DOA—dead on arrival.

We are all spiritual zombies—"the walking dead." God gives us spiritual life through the physical death of his own Son, which means...

I Can Be Forgiven for All My Sin

"God made alive together with him, having forgiven us all our trespasses" (Colossians 2:13). There's the magic word—*forgiven*. That word contains the only antidote to the poison of sin that flows through our soul.

But why couldn't God give Adam and Eve a get out of jail free card? Because a holy God can't just sweep sin under the rug.

Imagine that a friend borrows your car, backs it out of the driveway, strikes a gate, and knocks it down along with part of a retaining wall. Your property insurance doesn't cover either the gate or the wall. What are your options? You can demand that he pay for the damages, you can pay for the damages, or you can split the damages. Regardless of who pays, somebody has to pay. The debt doesn't just vanish into thin air.[10] That debt has to be either separated from your friend or it has to be separated from you.

The word *forgiveness* means to "separate." Every one of us carries our sin with us like a ball and chain. We need someone to separate that sin from us. That is what God did at the cross of Jesus Christ. One of the greatest verses in all of the Bible says, "As far as the east is from the west, so far does he remove our transgressions from us" (Psalm 103:12).

How far is east from west? If you travel west you can go around the world as many times as you want and you will never go east or if you go east you can travel the world hundreds of times and you will never go west. East and west have no connecting points. When God separates you from your sins, he separates them so far that they will never catch up with us again. We are forgiven.

Don't miss this quote: "And you, who were dead in your trespasses...God made alive together with him, having forgiven us all our trespasses" (Colossians 2:13).

How many of our sins were still out in the future when Jesus died? All of them. God had already factored in our sins and included them in Christ's death. We can know we've always been forgiven and are right with God because God has forgiven all of our sins—past, present, and future.

Free From Guilt

Paul tells us how, at the cross, God could forgive all our sins and still be God. "By canceling the record of debt that stood against us with its legal demands. This he set aside, nailing it to the cross" (Colossians 2:14). The word for *record of debt* means "something written with the hand" or "an autograph." In that culture, if you owed someone some money, you had to write out your own certificate of debt in your own handwriting and sign it.

Paul describes that record of debt as something that "stood against us with its legal demands." He was referring to the law of God that everyone has broken. Every sin committed, beginning with Adam, has resulted in a debt causing a massive spiritual deficit.

When my wife Teresa and I go out to eat, we usually pay with a credit card. We enjoy the benefit of the meal even though the meal hasn't yet been paid for. That credit card is a promise to pay off the debt in the future.

People living during Old Testament times charged their sins on spiritual credit cards known as animal sacrifices. They took their Visa cards to the temple in Jerusalem, and the priest would sacrifice those animals and their sin would be put on that spiritual credit card.[11]

Over the centuries that credit card bill continued to grow as sins were committed and animals were sacrificed. Still, the bill had not been paid, for God said animals could not pay for the sins of humans—they could serve only as credit cards.

I love this picture that illustrates what God does for us. Records of debt were written on papyrus, a paper-like material. The ink that was used had no acid in it and could not soak into that paper. Since the ink remained on the surface, you could take a wet cloth and just wipe it off. When Jesus died, we are told he "cancelled that record of debt." That word *cancelled* means "to wipe off." When Jesus Christ died on the cross, God wiped our debt clean.

Nailed!

Paul goes on to say, "This he set aside, nailing it to the cross" (Colossians 2:14). Two things were nailed to the cross that day—the body of Jesus and our sin. The hammer of our sins nailed Jesus to the cross. At the same time, the hammer of his forgiveness nailed our sins to the cross.

We owed a debt we couldn't pay. Jesus paid a debt he didn't owe. We have now come full circle. The first Adam tried to put himself where only God deserved to be. The second Adam put himself where we deserved to be. The first Adam tried to put himself in God's place. The second Adam put himself in our place. The first Adam passed the buck. The second Adam said "the buck stops here."

An old map of Jamaica is titled "Land of Look Behind." It goes back to their days of slavery. When slaves escaped they would head for the mountains. The government would send troops after them, and the slaves would frequently look over their shoulders afraid they were going to be captured. They gave this mountainous area the name "Land of Look Behind."[12] Imagine Adam and Eve as they left the Garden of Eden looking back, wishing they could undo what they had done, wipe the slate clean, and start over.

Jesus came to our rescue so we don't have to look behind us anymore. We can get out of the guilt trip forever because our debt has been paid in full.

Prayer for This Week: *Awesome God, in a world where so much is wrong, you are able to make it all right again. Begin with me by removing my guilt and reconnecting me to you.*

Question for This Week: Practice the power of confession. Write out a list of all that's wrong with you. If you can do it on a whiteboard or a mirror, even better. When you're done, confess it all to God—and wipe the list clean.

4

Happily Ever After

Scriptures for This Week

- Isaiah 9:1-7
- John 14:1-7
- Revelation 21:1-5
- 2 Peter 3:13-16
- Matthew 19:28-30

Back to the Future

Everybody loves a good celebration. Birthdays. Holidays. Marriages. Births. Victories. Every year the church celebrates two big days, Easter and Christmas, that look backward to two of the greatest events in history—the birth of Christ and his resurrection. Christianity is centered on the birth, life, death, and resurrection of Jesus, but it doesn't end there. After Jesus came out of the tomb and ascended to heaven, God was just getting started.

God is not about just the past or the present; he is also about the future. He is in the restoring and renewing business, and he is going to regain for us the paradise we lost in the Garden of Eden. Yes, Virginia, there will be a new heaven and a new earth where everything is all good. Followers of Jesus will spend eternity there. We are told what it means in God's eyes to live "happily ever after." The last chapter in the whole Bible is about restoration.

Have you ever heard somebody say, "I don't know what the future holds, but I know who holds the future"? That person isn't completely correct, or maybe they've never read the last chapter of Revelation. We *do* know something of what the future holds because around AD 95 on an island called Patmos, the One who holds the future took us back to the future. The resurrected Jesus pulled back the curtains of eternity and revealed to a disciple named John how God is going to restore everything the way it was supposed to be.

We Are Going to Live in God's Perfect Place

"Then I saw a new heaven and a new earth, for the first heaven and the first earth had passed away, and the sea was no more" (Revelation 21:1). We come full circle from the creation of heaven and earth in Genesis to the restoration of a new heaven and a new earth in Revelation. Eugene Peterson puts it this way:

> The biblical story began quite logically with a beginning and now it draws to an end...also with a beginning. The sin-ruined creation of Genesis is restored in the sacrifice renewed creation of Revelation. The product of these beginning and ending acts of God are the same, "The heavens and the earth" in Genesis and "A new heaven and a new earth" in Revelation. The story of the Bible that has creation at the beginning also has creation at the end.[13]

The picture here is not of a world brand-new but a world *re*newed. God is not going to dump this world into a trashcan and start over. He is going to *restore* this world to the way it was meant to be.

We live in a world that is polluted physically, morally, and spiritually. A perfect God lives in a perfect world and wants his people living in a perfect world as he did in the beginning. Everything around us—the atmosphere, the planets, even our resurrected bodies—are going to be upgraded beyond what you and I can imagine.

Then John adds a strange, unique detail: "And the sea was no more." My first thought when I read that was, *What a bummer!* I love the ocean. (No oysters in heaven? Seriously?) Then I found out one reason oceans exist.

Over 70 percent of the world's surface is covered with salt water. The average depth of the ocean is three miles. Why does this earth need all this salt water? Because the earth needs to be cleansed daily so that we can live.

This earth is bathed in what you might call an "antiseptic solution" composed of about 96 percent water, 3.5 percent salt, and about .5 percent of trace constituents. That salty brine of the ocean not only cleanses the atmosphere, but it also creates the rain we need.

Furthermore, the sea serves as a giant septic tank that absorbs and breaks down all the pollutants and waste that get washed into our streams and rivers that flow into the sea. The sun then heats the sea and brings out of it pure clean water-vapor clouds, which bring rain back to the land. We need this continuous cycle of cleansing and renewing on this earth, but on the new earth there won't be any pollution or waste and therefore no need for cleansing and no need for a sea. God thinks of everything.

We Are Going to Live in God's Perfect Presence

This new heaven and this new earth is going to have a capital city. "And I saw the holy city, new Jerusalem, coming down out of heaven from God, prepared as a bride adorned for her husband" (Revelation 21:2). God is the architect, the builder, and the interior decorator of this city.

It is a beautiful city. The word *adorned* gives us the word *cosmetic*. It means "to make beautiful." You have never ever seen a more beautiful city than this one. That is why she is called a bride. I've done a lot of weddings and I've never performed a ceremony for a bride who wasn't beautiful. Every bride is beautiful. How exciting it will be when God unveils this city to his people.

This city is an expansive 1400 miles wide, long, and high (Revelation 21:16). That is large enough to contain all the landmass from the Appalachians to the California coast and from Canada to Mexico. This city will be forty times the size of England, ten times the size of France, larger than India and that is just the ground floor.[14] Remember, the city stands as tall as it does wide. If God were to stack the floors in this city like an architect would in a building, this city would be over 600,000 stories tall. What is God saying? There will be plenty of room for everybody that loves him.

What makes this city so magnificent is who lives in it. "And I heard a loud voice from the throne saying, 'Behold, the dwelling place of God is with man. He will dwell with them, and they will be his people, and

God himself will be with them as their God'" (Revelation 21:3). For the first time, all of God's people will live in God's perfect presence. Our eyes will see him. Our ears will hear him. Our hands can touch him. Our lips can kiss him. He will never be out of sight. He will never be out of mind. He will be as he has always been, "God *with* us."

We Are Going to Live in God's Perfect Peace

"He will wipe away every tear from their eyes, and death shall be no more, neither shall there be mourning, nor crying, nor pain anymore, for the former things have passed away" (Revelation 21:4). John doesn't tell us only what is there; he also tells us what's not there. This place is going to be so different from anything we've ever experienced that what is absent is even more pronounced than what is present.

First, no sorrow exists there. As a pastor I can testify that nothing is more gut-wrenching than hearing the wails and cries of people whose lives have been decimated and whose hearts have been devastated by grief and sorrow. In heaven there will be no more tears, mourning, crying, or pain. No need for hospitals, hospices, or healthcare. No sadness…just gladness! Thomas Moore said, "Earth has no sorrow that heaven cannot heal."[15]

There will be no death. I love the way John wrote it, "Death shall be no more." Imagine a world with no cemeteries and no obituaries, no funeral homes or crematoriums. The darkness of physical death will disappear in the brightness of our eternal life.

Sorrow and death will cease because sin will disappear.

"But nothing unclean will ever enter it, nor anyone who does what is detestable or false, but only those who are written in the Lamb's book of life" (Revelation 21:27). Imagine a world where everybody is not just good but perfect. A world of no arguments, lawsuits, conflict, or confrontation. A world with no need to forgive or be forgiven. Everything is going to end even better than it began.

The Final Solution

I wouldn't mind moving to the new earth right now, but I have to solve three problems first: sin, sorrow, and death. They all came on that fateful day in the Garden of Eden. Adam sinned, death entered, and sorrow was the result. From that time to now, the cancer of sin has metastasized into death and sorrow. Neither science, nor technology, nor education, nor money, nor human ingenuity can ultimately solve any of these problems.

God sent Jesus to die on the cross to take care of our sin problem. Then he raised him from the dead to take care of our death problem. One day he is coming back to restore this world to the way it was meant to be to take care of our sorrow problem. That is in a nutshell the story of the Bible. The greatest news of all is God wants to make his story *your* story by his grace to you and your faith in Jesus. When those two things meet, God guarantees you will live happily ever after.

Prayer for This Week: *Dear Lord, I feel that tension of wishing for a better place, greater peace, and your unending presence. Thank you that eternal life begins now and that I can join you in each of these today.*

Question for This Week: Look back in your life to a time when something destructive occurred. How did beauty rise from those ashes? How has God recreated your "place" with his presence and with his peace?

Section Two

A Nation Is Born

No nation has a more storied beginning than Israel. Visions and dreams lead to a race and a nation destined to become a blessing to the entire world. The story takes us from deserts to dungeons and from crossing parted seas to traversing deep rivers. A promised land is reached with divine miracles and life-changing messages littered along the way. Read and be changed.

5

Yes, God

Scriptures for This Week

- Galatians 3:5-9
- Genesis 12:1-4
- Hebrews 11:8-12
- James 2:20-24
- Romans 4:13-25

Just Say Yes

Have you ever considered how a yes or a no can make such a profound difference in your life?

One man's yes to God forever changed the world. His yes gave birth to the world's greatest nation, which gave birth to the word of God and the Son of God and shows all humanity how we can experience the spiritual rebirth we need to have a relationship with God. We know this yes was a big deal for several reasons. Two chapters in Genesis record creation, one chapter records the fall of the human race, eight chapters record the history of the world from creation to this yes-man. Then thirty-eight chapters deal with this yes-man.[16]

His name is Abram when we first meet him (God later changes his name to Abraham), and next to Jesus he is perhaps the greatest person in the entire Bible. He is mentioned 308 times in Scripture (234 times in the Old Testament and 74 times in the New and quoted in 27 books (16 in the Old Testament and 11 in the New). His name is known worldwide, and he is revered by the three major religions—Christianity, Judaism, and Islam.

The first 11 chapters of Genesis recall creation, the fall, the flood, and the Tower of Babel, covering a period of roughly 2000 years. The last 39 chapters all focus on Abraham and his family covering some 350 years.

We have more detail about Abraham than about the origin of the universe. Why is so much attention given to this man?

Abraham is the prototype of how everyone can have a relationship with God, and he becomes the father of the nation of Israel because of his yes to God. A yes to God is always the best and right answer to whatever he asks you to do. Abraham's yes teaches us some valuable lessons.

God Reveals Himself Personally Through Grace

The next few words seem innocuous, but signal a shift in history. "Now the LORD said to Abram..." (Genesis 12:1). Up to this point the history of the human race was just plain sordid. Since Eden, sin's cancer had spread so that God regretted his creation and sent a worldwide flood of destruction, saving Noah and his family alone. Life went on as usual until the building of the Tower of Babel, a monument to human pride and idolatry. God upsets that applecart and introduces a multiplicity of languages, scattering the human race all over the earth and destroying cross communication.

Abraham lives in a world with no connection to God, no revelation from God, a world where people are alienated from each other and separated from God. It was a world in spiritual darkness with no light at the end of the tunnel. Then God shines the light of his word to this one man—and a most unlikely man at that.

Abraham was from Ur of the Chaldeans (Genesis 11:28), one of the most important cities of the ancient world. It was a center for mathematics, astronomy, and commerce with a university and library, and a mecca of paganism, centered around the moon-god Nanna and the goddess Ningal. Abraham was an idolater from a city of idolatry. When God came to Abraham he was a pagan, unbelieving Gentile. Nothing about him seems religious or righteous.

Abraham was not looking for God, but God was looking for him. Nothing in Abraham would have caused God to look for him or speak to him. It was a calling of grace. From this momentous encounter we learn that grace gives us a place with God. We don't seek God; God seeks us. God always makes the first move in every human relationship. Grace is always the starting point with God.

We Respond to God Positively Through Faith

The then-unknown God tells this pagan idolater something that puts Abraham between the biggest rock and the hardest place he had ever been. "Go from your country and your kindred and your father's house to the land that I will show you" (Genesis 12:1).

Abraham is seventy-five years of age, which was the prime of life at that time. He has a beautiful wife, a successful business, he's surrounded by family and friends, and God says to him, "I want you to pack nothing—leave everything and go." God doesn't tell him where he is going, how long it will take to get there, what he is going to do once he does get there, how long he is going to stay there, nor what is going to happen to him once he gets there. It's just, "Pack up, get up, and leave."

Because of what God says next, we cannot call this blind faith or a leap in the dark.

"And I will make of you a great nation, and I will bless you and make your name great, so that you will be a blessing. I will bless those who bless you, and him who dishonors you I will curse, and in you all the families of the earth shall be blessed" (Genesis 12:2-3). God begins his relationship with Abraham through a promise and a question: "Abraham, do you trust my word or not?" The ball is in Abraham's court, and unlike Adam he gets it right. "So Abram went, as the Lord had told him..." (Genesis 12:4). Abraham's faith met God's grace and set off a chain reaction that would produce divine blessings that continue to this present day and for all eternity. But the story isn't finished.

"And he brought him outside and said, 'Look toward heaven, and number the stars, if you are able to number them.' Then he said to him, 'So shall your offspring be'" (Genesis 15:5). God takes Abraham out to do some stargazing. Though Abraham's wife, Sarai, is past childbearing age, God says, "You are not just seeing stars. You are seeing your family." What happens next is a watershed both in biblical and human history. "And he believed the Lord, and he counted it to him as righteousness" (Genesis 15:6). Abraham, at that moment, went from being a pagan to a believer. This verse gives us the blueprint on how to have a relationship with God. To be right with God, you must have the righteousness of God, and the righteousness of God comes only through faith.

No temple, no tabernacle, no church, no law, no Ten Commandments. A relationship with God doesn't come through religion or personal righteousness. But when our faith meets God's grace, God counts it as righteousness. Faith is the key that unlocks the door to God's house, the passport that makes you a citizen of God's kingdom, the password that gets you into God's family. Faith is the yes that leads to one last principle.

God Rewards Us Powerfully Through Blessing

God promised Abraham three things. First, he promised Abraham would be the father of a great nation—the nation of Israel. From that nation we got the prophets; from the prophets we got the Old Testament; from the Jewish people we got the Savior of the world. Promise kept; blessing given.

Second, God promised Abraham a great name. Again, you can't go anywhere in the world where his name is not known. He is seen by the Muslim, the Jew, and the Christian as the father of their faith. He is still the hero of the Hebrews, the jewel of the Jews, the brightest star in the Hebrew heaven. Promise kept; blessing given.

Then, God promised Abraham he would make him a great blessing and that through him, "all the families of the earth shall be blessed." How has Abraham blessed all the families of the earth? Through his descendant, Jesus Christ. Though Abraham didn't understand it, and though many of the prophets could only predict it, we now know that through the Son of God, the greatest blessing came to the entire world.[17]

What Is Your Answer?

Do you know why we should always say yes to God? God wants to work through our yes to accomplish his best. When we say yes to God, we get blessed and we become a blessing.

Do you realize that every blessing in your life has come as a result of somebody saying yes? You are alive right now because your mother said yes to giving you life. You enjoy the freedom you have today because men and women said yes to defending this nation. You are alive today because God said yes to giving you another day. You can have eternal life when you say yes to Jesus Christ.

It is not uncommon for naval submarines and ships to sail under sealed orders. The captain is given an envelope that is opened only after the ship leaves port. Rather than unveiling the entire course, the directions give coordinates to the next stop. Once they reach the specified location, they radio for further instructions and the process continues. The ship navigates from point to point with no revelation of the final destination. There are orders and a plan. The captain's only job is to say yes to every order he receives.

When we say yes to God, he takes care of the rest. When Jesus said yes to God, he accomplished the best thing ever for the world. God wants to use our yes to accomplish his best. What is your answer?

Prayer for This Week: *Lord, you are the great guide, the all-knowing shepherd who never leads his people astray. Give me the courage to say yes to you in new ways that will extend your blessing.*

Question for This Week: Describe the ways in which your own Christian faith affects the world and leaves a legacy.

6

In the Crosshairs

Scriptures for This Week

- Romans 12:17-21
- Genesis 45:4-7
- Genesis 50:19-21
- Acts 7:9-10
- 1 Peter 3:8-12

God Is Desiring His Praise from Your Life

Have you been treated unfairly? Experienced an unjust circumstance? Been dealt a bad hand? Is there someone who is the cause of all your trouble and have you daydreamed about turning the tables? The story of Joseph is one you may relate to (Genesis 37–50).

Joseph lived through some difficult situations. When Joseph and his brothers were all still living at home in Canaan, they tossed him into a pit and sold him into slavery that landed him in Egypt. After that, Joseph was falsely accused of rape and thrown into the Pharaoh's prison for thirteen years. But in a positive turn of events, Joseph became the prime minister of Egypt and led the country through years of prosperity. A famine arose in the land, and Joseph was making tough choices. In the midst of this, in walked his travel-weary brothers looking for food.

These brothers who had sold him were now there to buy from him. The same ten brothers who had thrown him into a hole now needed him to pull them out of one. This plot has more twists and turns than a Texas tornado, and Joseph needed to keep some perspective.

Joseph faced a choice we all face: When wronged, do we respond with bitterness or forgiveness? Revenge seems to be one of the sweetest and most satisfying acts of life. Isn't giving them what they deserve for giving you what you didn't deserve the right thing? The answer to that question depends on whether you believe this statement: If God is in control of your life, then you can praise him for your friends and trust him with your enemies. What does God desire of you in those pivotal moments of pain? Praise and trust.

God Is Arranging His Prospects in Your Life

"What goes around comes around" will be true in your life one day. That father who neglected you growing up will need you to care for him in his old age. That spouse who walked out on you will need your help down the road. One day you may be able to fire the person who wouldn't hire you.

When you have someone in the crosshairs, do you take the shot?

A portion of Joseph's story shows us how he sets his brothers up. However, he isn't setting them up for evil but for good. He knows they need to come clean and be broken before God. He accuses them of being spies, puts them in prison, frees them, and then sends them home with food if they'll bring back one final brother. When they return with Benjamin, he throws them a banquet, gives them more grain, and then sets them up one more time, making them look like thieves in spite of his kindness.

When he nails them with the goods (a silver goblet from his banquet), the brothers come clean. "God has uncovered your servants' guilt" (Genesis 44:16 NIV).

Now we get to the good part, one of the greatest moments in the entire Old Testament, the climax of a story that has taken decades to tell. Joseph made himself known to his brothers, and then broke down in tears from all the loss. His brothers stood there afraid, the color draining from their faces. Yet, Joseph doesn't banish them to prison and poverty. Instead he says, "I love you. I forgive you. I accept you" (Genesis 45).

When he said, "Come close to me," he was saying, "I love you." When he called himself, "Joseph, your brother," he was saying, "I forgive you." When he said, "Don't be angry with yourselves," he was saying, "I accept you."

How did Joseph do it? How could he forgive and forget all that these brothers had done to him? How could he respond with forgiveness rather than with bitterness?

God Is Fulfilling His Plan in Your Life

In Genesis 45, Joseph echoes a faith-filled statement: *God sent me.* Into that pit in the desert, *God sent me.* Into slavery, *God sent me.* Into that false accusation of rape, *God sent me.* Into that unjust prison for thirteen years, *God sent me.* Everything Joseph believed could be summarized in two phrases: "You sold me...but God sent me."

Later, when Jacob died and the brothers were afraid that Joseph would now take his revenge, they started all over again begging for their lives. Joseph makes this great statement in Genesis 50:20 (NIV): "You intended to harm me, but God intended it for good."

In those unfair circumstances in your life, do you know what God is saying? He's saying, "Everything is going according to plan."

God uses three things to fulfill his plan for us: pain, problems, and people. God could have prevented the brothers from selling Joseph. God could have prevented Joseph from being falsely accused. And God could have prevented Joseph from being thrown into prison. But it was all part of his plan. One of the things that can rescue you from bitterness and revenge is to remind yourself, *God is fulfilling his plan in my life.*

God Is Accomplishing His Purpose in Your Life

God isn't caught off guard when things go wrong in your life. He isn't surprised the way that you are. Not only is everything that happens in your life going according to God's plan, but it is going to accomplish his purpose.

You may need to be patient. It took Joseph a couple of decades to understand God's purpose, but here's what he discerned: "God sent me ahead of you to preserve for you a remnant on earth and to save your lives by a great deliverance" (Genesis 45:7 NIV). God's purpose was to save their lives, the lives of the ones who had harmed him. But that's not all. Joseph said, "God intended it for good to accomplish what is now being done, the saving of many lives" (Genesis 50:20 NIV). God's purpose was to save *many* lives.

When Joseph was sold into slavery in Egypt, he didn't know that one day a famine would come that could destroy the entire nation. He didn't know that he'd be placed in a powerful position to help save that nation.

Joseph didn't know that in a hard confrontation, he'd preserve his family so that the nation of Israel could be born and the world could have a Savior. God doesn't love your hardship, but God does love life with his people and works his purpose so that we all can have it.

If you understand that God takes both the good and the bad, both friends and enemies, both fairness and unfairness to accomplish his purpose in your life, then you cannot be bitter. Joseph doesn't respond out of bitterness. Joseph doesn't impart more fear. He laid aside thoughts of revenge and put his brothers' fear to an end. "Don't be afraid. I'm not God." Like the book of Proverbs says,

> Don't say, "I'll pay you back for the wrong you did."
> Wait for the LORD, and he will make things right.
> (Proverbs 20:22 NCV)

What if making things right isn't about repayment but renewal? No matter what other people do to you, payback doesn't belong to you but to God, and how that looks is up to him. If you could see God's big picture for just a day and how everything happens in order to accomplish his purpose, then you could always say the same thing about others that Joseph said about his brothers: "You intended to harm me, but God intended it for good" (Genesis 50:20 NIV).

God Is Keeping His Promise in Your Life

Joseph made another statement to his brothers that they didn't pick up: "I fear God" (Genesis 42:18). Why did he say that? It goes back to something that occurred just a few verses earlier when his brothers first came to him in Egypt and bowed down before him. We are told, "Then he remembered his dreams about them" (42:6-9). Joseph remembered the vision God gave him that all his brothers would bow at his feet. God had kept his promise, and Joseph stood in awe of it.

Joseph's life is one long illustration of one of the greatest verses in the New Testament: "And we know that in all things God works for the good of those who love him, who have been called according to his purpose" (Romans 8:28 NIV).

Yes, God uses pain, problems, and people to accomplish that purpose and that is why you can even bless your enemies. That is why you can return good for evil, because you know that no matter what anybody else does to you, God will take it and is taking it and using it for good.

You're not the powerful leader of a country, and you probably haven't been sold into slavery or had to fight serious criminal charges. Or maybe you *have.* The presence of problems never means the absence of God. And when people are doing their worst to you, God is doing his best for you.

The next time you get somebody in the crosshairs and you're tempted to squeeze the trigger, just remember God is using that person to fulfill his plan, accomplish his purpose, and keep his promise in your life.

Prayer for This Week:

Father, thank you for your attention to the details of my life. You heal the broken places with your goodness. Show me how to love in spite of loss and to stand in awe of your promises.

Question for This Week: What is the difficulty you're facing that needs God's perspective and how can you work with God to accomplish his purpose?

7

The Way to Freedom

Scriptures for This Week

- Psalm 105
- Exodus 2:23-25
- Exodus 12:1-17
- 1 Corinthians 5:6-8
- John 1:29-34

Remember God's Story

My favorite subject in school was always American history. To this day, I am always reading some book on the subject. Our nation's founding is one of the most fascinating stories in all of history, and it has the fingerprints of the providence of God.

No nation, however, has a more fascinating history than the nation of Israel. From God's call and covenant with Abraham to Abraham's miracle son, Isaac, the father of Jacob and Esau, to Jacob's twelve sons, we see God's hand at work. We then read how God raised Joseph to power in Egypt, redeeming and restoring what was a real family mess. The family remains in Egypt so, at this point, the nation of Israel doesn't exist. But the family is growing and growing.

A new Pharaoh soon rises to power, one who doesn't know the story of Joseph (or Jacob or Isaac or Abraham). He knows, though, that Joseph's family now numbers 600,000 men, plus an untold number of women and children (see Exodus 12:37). He and his advisers are worried that they might be overtaken by these Hebrews, so he enslaves them and kills the firstborn males.

The family, too, has long forgotten the God of their ancestors. They have lost all hope that they will ever be freed. They are under the thumb of the most powerful nation with no way of escape. When you're enslaved, you need freedom.

Watch for God's Leading

In the fright and horror of the Pharaoh's killing spree, one Hebrew baby is spared. His name is Moses. In an ironic twist, God raises Moses up as an adopted son in Pharaoh's house. He then empowers him to be the deliverer of the Hebrew people, who by this time have been enslaved for four hundred years. It is not going to be an easy task. Significant acts never are.

This brings us to what the nation of Israel still considers one of the two greatest events in its history. This event was so critical to this nation that God even changed the calendar, making this day the beginning of Israel's religious year. It becomes the basis of one of the greatest celebrations the nation has observed ever since: the Passover.

This is the clearest picture of redemption in the entire Old Testament. This story teaches us that no one is beyond God's redemption and forgiveness. We see in this account both the birth of a nation in a night and the freedom of a nation in a day after four hundred years in bondage.

You may be in bondage today to pornography, drugs, alcohol, bitterness, lust, or anger. Perhaps you have tried to get free from these things, but the keys to your shackles don't work. I'm telling you freedom awaits you. You can find a way out.

Accept God's Direction

After four hundred years of making bricks, being ordered around, told when to get up, when to go to bed, what to eat, and when to eat it—Israel's emancipation proclamation is about to be enacted. The Hebrews are about to become a free people. Here are the directions that God gives to Moses to give to the Israelites: "Tell all the congregation of Israel that on the tenth day of this month every man shall take a lamb according to their fathers' houses, a lamb for a household" (Exodus 12:3).

The Israelites are in slavery and bondage to the most powerful king and the most formidable army on earth. If they were ever to defeat this army, it would take a legion of angels to do it. Yet, God's plan is to first have the people collect lambs, the most meek and defenseless creatures on earth.

The lambs were to be selected on the tenth day of the month, observed and examined for four days, and then each lamb was to be killed at twilight. They were to take the blood of their lambs and paint it on the doorposts of their houses, because it would be their protection against God's death angel that was going to pass through the land this night (Exodus 12:1-13). It sounds fantastical and ludicrous. But after all that had gone on before this (plagues of frogs and flies and killer hail), the people were open to God's direction.

God's direction is not up for debate or discussion. It is his way or no way. Israel had to learn on this night, as we must learn on this day when we are out of options, that God is not only our best way out, he's our only way out.

Follow God's Provision

It is one thing to be told what to do, but another to do what you have been told. To accept God's direction you've got to apply God's provision. It wasn't enough just to slay a lamb or collect its blood in a bowl. The blood of that lamb had to be painted on the doorposts of the house. If it wasn't, the Hebrews would suffer the same fate as the Egyptians. They were to obey what Moses told them to do.

A locked door wouldn't save them. A heavily guarded door wouldn't save them. Only blood on the door would work.

God did not say, "I will pass over you if you are a religious person or a righteous person or a respectable person." Only the blood on the door would work.

A baptismal certificate, a giving receipt, or a resume of good works doesn't work for us either. Only the blood of the Lamb works. No half-beliefs or substitutes are allowed.

Maybe some were animal lovers or maybe their children cried, "Daddy, why are you killing our lamb?" Regardless of the feeling the Hebrews may have had—this act was ridiculous, gross, or confusing—they had to obey God.

However, *we* can see the logic. We can connect that this important moment was pointing toward a future Lamb, one who would pay the debt of sin and offer freedom and redemption to anyone willing to apply

God's provision. "For Christ, our Passover lamb, has been sacrificed" (1 Corinthians 5:7).

History was made that night by people who believed and followed God. You can believe what God says, but it doesn't matter if you don't do what God says. You can accept God's option as being true, but it won't work unless you apply God's provision and let it work in your life.

Experience God's Freedom

What God did on this night was so important that he told the budding nation of Israel that they should never, ever forget it: "This day shall be for you a memorial day, and you shall keep it as a feast to the LORD; throughout your generations, as a statute forever, you shall keep it as a feast" (Exodus 12:14).

When God frees you from whatever is binding you, a new day dawns and a new life emerges. Passover marked a new beginning for these Jewish people and bound them together as one nation under God. From then until now, every time Jewish believers would hear the words *redeem* or *redemption*, they would think of the Passover. God had delivered them through the blood of the lamb, and he delivers us the same way today.

Do you remember how the lamb had to be perfect? How every part of that lamb had to be examined over a period of time to make sure there was no blot or blemish? Jesus Christ, the Lamb of God, was examined for thirty years. The Sadducees, Pharisees, Herodians, and synagogue leaders all posed hard questions to Jesus. Even Pontius Pilate examined him and concluded, "I find no fault in him." Jesus was *the* perfect Lamb.

When you study the Passover you are not just looking into a window of what God did then. You are looking into a mirror of what God is doing today. They were saved by the blood of a lamb—not a single Hebrew home lost a child—and we are saved in the same way.

Every one of us was born with sin over the doorpost of our heart. Once we place our faith in Jesus, our sins disappear. When God looks at your heart, he either sees your sins or Jesus's blood. The only way to freedom and to eternal life is by the blood of God's Lamb.

Prayer for This Week: *Holy God, you are my only maker and my only savior. Help me to remember your story and to watch for your leading as I seek to follow your path to freedom.*

Question for This Week: Write out your story with God. At what points has he freed you from imprisonment? Where can he free you still?

8

Catch-22

Scriptures for This Week

- Matthew 19:16-30
- Exodus 14:13-31
- Psalm 66
- Nehemiah 9:5-12
- Isaiah 63:11-14

Boxed In

Over fifty years ago, Joseph Heller wrote a novel about fighter pilots in World War II who were facing missions of increasing danger and frequency. A pilot who understood his peril would go to great lengths to be released from service, and the only way to do so was to request a hearing that would declare him insane. The catch was that only a sane man would know well enough to request such a hearing. Caught in this contradiction, he was never released. It's what Heller called a catch-22.

If you are in a predicament, it will appear that every path, every decision will lead you to doom. Your job, your marriage, and your kids can all present you with situations where it feels as if every direction is a dead-end street. If I were an attorney who specialized in suing doctors for medical malpractice, and then I discovered that I needed surgery, I would be in a major predicament.

The most involved predicament the nation of Israel ever endured also became the most celebrated event in Jewish history. Two feature films have been made about the event that we call the exodus. In the previous chapter we talked about the Passover, but this is what happens next.

After the children of Israel leave Egypt, God leads them toward the Red Sea. He parts the sea and the children of Israel pass through. He then closes the waters back on the Egyptian army and they all drown. God saves the day and gets the glory. This is what the story is about—not the situation, but the Savior.

Right Where God Wants Us

"Then the LORD said to Moses, 'Tell the people of Israel to turn back and encamp in front of Pi-hahiroth, between Migdol and the sea, in front of Baal-zephon; you shall encamp facing it, by the sea'" (Exodus 14:1-2).

That's a lot of words I can't pronounce, but what do they mean? Baal-zephon was a geographical cul-de-sac, a dead-end street. To the north were huge Egyptian fortresses—massive stone structures that could not be attacked. To the south lay nothing but the Egyptian desert with no protection, no water, and no food. To the west was Pharaoh and his army. To the east lay the portion of the Red Sea that today is called the Gulf of Suez. This was the catch-22 of all catch-22s. Stay put and be defeated or move any which way and die.

The children of Israel have just escaped from 430 years of slavery. They have followed God out of Egypt and are painfully aware that this decision has led them into a corner. This wasn't a navigational error. They hadn't miscalculated or taken a wrong turn. God had led them to this dead end. God will do that so we will learn to trust him and follow his ways. We never quit learning to trust him.

The bad news is that God will lead us to Red Seas, but the good news is that God goes with us and before us. Begin every day signing a Declaration of Dependence upon God because if he leads you that day to a place of desperation and despair, you will stay there until it becomes a place of complete dependence on him. Depend upon God not only to lead you wherever he wants you to go, but also to make a way out once you get there.

Go Where God Leads You

"Moses stretched out his hand over the sea, and the LORD drove the sea back by a strong east wind all night and made the sea dry land, and the waters were divided" (Exodus 14:21). You will never experience the greatness of God, the power of God, the love of God, or the glory of God until you allow God to put you in a place where only he can make a way out. He can resolve the catch-22.

The Israelites could hear the hooves of horses thundering after them. They could see the spears and the swords glinting off the setting sun. Pharaoh himself pursued them with passion. They likely judged this to be the final moment of their lives—that is, if they were looking only at the circumstance.

If you were just looking at the circumstance and not at God, you might be tempted to yell "Run!" or to wave a white flag. Many of us would shake our fist at heaven and call out, "Why do I even bother listening to you?"

Moses doesn't do any of that. Instead, in Exodus 14:13 (my paraphrase) he decides to watch what God will do, and he urges his people, "Be confident! Fear not! Don't run! Be calm! Stand still and stay firm! Just watch and you will see the salvation of the Lord!" In this entrapped moment, Moses did not panic. He had done all he could do and he knew to wait and watch.

Several years ago God led me to start a church with a core of about two hundred people. I led them away from a strong, stable church to a high school cafeteria. I knew God led me to do it, yet I was consumed with the cost. Then they realized that I had done everything God had commanded. I needed to watch and trust God. Two days later, two men who had bought property called to say they were giving it to us. Our church is living proof that when you are standing before a Red Sea in your life, that sea will part.

Look for and listen to the voice of God. He will speak to you. He will show you what to do, but once you've done all you know to do, then you must wait and watch.

Do What God Tells You to Do

God was not going to make it easy for the children of Israel to make their escape; they needed to trust him. He said, "And I will harden Pharaoh's heart, and he will pursue them, and I will get glory over Pharaoh and all his host, and the Egyptians shall know that I am the Lord" (Exodus 14:4). God wants the glory and he gets it.

Pharaoh charges with his best fleet of chariots ridden by his best men so that Israel could experience his worst. Focusing on this threatening Delta Force might overshadow the way out of the catch-22, but the children of Israel kept their eyes on God and saw his best. Pharaoh has Israel right where he wants them, but so does God, and God says, "Go into the sea." When they do, the miracle begins.

God made his way out clear. These two-and-a-half million Israelites didn't make their way through a compact canyon of water. God was much bigger than that. If they marched two-by-two, their line would be eight hundred miles long and would require multiple days and nights to get through it. To walk through it in one night as they did, they had to walk five thousand abreast in a three-mile-wide space in that sea.

In comparison, the six-hundred-chariot Egyptian army pursued them looking a little small. When God removed his hand from the waters, a divine dam broke and the entire Egyptian army drowned. The greatest thing that happened was not the Red Sea parting or the Red Sea closing, but that God had kept every promise he made. The Egyptians acknowledged the God of Abraham in their last words, "'Let us flee from before Israel, for the LORD fights for them against the Egyptians'" (Exodus 14:25). And then they were wiped out just as God said they would be.

After 430 years of forgetting God, the children of Israel came back to believing God. He didn't want them to think they could succeed on their own power. What was most important to God was that everything fade away in the light of his glory and grace.

Believe What God Says He Will Do

Now Moses had the task of leading this huge crowd of people through a wilderness that would daily require fifteen thousand tons of food, four thousand tons of firewood, and eleven million gallons of water. Every time they camped, they would need a campground two-thirds the size of Rhode Island (roughly 750 square miles). Do you think Moses had this all figured out before he left? Not at all. What in the world was he doing? He was just going where God led him to go, doing what God told him to do, and believing what God said he would do. And in the end, God brought his people all the way to the Promised Land.

Now I don't know what Red Sea you are facing today. Maybe you are at an impasse in your marriage. Maybe you are facing a giant financial wave that is about to overwhelm you. Or maybe you need God to part a relational Red Sea between you and a relative or a friend. You can't possibly have it all figured out. Do what you know you should do while you look to God to solve your catch-22. He's already solved it in a greater way than you ever could.

What the exodus is in the Old Testament, the resurrection of Jesus is in the New Testament. The exodus is a picture of what Jesus has done for us. We faced a Red Sea called sin. Behind us was an enemy called death. But Christ held a cross over the sea of sin and he parted it. As our resurrected Lord, he put death to death so he could lead us to a promised land where we will live with him forever and ever. This is the glory and grace of God. This is what the story is about.

Prayer for This Week: *Lord, you are the God who sees and the God who saves. Help me to turn to you in my difficulties so that I don't miss the miracle.*

Question for This Week: Think of a situation that you're struggling to make sense of and note the various solutions you might choose. Which way through it would glorify God alone? What are you going to do next?

9

The Need to Succeed

Scriptures for This Week

- Joshua 1:1-9
- Proverbs 16:1-3
- 1 Kings 2:1-4
- Romans 12:1-2
- Isaiah 41:8-10

An Unlikely Success

The most popular Bible app, YouVersion, allows users to read the Bible, take notes, and even share verses. At the end of every year it reports on the most popular Bible verses that were shared. Among the top ten in 2013 was this verse from the book of Joshua:[18] "Have I not commanded you? Be strong and courageous. Do not be frightened, and do not be dismayed, for the LORD your God is with you wherever you go" (Joshua 1:9).

Why did this Old Testament verse go viral? The story it's in couldn't be more different from our modern lives. The book of Joshua is the story of people who had rebelled against God and their leader, Moses, and were left to wander in a Middle Eastern wilderness for forty years. When we encounter this verse, many of the people have died off, including Moses, and now Joshua is being charged with bringing those who remained into the Promised Land.

Joshua needed to advance, but he didn't have a lot to work with. These people were seasoned desert nomads not battle-tested warriors. He had no special forces, no trained army, few weapons, and no battle plan. They faced at least seven known nations of hardened warriors, every one of which was bigger, stronger, and better equipped than this ragtag bunch of Jewish people. Yet, Joshua had been given his marching orders in a verse that went viral nearly thirty-four hundred years later.

With that verse guiding him, Joshua went on a years-long conquest that started with a supernatural river crossing and included secret patrols, stolen plunder, terror, toil, and tragedy. The encouragement of that verse was the secret to Joshua's unlikely success.

Success Is Experiencing the Presence of God

Who gave the greatest speech you've ever heard? Martin Luther King Jr.? Gandhi? Winston Churchill? What was it about? When God gave one of the greatest speeches in history to Joshua, it centered on the words *success* and *prospering*, two things everybody wants to do. If you go to Amazon, you will find thousands of books on how to be successful. Everybody wants to know the secret of success.

The good news is that the secret to success is not so secret. God wants us to be successful, but only in his way. In Joshua 1, God divulges his secret of success: "Just as I was with Moses, so I will be with you. I will not leave you or forsake you" (Joshua 1:5b).

The late nineteenth-century Scottish minister George MacDonald once said in a sermon, "In whatever man does without God, he must fail miserably—or succeed more miserably."[19] Do you know why that statement is true? Without God, all success ends in ultimate failure.

Suppose we could build our own man and we made him a combination of Mark Zuckerberg, Tiger Woods, Brad Pitt, and Barack Obama. You would have one of the richest, most famous, handsome, and powerful people in the world. This man could buy anything, go anywhere, meet anybody, and would live on top of the world. Next, suppose I told you that this man was missing the presence of God in his life. He has no connection to the Creator whatsoever and he dies that way. Was he successful? I say no.

If you're successful in life, you will have God inside you while you live and beside you when you die. C.S. Lewis said, "He who has God and everything has no more than the man who has God alone." The same God who promised he would be with Joshua has promised to be with you.

Success Is Obeying the Principles of God

If you need to succeed, remember that it pays to obey. God tells Joshua that if he will do whatever the word of God tells him to do, success will follow him wherever he goes. He says that a key to success is found in how we adjust to what God wants.

> "Only be strong and very courageous, being careful to do according to all the law that Moses my servant commanded you. Do not turn from it to the right hand or to the left, that you may have good success wherever you go" (Joshua 1:7).

When we think of success, we think of position, of power, of prestige, of possessions; but in God's world success means to do what is right. In God's eyes, the way we respond to his word determines whether we are a success or a failure.

In verse 8 God gets specific in telling us what we are to do with his word: "This Book of the Law shall not depart from your mouth, but you shall meditate on it day and night, so that you may be careful to do according to all that is written in it. For then you will make your way prosperous, and then you will have good success."

How do we apply this verse to ourselves? In at least these three ways.

1. You must look it up.

Ingest and digest the Bible to the point that the words are always in your mouth. If your heart is full of God's truth, your mouth will speak God's truth and say the things you should and not say what you shouldn't.

2. You must let it in by meditating on it.

The word *meditate* suggests the image of a cow chewing its cud over and over. When we meditate, we run a truth around in our mind until we begin to see life from God's viewpoint. A mind filled with the word of God leads to a heart full of the love of God.

3. You must live it out.

Do what it says. Do you know what the real prosperity gospel is? It is not, "God wants everybody to be rich." The real prosperity gospel is, "God wants everybody to be obedient." That leads to true success.

The proof that you believe the Bible is to obey the Bible. But this has to be an all-in, zero-tolerance, total obedience. This is when the Bible comes alive. This is when we see God at work. Obedience is our success.

Success Is Fulfilling the Purpose of God

Do you remember from chapter one those inquiries into our purpose and personhood? Who am I? Why am I here? Where am I going? Have you been thinking on them as you've been reading? Joshua is about to find out his answer to, "Why am I here?"

> "Be strong and courageous, for you shall cause this people to inherit the land that I swore to their fathers to give them" (Joshua 1:6).

Joshua was the reason the people would inherit the Promised Land. He was going to fulfill God's purpose established from the time of Abraham. This was Joshua's calling and what he was born to do.

The greatest tragedy that I can think of is to go through life and never know your purpose. Only three types of people exist today.

- Those with *no purpose* in life. They drift through life, go to school a little, get a job, switch jobs, find a spouse, switch spouses, move from house to house, retire, and die.
- Those with the *wrong purpose* in life. Maybe they are super-achievers or career ladder-climbers who live a life with little or no thought of God and die without him.
- Those who have found the *right purpose* in life. They believe that God put them on this earth to fulfill his purpose and they are doing what they believe that purpose is.

God guarantees to fulfill only his purpose for your life. We don't create our purpose, we discover and pursue it. Joshua knew he had nailed it; he had the presence of God, he obeyed the principles of God, and he was filled with the purpose of God. Success was guaranteed.

An Irresistible Success

Just look at the way God brought Joshua from an unlikely success to an irresistible success. He didn't do it in a human way, picking and choosing what works based on studies and surveys. He did it God's way.

Listen again to what God said to Joshua in verse 5: "No man shall be able to stand before you all the days of your life. Just as I was with Moses, so I will be with you. I will not leave you or forsake you."

Did you hear what God said to him? God said, "If you will recognize my presence, obey my will, and fulfill the purpose I have put you on this planet to fulfill, *no one will stand against you.* You will be an irresistible force, an immovable object. Every foe you meet will be the foe you beat." Nothing and no one can stand against anyone who stands with God.

The Bible is not about your personal fulfillment, accomplishments, or happiness. The Bible is about God's presence with you, how you fit into his plan, and how you can be fulfilled through his purposes, not your own. God will feed your need for success with the only success that matters—his.

We were put on this earth to experience the presence of God, obey the principles of God, and fulfill the purpose of God. When we do, success is guaranteed.

Prayer for This Week: *Father, thank you for leading me to you, the One who gives me my purpose. Keep me in your presence as I seek to do what is right in your eyes and for the world.*

Question for This Week: What is God's purpose for you? How is it different from the purpose you created for yourself?

10

Out on a Limb

Scriptures for This Week

- Proverbs 2:1-5
- Judges 19:1-30
- 1 Peter 4:1-6
- Judges 21:25
- James 1:19-21

Right and Wrong

An atheist once gave this view of morality: "I have been told that without God there can be no morals and that as an atheist I can have no morals. I disagree. I believe in love, hope, honor, loyalty, honesty, trust, respect, etc. Those things don't come from God. They come from within and from human interaction. If you need God to tell you what is wrong and what is right and you can't figure it out on your own, then you may be part of the problem."

I disagree. You cannot have true morality without God. When you try to make right and wrong a matter of human choice or human reason, you are out on a limb that will break every time. Only with God can you know what is right and what is wrong and only with God can you tell the difference.

A story in the Bible tells us what happens when we remove God from our ethics. I warn you, it's a gruesome story of an unprincipled time and unethical exploits. It occurred when the nation of Israel was still unorganized with no central government, just twelve tribes functioning as separate jurisdictions. As I retell it, we'll see the ominous, developed, national life without God. You see, they *did* have a king (God) and they did have a law (his Commandments), but they discarded and disobeyed both.

Believe in Moral Values

I am not saying you must believe in God in order to believe in what is good, that you cannot formulate good values without God, or that you must believe in God to believe that morality exists. The question is not the fact of goodness but the *foundation* of goodness.

God has given us that foundation in his commandments. Psalm 119:160 says, "The sum of your word is truth, and every one of your righteous rules endures forever." News commentator Ted Koppel once said, "There is harmony and inner peace to be found in following a moral compass that points in the same direction regardless of fashion or trend."[20] God has provided that moral compass in his word. What he tells us he tells everybody, and what he tells at any time he tells for all time.

This means that even the most wicked people are not devoid of a value system; it's just one founded on self. In Judges 19, we read of a Levite, a member of the priesthood and a custodian of God's law, who plugs into a depraved value system. He's not a righteous man and he takes a concubine, a legalized mistress. This concubine then cheats on him, and to escape his wrath, she flees to her father's house in Bethlehem.

Four months later, he goes to get her and her father welcomes this apparent son-in-law. They party it up for days. When the son-in-law leaves to take her home, they journey into the evening to a town called Gibeah. The custom of the day was to offer hospitality to someone sitting alone in the city square, but no one in Gibeah did this for this weary couple. At evening, an outsider, an Ephraimite, takes them into his home. They lodge with him, pull out the wine, and start to get happy. This is where the story gets grisly. The "worthless fellows" of the city storm over and demand that not the concubine but the Levite be handed over for their sexual pleasure. The host says, "You can't have the man, but take my virgin daughter and this other woman. I don't care at all what you do to them."

This scene is vile and reprehensible. It would be hard to find anyone who can sympathize with the perpetrators in this story. A universal moral value shouts, "This is wrong!" If a universal standard of right and wrong exists, someone with universal authority has established it. Humans have opinions or a pretense of power, but they don't have universal leverage. Without an objective right or wrong, we do what is right in our minds.

Live by Moral Virtues

Over the last several decades, anthropologists have done an exhaustive survey of the various cultures of the world, and they have found that morality is universal. Scholars have never found a culture, past or present, that doesn't have some system of morality. The standards of morality may differ from one culture to another or even within a culture, but every culture knows the difference between what ought to be and what ought not to be.

Jesus said that the moral virtues we should live by can be summed up in one word—*love*—and it should flow both vertically to God and horizontally to our neighbor. When you follow this righteous rule, you will also find loyalty, honesty, love, generosity, and sacrifice—all that is good and right. This flow of love was absent in this story.

This Levite coward sleeps through the night while his concubine is raped and abused. In the early morning, she is released and falls down at the door of the house. When the Levite finds her lying on the stoop, she's dead. The man is now angry, not over her abuse, but over his loss. The hospitality toward him has been violated and revenge must be taken. To recruit his fellow Israelites to his cause, he cuts his dead concubine into twelve pieces and sends one to every tribe.

If you were to open a box in the mail and find a head or a foot, it would get your attention. Eleven tribes are ticked off, and they commit to see that justice is done. Forming an army of 400,000 men, they storm the city and demand to execute the perpetrators, but the Benjamites defend them. The Benjamites are willing to fight for what is wrong, and 2000 Israelites are killed in the conflict that ensues. In the end, the tribes of Israel kill every one and every animal in every town in the region of Benjamin, except for 600 Benjamites who escape. When God's goodness isn't anywhere, it is absent everywhere.

Avoid Moral Vacuums

After all of this, the Israelites find themselves with a decision to make. They realize they have almost wiped out an entire tribe and they need to repopulate it. Their own thinking leads them to go into one of their cities and kill every man, woman, and child except for 400 virgins and give them as wives to the Benjamites. Afterward, they went into Shiloh and kidnapped 200 more women, forcing them into marriage.

Somebody has called this story "the sewer of Scripture" because it may be the most disgusting and degraded story in the Bible. There's not one admirable character, noble act, or hero. In the end, after the rape, the killings, the genocide, the mutilation, and the indifference to all of it, everybody just goes back to business as usual. How do you explain this? Judges 21:25 sums it up, "In those days there was no king in Israel. Everyone did what was right in his own eyes."

These three chapters give us the ugliest story in the Bible, and yet at every stage people were doing what they thought was right. As far as the men of Gibeah were concerned, rape was all right. To the farmer and the Levite, homosexual rape was unthinkable, but heterosexual rape was acceptable. The men of Benjamin thought it was right to defend what was wrong. The Israelites thought it was right to massacre innocent men, women, and children and kidnap women and force them into marriage. It never occurred to any of them they were doing what was wrong.

We Will Be Judged by a Moral Vision

God is necessary for true morality. Rightness and wrongness is founded on God, and only with God can we know that evil and wrong will be punished and goodness and righteousness will be rewarded. With God we know that the scales of justice will be balanced.

Suppose you could have morality without God. What good is morality without accountability? If no afterlife exists, what difference does it make whether you live like Mother Teresa or Adolf Hitler? Without God those rapists got away with it. Those who were guilty of genocide got away with it. Without God, militant terrorists, crooked politicians, and religious hypocrites all get away with it.

Without God, you are out on a moral limb. Jesus defines and declares right and wrong from the cross. The wrong is what he died for so that we could be made right. He alone decides which is which. When we look to Jesus and live by his word, we will not only know what is right, we will do what is right in the only eyes that matter—the God whose compass is love.

Prayer for This Week: *Holy Father, show me where I'm blind to my immorality. Open me up to the wisdom in your word so that I might live with moral virtue.*

Question for This Week: In what ways has your moral compass pointed you in ways separate from the trends happening around you? Were you motivated by God's goodness or your own?

11

The Beauty of Suffering

Scriptures for This Week

- Psalm 123
- Romans 5:1-5
- Job 36:13-21
- 1 Thessalonians 1:2-7
- Job 42:1-6

A Compassionate Picture

The country mourned in 2015 when we saw the heartbreaking photo of Aylan, the three-year-old boy whose body washed ashore during the Syrian refugee crisis. Photos depicting Ebola victims, acts of terrorism, and natural disasters make us want to cry long cries and ask big questions.

I often ask why people suffer. It's okay to ask this, and when we do, God hears us and he takes our question seriously. It touches him so deeply that he offers us a picture of it in an entire book titled Job. As we ask, appeal, and even accuse God regarding our sorrows, I envision God pointing to Job and asking, "Does your pain look this way? Is your devastation like his?"

Many believe Job is the earliest book of the Bible to have been written. Job lived about four thousand years ago, perhaps at the time of Abram, and he lived one of the most blessed and cursed lives in human history. When we read Job's story, we feel his grief, anguish, and frustration. We are connected to a universal struggle, and we begin to feel God's comfort. "I get it. Let's go through this together. I've been there before." God is all about showing himself to us.

No Free Passes

Job was someone special. Job 1:3 says, "this man was the greatest of all the people of the east." He was called righteous, blameless, and upright. No skeletons hid in his closet. The IRS and the FBI put together could find no blemish on his character. Even God himself said, "There is none like him on the earth" (Job 1:8). If we could earn a free pass from suffering, Job should be first to receive one.

Job was also blessed with eleven thousand animals, scads of servants, money, land, and houses, but they couldn't compare to the amount of faithful trust he had for the Lord. He rose up early and offered prayers and sacrifices for *each* member of his household in order to ensure their right standing before God.

God allowed the devil to take away everything that Job found precious. In one day, most of his animals, servants, and all ten of his beloved children, the ones he prayed for daily, died. Then, to add misery to his calamity, Job himself was covered with painful sores from head to toe.

No one is excused from suffering. No man in the Bible, other than Jesus Christ, ever suffered more than Job, and other than Jesus, no man ever suffered more unfairly than Job.

To handle the problem of pain and suffering in life, we must accept that God uses suffering always for our good and for his glory.

Detecting God's Goal in Suffering

There has never been a person alive who hasn't experienced suffering and asked the heavens, "Why?" "Why me?" "Why now?" "Why them?" Maybe you've asked it recently. Maybe you've asked it just today. The Greek philosopher Epicurus said,

> "Is God willing to prevent evil, but not able? Then he is not omnipotent.
> Is he able, but not willing? Then he is malevolent.
> Is he both able and willing? Then whence cometh evil?
> Is he neither able nor willing? Then why call him God?"[21]

When you think like this, you're saying, "There can be no possible divine purpose for suffering." But just because you cannot see a purpose in something does not mean that something does not have a purpose.

Job's wife encouraged him to curse God for having to endure such suffering. Job, taken aback by her foolishness, replied, "Shall we indeed accept good from God and not accept adversity?" (Job 2:10 NASB). He was saying that if God exists and is good and powerful, then we must believe not that he is the cause of our pain, but that there may be a purpose for it.

In Job 42:2-3, Job acknowledges three things about God:

1. God controls this universe and nothing can frustrate his eternal purposes.
2. Everything has a divine purpose. Not one molecule in this universe is without a design.
3. We don't always understand God.

You never have to *understand* what God is doing if you can *trust* God to control rightly. When you are going through adversity and pain and suffering that you don't understand, knowing all the answers is less important than knowing the One who does.[22]

God not only gives us the good, he also allows us to suffer the bad. This is because God is interested in our holiness and in his glory before he's ever interested in our happiness. Our own wisdom can't reconcile this, but the promise implies a purpose.

Expecting God's Grace in Suffering

If we can accept that God is more interested in our holiness than our happiness, then we can begin to accept that God's grace, not our suffering, is the point.

If you go to a jewelry store to buy a diamond ring, that jeweler will take a piece of black velvet and lay the diamond down on it. Why doesn't he lay it on a sheet of white paper? Because he wants to do everything he can to draw your attention to the beauty of that diamond.

God is the jeweler and this fallen world is the black velvet. The Bible says that God is a God of mercy, grace, and love. But how would we know God's attributes if there were no sin, sorrow, or suffering?

In eternity past, before this world was ever created, before evil was ever allowed to exist, God was known by his angels as omnipotent, omniscient, omnipresent, all powerful, and all knowing, but they knew *nothing* of the love of God, the grace of God, the mercy of God, and the compassion of God. Neither do we.

In order to demonstrate more of himself, his attributes and his nature, God created our world, and he created us with the freedom to decide whether we will love and obey him. Because we chose not to obey, this world became like that black velvet backdrop against which the beauty of his grace, mercy, and love could be seen.

How could a merciful God ever show mercy in a world without sin? How could a comforting God ever comfort a world that never hurts? How could a gracious God ever show his grace to a world that didn't need his forgiveness and his love? We would miss all those characteristics and some of our favorite things about God.

Take comfort—evil may be present but evil doesn't prevail. All suffering, sorrow, and sin is temporary. On the other side of eternity, we will all be able to look and say, "So that is what God's grace looks like. That is what redemption looks like and what it means to be healed. So that is what our God is like. Apart from suffering, sorrow, and sin, I would have had no idea."

Reflecting God's Glory in Suffering

The most important and most neglected part of this whole problem is that everything that was made exists for the glory of God. Everything we do or say is to be done for his glory. God, who is all knowing and all powerful, created a world that he knew would rebel against him and be filled with evil. Therefore, there must be something about evil and suffering that can glorify God. Listen to this from Psalm 50:15, "Call upon me in the day of trouble; I will deliver you, and you shall glorify me."

If the most important value in life is our comfort, our well-being, our welfare, our health, our prosperity, then suffering and evil make no sense. But the supreme value in the entire universe is none of those things. It is the glory of God.

If you focus on the problem of suffering, you will never come to a satisfactory answer for why it exists. God does not call us to focus on the problem of suffering; he calls us to focus on the promise of suffering.

Suffering is temporary and can be used to strengthen our faith and can give God glory. So when bad things happen to us, instead of asking why, we need to ask, "Lord *what* do you want to do with it?"

The answer to the *what* question is that God wants you to *grow* your faith in him. The existence of evil does not eliminate the possibility of God. The existence of God guarantees the elimination of evil.[23] We can't allow suffering to weaken our faith but to strengthen it. If he decides that on our behalf the current trial is worth it, then we can trust that in some way our suffering is *for* us and that God will use it for good and for his glory.

Prayer for This Week: *Lord God, I am hurting and know that a purpose for my suffering exists. Do not waste this time. Make me more like you that I might shine against the darkness.*

Question for This Week: Thinking about your current struggle, how can you reframe it and consider how it might come with a promise?

Section Three

Wise Kings

God gave Israel the two greatest kings who ever lived—David and Solomon. One was a champion of warfare, the other a champion of wisdom. Together this father-son combo takes us far beyond the political side of royalty to the spiritual side of life. By practice and precept, they offer a glimpse into how to make wise choices in the journey of life. Read and be changed.

12

How to Say Yes to the Giant

Scriptures for This Week

- Deuteronomy 31:1-6
- 1 Samuel 17:33-37
- 1 Chronicles 16:34-36
- 2 Chronicles 32:6-8
- 2 Corinthians 4:7-12

The Greatest Yes

Richard Branson has founded more than four hundred companies under the Virgin Group and is the twelfth richest billionaire in the United Kingdom. He's created a record company, two airlines, a space tourism company, owns his own island retreat, crossed the Pacific Ocean in a balloon and the English Channel by kiteboard. When asked how he has accomplished so much in his life, he said, "If someone offers you an amazing opportunity and you are not sure you can do it, say yes. Then learn how to do it later."

One Bible story tells of someone with the spirit of Richard Branson but with even more courage. The story takes place in the Valley of Elah, where Israel and her mortal enemy, the Philistines, are camped on adjacent mountains. The heavyweight champion of the Philistines was a giant named Goliath. He challenged any man in Israel to a winner-takes-all match. But no one bit.

You may know how a teenage country boy named David volunteered to go out with a sling and a stone, killed this giant, and accomplished probably the greatest upset of any contest in the history of mankind.

This story tells of the power of a single word: *yes*. The greatest yes is the yes you say to God whenever he calls you to do anything for him. I challenge you to dream about the places in your life where you might need to say yes and unlock the potential God has for you.

Let No Man's Heart Fail

In 1 Samuel 17:3 we see the original Bigfoot. He stood nine feet, six inches tall and wore a bronze T-shirt that weighed 175 pounds and carried a spear the head of which weighed 25 pounds. Verse 24 shouldn't be too surprising: "All the men of Israel, when they saw the man, fled from him and were much afraid."

Goliath was a big man with a big mouth, and everybody was talking about him. But David enters the story talking about God. Everybody else is majoring on Goliath and David is majoring on God. Somebody shows up who cares more about the glory of God than about the girth of the giant.

David has never fought a battle, never wielded a sword, and never picked up a shield in his life. Yet his words might be the most courageous words a man spoke in the Bible: "Let no man's heart fail because of him. Your servant will go and fight with this Philistine" (1 Samuel 17:32). Because David said yes to fighting this giant, he went on to become the greatest king who ever lived, ruling the greatest kingdom that has ever existed.

We will face giants. The only way to fight those giants is to realize our story isn't about all of our giants. It's about God.

What was it that moved David to do what no one else would do? What was it that separated this courageous fellow from the cowards? The answer is that David had already experienced God's power.

I Have God's Power Behind Me

David could face the fearful present because of what he remembered from a frightening past. He recalled how with nothing more than a staff, a slingshot, and his bare hands, he had killed a bear and a lion by the power of God (1 Samuel 17:34-37).

Do you know why we fear our giants? We forget what we ought to remember and we remember what we ought to forget. We tend to remember our failures and forget our victories. We tend to remember our low points and forget our high points.

If you remember what God has done for you, you will trust what God will do for you. But if you forget what God has done for you, you will doubt what God will do for you.

Hindsight gives a lot of insight, and David said to Saul, "God has a perfect track record. He always comes through. He never fails. God can give me victory today because he gave me victory yesterday. He is no different today than he was yesterday."

I Have God's Presence Beside Me

Saul says, "Go, and the Lord be with you!" (1 Samuel 17:37). When David was ready to step out to the fight, Saul seemed to acknowledge that our only real hope is the presence of God.

Have you ever over prepared for an event? Maybe you over packed for a trip or studied far more material than the final exam required? If so, then you know the weight those extra provisions add. David knew this task was so important that he needed to travel light. He took only his staff, five smooth stones, his slingshot, and the presence of God.

Goliath had a shield and a sword, his armor and his army. All David had was God, and that is all he needed because David understood something that nobody else on either side understood: "The battle is the Lord's."

When we go into a battle, we take our best arguments, our best defense, our best game face. We go in as if it all depends on us. We want to wow with our presence and preparation. But we are just fighting for ourselves. David had another perspective. David was not fighting for God; God was fighting for David. David would not kill Goliath for God; God killed Goliath through David.

You never go to battle alone; you always go to battle with God. The way to do this isn't to focus on the opposition but to focus on God. The only thing David ever notes about Goliath is that he is an "uncircumcised Philistine." He doesn't ask any other details about Goliath. It doesn't matter, because he knows God so much better.

Do you know how many times David talks about God? Nine. His

God thoughts outnumbered his giant thoughts 9-to-1. You would face life differently if your God thoughts outnumbered your giant thoughts. You'll have the courage of David if you know every day as you get out of bed, "I have God's presence right beside me 24/7."

I Have God's Purpose Before Me

Have you ever watched a movie, and when the credits roll you wonder what the whole production was even about? When you gather with your friends afterward, everyone has a different take, and while some angles make sense, you never feel like you got it?

The plot isn't as important as the purpose. When you see *why* David was willing to risk his life, then you understand what the story is about. The purpose of the battle was not to prove that David could kill a giant, nor was it to prove that we can kill ours. It was to show us that God always wants to save.

This is not a story about a shepherd. This is a story about a Savior. This is a story about Jesus.

Look at these parallels. The giant came out to taunt Israel for forty days; Jesus fasted forty days in the wilderness before facing the devil. David kneels at a brook and picks up his stones; Jesus knelt in a garden and picked up his cross. David faced a giant named Goliath; Jesus faced the giants of sin and death. But although David lived, Jesus died. Although David later died, Jesus rose from the dead never to die again.

In the same way, our story, our battle, our struggle isn't about us. It's about Jesus's saving activity in our lives and in the world around us. If we're paying attention to his presence and remembering his power, we'll catch a glimpse of his purpose as he defeats the giants.

Giants are God's reminder that if we will take care of our faith, he will take care of the fight. If we will be concerned for his glory, he will be concerned for the victory.

You can recognize a giant if you hear things like...

- You are not worthy to be forgiven.
- You are not good enough to be used.
- You can't work this marriage out.

- You will never get control of your temper.
- You will never overcome bad habits.
- You will never be forgiven for that.
- You can never change.

Those are giants. The good news is that Jesus has already defeated them. Jesus said yes to the cross so we can say yes to Jesus. This frees us to say yes to all God has for us. Every day as you go to battle, remember that you have God's power behind you, God's presence beside you, and God's purpose before you.

Prayer for the Week: *Lord God, thank you for including me in your story. Help me turn my focus from my fights to my Father so that I might be courageous in the midst of everything that wants to conquer me.*

Question for the Week: Are you taking up challenges that don't belong to you? How can you join God in the battles that accomplish his purpose instead of yours?

13

Just the Two of Us

Scriptures for This Week

- Psalm 1
- Psalm 37:3-7
- Ruth 2:11-12
- 1 Corinthians 1:20-25
- Psalm 130:1-6

Spending Time Together

Teresa and I have been married for over forty years. I love our marriage. Sometimes, though, our schedules, work, projects, family, and other things cause us to spend more time with other people than we do with each other. She never fails to let me know when she's reached her limit by saying, "We need some time away for just the two of us." I'm pretty quick to agree and we get busy planning.

Just as a husband and wife need time together, all intimate relationships—friends, parents and their children—benefit from one-on-one time. We also need time together with our Father in heaven. We need to bathe him in loving worship while he wraps us in love. Call it whatever you want—a quiet time, a devotional life—we need that time alone with God.

God, too, desires this time with us. He wants us to spend time with him so badly that he paid in order to get it. He sent Jesus to remove every barrier, tear down every wall, bridge every gulf, unlock every door so that we could have a personal relationship with him. Teresa and I got married because we couldn't bear to live life apart. In the same way, God wants us to have unrestricted access to him, anywhere and anytime we want. God has a personal side and he wants us to know it.

Our schedules do get in the way. People have always been busy. King

David was a full-time king and ran the most powerful nation in the world, but he made spending time with God in personal and private worship a priority, and he shows us why.

Spending Time with God Causes Me to Reflect God's Character

Whenever I am alone with Teresa, just spending time with her, I am delighting in her and her alone. David tells us that delight is important: "Delight yourself in the Lord" (Psalm 37:4). *Delight* means "to take pleasure in." You cannot delight in something or someone you don't know. Everything that David is going to say in the next several verses hinges on this concept of delighting in the Lord.

We can delight in the Lord because the better our relationship is with him, the better our relationships with other people will be. Have you noticed that the more you spend time with other people, the more you become like them? You find yourself using their phrases, seeing their point of view, and adopting their idiosyncrasies. Likewise, as you spend time with God, he changes you so that you become more like him. The benefit is that the more of God you have in you, the more other people will respond favorably to you. Spending time with God gives him the chance to change you so he can use you to change other people.

Years ago Merv Griffin interviewed Charlton Heston, who played the part of Moses in *The Ten Commandments* and also starred in *Ben-Hur.* Griffin asked Heston if any of the characters he had portrayed in his religious movies had changed his spiritual outlook. Heston thought for a moment and then said, "Playing Moses changed my spiritual outlook. You can't walk barefoot down Mt. Sinai and be the same person you were when you went up." You cannot spend time with God, get close to God, know God better, and love God more and be the same person.

Spending Time with God Allows Me to Receive God's Blessings

Have you ever read any version of *Aladdin and the Magic Lamp*? All Aladdin had to do was tell the lamp what he wished for and it would give him his desires. Sometimes we treat God like that and we believe it's right because David goes on to say, "And he will give you the desires of your heart" (Psalm 37:4b). But that is not what this verse means.

There are at least three types of desires that we can have. One is a selfish desire—we want something that God may not want for us, but we go ahead and take it and then blame God for it. Other times our desires are satanic—we want what the devil wants us to want. And sometimes we have sanctified desires—when our desire is the same as God's.

Delight needs to come before desire. When you delight in the Lord, your desire will be his desire. One of the greatest questions you can daily ask God is, "Lord, what is the desire of your heart for my heart?" When you delight in the Lord, your heart will be tuned to his. Then he can give you what he wants to give you because you both desire the same thing.

When you want what God wants, God will always give you more than you want. Do you remember when God told King Solomon, "Ask for anything that you want and I'll give it to you" (1 Kings 3)? And rather than ask for riches and honor, Solomon asked for wisdom. Not only was that what God wanted him to want, but the Scripture goes on to say that God also gave him riches and honor.

God does not want what is good for you. God does not even want what is better for you. God wants what is best for you. When you spend time with God learning what he wants, you always get God's best.

Spending Time with God Moves Me to Rely on God's Power

Water boils at 212 degrees Fahrenheit at sea level, but at 211 degrees it's just hot water. One extra degree, an increase of less than one-half of 1 percent, can make the difference between a pot of warm liquid and a bubbling caldron of tremendous power. One-degree difference can create a full head of steam with enough power to move a train weighing several tons.

Without God, you will always be a degree short in whatever you are trying to accomplish. That's why the greatest thing you can ever do with your business, your goals, your ambitions, your plans, your desires, your family, your life is to commit it to the Lord and to trust him with it. Let him have it, and he will do more with it than you ever could alone.

David tells us, "Commit your way to the Lord, trust also in Him, and He will do it" (Psalm 37:5 NASB). The word *commit* means to take a burden off your shoulders and roll it onto someone else. We are to roll our way onto the Lord. We are to commit to him and to trust in him.

God is not concerned with what you can bring to pass in your life. Your efforts don't have the power that his do. The things that God wants you to do for him are the things only he can do through you. When we commit all our works and all our ways to the Lord, we are told "and he will do it." Do what? Whatever is best for you. He will bring about everything in your life that will be for his glory and for your good.

Spending Time with God Teaches Me to Rest in God's Will

Next, David tells us to take a chill pill: "Rest in the Lord and wait patiently for Him; do not fret because of him who prospers in his way, because of the man who carries out wicked schemes" (Psalm 37:7 NASB).

Three times in the first eight verses of this psalm we are told "fret not." You find that phrase in verses 1, 7, and 8. When you spend time with God, you get to know God better, trust him more, and love him best. When you know him and trust him and love him, you can rest in him. Don't get worked up with anxiety. Wait patiently for him to work things out in your life. This is one of the powerful benefits of personal, private time in worship with the Lord—it teaches you to replace worry with worship.

If you spend time with the Lord, you'll understand that you can delight in the Lord, commit your way to him, trust in him, and rest in him, even with all the competing distractions. Will you realize the importance of personal time with God, just the two of you, and spend that time with him? If you will, it will make the rest of your time more gainful, your relationships more glorifying, and your heart more like his.

Have a time every day where just you and God meet. Then watch God transform your life.

Prayer for This Week: *Lord, teach me to delight in you. Help me to set aside time to know you, worship you, and rest in your great love for me.*

Question for This Week: In every part of your life, do you want your way or are you willing to ask God to do it his way?

14

The Way to the Will

Scriptures for This Week

- James 1:2-8
- Proverbs 1:1-7
- 2 Chronicles 1:1-13
- Job 12:7-13
- Proverbs 24:3-7

Decisions, Decisions

In the 1940s, Pastor Reinhold Niebuhr wrote a prayer that affected the world:

> God, grant me the serenity to accept the things I cannot change,
> the courage to change the things I can,
> and the wisdom to know the difference.

While that is a great prayer, it needs a second verse:

> God, give me the will to change the things I can,
> the courage to make those changes,
> and the wisdom to make the right changes.

The challenge we all face every day is confronting the things we can change and making the right decisions about those changes. Life comes down to decisions. Spent money you wish you had never spent? Bought a car you wish you had never bought? Made an investment you wish you had never made? Entered into a relationship you wish you had avoided? Accepted a job you wish you had never taken?

We all can look back at life and see where we made both good decisions and poor decisions. From God's perspective, they are wise decisions or foolish decisions. Just as every parent wants to train their children to make wise decisions, God wants his children to choose wisely. And the wisest decision is to seek and use God's wisdom for every decision.

Acknowledge Its Power

What's the wisest decision you have made this month? How about yesterday? How do you know? Perhaps it produced a positive profit, an exceptional experience, a renewed relationship?

If we're going to be wise about seeking wisdom, we need to know what we're looking for. Wisdom is not always caution or cleverness. It's not even great nerve or knowledge. Someone once said wisdom is the right use of knowledge. Knowledge is knowing a tomato is a fruit. Wisdom is not putting it in a fruit salad.

We are living in a world that is swimming in knowledge but thirsty for wisdom. The amount of knowledge we have at our fingertips today has led to a phenomenon called "information overload." Human knowledge is doubling every thirteen months.

Many people know a great deal and are the greater fools for it. There is no fool greater than a knowing fool.[24] Wisdom is not just intellectual knowledge but applied, practical, hands-on living. Wisdom, like foolishness, is something you can extend to every area of your life.

In the book of 2 Chronicles, we read about a great king, Solomon, who did not ask God to make him smart enough to make a living. He asked God to make him wise enough to make a life. God gives you wisdom not so you can show others how much you know but so you can show others how to live.

Admit You Need It

Nobody understands more the importance of making wise decisions than a king, and one of the greatest kings who ever lived was Solomon. He watched his father, David, skillfully govern his people. He was beloved, educated, literate, and went on to become a prolific writer. Later, Solomon wrote a book called Proverbs, a letter to his son on how to live a life of wisdom. He advises his son: "For the LORD gives wisdom; from his mouth come knowledge and understanding" (Proverbs 2:6).

In our story in 2 Chronicles 1:1-13, Solomon is just twenty years old and has just been inaugurated. His office furniture hasn't even been moved in yet. He is still riding the high of his new position and hasn't appointed anyone to his cabinet, when one night God offers him another incredible opportunity.

God says, "Ask for whatever you want me to give you" (2 Chronicles 1:7 NIV). Solomon has just been given carte blanche by the God for whom nothing is impossible. This young king recognizes this and makes a decision that, in turn, makes him a great king.

I am pretty impressed with this young man. He was already wise enough to realize he *wasn't* wise enough. In his humility, he discerned two things. First, he did not have what it took to make the wise decisions a king must make. Second, God did.

Ask for It

To make a wise decision you first must admit that you can't. Benjamin Franklin said, "The doorstep to the temple of wisdom is the knowledge of your own ignorance."[25] Often, we make bad decisions and invite heartache because we refuse to admit that we need advice.

What would you ask God for if he said to you, "Ask for whatever you want me to give you"? An egotistical person would ask for fame. A materialistic person would ask for wealth. An ambitious person would ask for power. A bitter person would ask for revenge. But listen to how Solomon responds to God's offer: "Give me wisdom and knowledge" (2 Chronicles 1:10 NIV).

The order that Solomon put those words is important. You can have a lot of knowledge and a little wisdom, but if you have a lot of wisdom, you have a lot of knowledge.

You can do what Solomon did. You can ask for something bigger than fame, wealth, power, or revenge. Anytime you want wisdom you can ask for it. About eight hundred years after Solomon's dream came true, the brother of Jesus wrote: "If any of you lacks wisdom, let him ask God, who gives generously to all without reproach, and it will be given him" (James 1:5).

You don't have to be a king to need wisdom and you don't have to be a king to ask for it. The same deal God made with Solomon he will make with you—"wisdom and knowledge will be given you."

Our problem is we have enough knowledge to make foolish decisions, but we don't have enough wisdom to make wise decisions. God doesn't give wisdom to the people who think they know it all. He gives it only to the person who admits he doesn't know enough.

Apply It

God has a monopoly on wisdom. His wisdom is so far above our own that it makes ours look like foolishness. The apostle Paul even said, "The foolishness of God is wiser than human wisdom" (1 Corinthians 1:25 NIV). If God were capable of a stupid thought, that stupid thought would still be wiser than the wisest thought a human could ever conceive.[26]

But God doesn't give us wisdom to show what we know but to show others how to live. That brings us again to a definition of wisdom. Wisdom is seeing life through the eyes of God and living life in the will of God. And where do you find this wisdom? And how do you discern this will? The great news is God's will and wisdom is found in his word.

Getting into God's word daily is so important for making wise decisions because the choices you make end up making you. Choose to get to know God's word and it will change you, the way you think, and the things you care about. Knowing God's word helps you make the decisions that daily impact your health and happiness—how you manage your time, how you handle your money, and how you deal with temptation. When you make poor choices, you reap consequences, but wisdom teaches you the lesson before you make the mistake.

As you make your choices, tap into the One who can guide you toward wisdom. Before you make any major decision, ask what God's word says about the wisdom of this decision and what God's will would have you do.

You will either suffer the consequences of foolish decisions or enjoy the fruit and blessings of wise decisions. The wisest advice you will ever hear is this—give your life to Jesus, get under the authority of God and his word, and act on his wisdom.

Prayer for This Week: *Father, I am thankful that you lavish wisdom on me. Soften my heart to see where I'm foolish and strengthen my heart to follow your truth.*

Question for This Week: Where are you missing the wisdom of God? Ask two friends who know you well to give you some insight into situations where you might not be in tune to God's wisdom.

15

Getting into Position

Scriptures for This Week

- Proverbs 12:23-28
- Romans 12:1-3
- Proverbs 3:5-6
- Proverbs 16:1-3
- Isaiah 30:19-21

Wishing for a Do Over

When you walk in a cemetery, you'll see on the headstones someone's name, their date of birth, a hyphen representing that individual's *entire* life, and then their date of death. We tend to notice the two dates, but God looks at the hyphen. You and I are moving along our own short line. If you want your life to count today and last beyond tomorrow, you want to make sure the line you're on is pleasing to the Lord.

You can live with one of these mottos:

- "I do what I want to do." This is where most of the world lives today.
- "I do what I think I ought to do." This is where most Christ-followers live, but it's not the best motto.
- "I do what God leads me to do." This is where God wants all of us to live.

I use the first motto at times in my life, and it winds up being a major cause of conflict. When I face a big problem, I too often default to the second motto and make hasty decisions. That costs me too. But when I follow the instruction in this chapter on knowing and doing God's will, it remedies both of those problems.

You are who you are, what you are, and where you are in your life right now because of the choices you have made: your major in college, the person you married, your work, and where you live.

Every one of us would love to take back some decisions. We would all love do overs. We golfers would all like some mulligans. Others might wish for a remodel or a makeover, an upgrade or a cure. Whatever you call it, God calls it redemption, and it's the cry of every heart in our broken world.

What Is God's Will?

One of the top questions I'm asked is, "How can I know God's will?" or "What *is* God's will?" We may have a desire to know it, but we struggle to do so. God wants to guide and lead you in whatever you're stumbling through. God wants you to know his will. Ephesians 5:17 (NIV) says, "Therefore do not be foolish, but understand what the Lord's will is."

In the Bible God's will is spoken of in three basic ways: God's providential will, his practical will, and his personal will.

God's providential will consists of those things that God is determined to make happen that nobody can stop. Jesus's virgin birth, his death on the cross, and his second coming are all a part of the providential will of God.

God's practical will is his moral will—what he considers right and wrong for us to do. I'd say 95 percent of the will of God for our behavior has been revealed in the commandments in the Bible.

The Bible also speaks of *God's personal will.* Do I take that job? Do I go to this college? Do I date this person? Should I invest my money or make this purchase? Being serious about God means we seek to know his will in every area, including these daily decisions.

As a general rule God does not speak audibly, but I do believe that God still speaks. He speaks clearly enough that we can know his will in almost any situation. But first we must get into position to let ourselves be guided in order to follow his will. The real problem is not in finding God's will. The real problem is doing it.

Trusting God as Our Mentor

Proverbs 3:5-6 are among the most quoted verses in the Bible. We love the comfort they provide, but following their instruction is not so appealing.

The first step in knowing God's will begins with complete trust in God: "Trust in the LORD with all your heart" (Proverbs 3:5). If you don't have a relationship with God through Jesus, you cannot know God's will for your life. That's a hard truth, but take comfort because he's going to be your faithful partner in everything you do after that.

The word *trust* means to "lie down upon" or to "stretch out on." You probably don't question stretching out on your bed at night. Nobody sleeps with one foot on the floor. You just trust the bed to hold you. That is the first key to beginning to understand God's will for your life. You've got to put your complete trust in him.

God wants to be our mentor, but a mentor is effective only if you trust him. My mentor was Adrian Rogers. The first time I ever went to visit Dr. Rogers I made up my mind beforehand that whatever he told me to do I was going to do it. I trusted him and entered his office believing that what he would tell me to do would be best for me. He told me to start a file of great truths, illustrations, quotes, and stories. Thanks to him, I have an extensive system that has made me a better preacher.

I decided to act on Dr. Rogers's will before I knew it, and we must decide to do the same with God. God won't offer you his will as just one of the options for you to choose from. He will not show you his will until you say, "All systems go!"

Following God as Our Model

Proverbs goes on to say "and do not lean on your own understanding" (3:5b). When you make decisions, do you lean on your own ideas or on the insight of others? It's not possible to lean on yourself. You cannot manage your life on your own, make your own decisions, and get it right. Why? Because you don't know the future. But God is already *in* the future and we can lean on him.

Proverbs continues, "In all your ways acknowledge him" (3:6a). Today, if you acknowledge something, it means you pay lip service to it or you nod, wink, or smile politely. But here, *acknowledge* means to "focus on something and follow it." We could read this verse as, "In all your actions focus on God and follow him." Be laser-focused and chase down his practical will.

I went to college with my life planned out. Major in accounting. Go to law school. Get a high-paying corporate job. Be financially independent by forty. Retire and become the head football coach at the University of Georgia.

For three summers I couldn't land a job in either law or accounting. But different churches kept asking me to be a summer student minister and so I did. During those summers God grew my heart with joy for the ministry that led me to where I am today. I had no clue that he would send me to seminary rather than law school, but by taking those summer ministry opportunities, God was getting me ready to know his unknown will.

Put yourself in a position to be able to hear God's voice. When you are living out God's practical or moral will, he will show you his personal will.

Obeying God as Our Master

Up to this point in the passage it has all been about what we are to do. Now notice God's part: "And he will make straight your paths" (Proverbs 3:6b). This means that he directs your path and shows you his personal will for your life. By trusting him as your mentor and following him as your guide, you can be confident he'll guide you even when you feel like you're in the dark. Listen to this tremendous verse from Isaiah.

> "I will lead the blind by ways they have not known,
> along unfamiliar paths I will guide them;
> I will turn the darkness into light before them
> and make the rough places smooth.
> These are the things I will do;
> I will not forsake them."
>
> (Isaiah 42:16 NIV)

When you agree to follow God's guidance no matter what—even if it means changing your major, leaving your boyfriend, refusing a higher paying job, or having some hard conversations—then he will fill in the details of what to do. God's will is neither a mystery nor mystical.

When you put God in his rightful place, he will put you in the right place. That doesn't mean that life will always be easy or tough times won't come. It does mean that you will always be where God can protect you and provide for you as you walk in the paths he directs.

Prayer for This Week: *Almighty God, you know the way I should live, and you are present in every one of my choices. Give me a complete trust in you so that I can see the path you are leading me down.*

Question for This Week: Write out a statement that expresses what you believe is God's personal will for you in one of your current decisions. Spend some time determining if it conflicts in any way with God's providential or practical will.

16

Difference Maker

Scriptures for This Week

- Ecclesiastes 3:10-14
- 2 Timothy 4:1-5
- Colossians 3:22-25
- Ecclesiastes 12:13-14
- Romans 15:13

Finding What I'm Looking For

In a small unscientific survey I conducted, I found that one of the biggest questions on people's minds is, "If God is real, what difference does he make?" At the heart of this question is the issue of meaning, "What meaning can God give to my life?"

In a previous chapter, we met Solomon near the beginning of his reign as king of Israel. Solomon wrote some great books in our Bibles: Proverbs, the Song of Songs, and Ecclesiastes. Portrayed as the wisest man who ever lived, he asked this same question, "What is the point of life without God?" For a time in his life, he attempted to live life without God. But at the end of his life, Solomon wrote about his regrets.

The key to Ecclesiastes is written right in its beginning. Meaninglessness. This word shows up *thirty-three* times in this one book. In effect, Solomon is saying, "Life without God is a big fat zero. Nothing times nothing equals nothing." What is the difference God makes? Only God can make the matter of life matter.

God Gives Meaning to Life

A recent survey conducted by scientists from Johns Hopkins University asked almost eight thousand students at forty-eight colleges what they considered most important about their life. Three-fourths said their primary goal was "finding a purpose and meaning."[27] Solomon's address in Ecclesiastes sings the same tune: "If all there is to life is life, then life means nothing."

What would life mean without God? If our lives are doomed to end in death, then not only does life not matter, it doesn't matter how we live. The scientist working in a lab trying to advance human knowledge, the doctor trying to find the cure for cancer to alleviate pain and suffering, the diplomat working overtime to promote peace in the world, and the soldier sacrificing to protect his country and keep people free participate, Solomon says, in work that means nothing without God.

Take a look at what gives you meaning. Add up all your title deeds, stocks and bonds, all the times you get your name in a newspaper, all your money, promotions, and achievements. Without God, it is one big zero. Solomon says that

> Nobody remembers what happened yesterday.
> And the things that will happen tomorrow?
> Nobody'll remember them either.
> Don't count on being remembered.
>
> (Ecclesiastes 1:11 MSG)

Your life is inconsequential. Life without God for everyone on this planet is like my daily exercise routine—spinning wheels, running in circles, climbing ladders but going nowhere.

Only God gives meaning to life. And people need to hear about this God so they can know him and make an eternal decision that will change their eternal destiny.

God Gives Morality Its Foundation

One of my favorite authors is my friend Ravi Zacharias. Several years ago he spoke at the University of Nottingham, England, and a rather exasperated student in the audience was attacking God over the whole idea of evil and suffering.

It is a humorous conversation, because as C.S. Lewis once said, "There is nothing so self-defeating as a question that is not fully understood by the one who is asking it." This student asked Ravi, "How can there be a God with all the evil and suffering that exists in the world?" Here's how their conversation went from there:

> *Ravi Zacharias:* "When you say there is such a thing as evil, are you not assuming there is such a thing as good?"
>
> *Student:* "Of course."
>
> *RZ:* "When you assume there is such a thing as good, are you not also assuming there is such a thing as a moral law on the basis of which to distinguish between good and evil?"
>
> *Student:* (Hesitating) "I suppose so."
>
> *RZ:* "If then there is a moral law, you must posit a moral law-giver, but that is who you are trying to disprove and not prove. If there is no moral lawgiver, there is no moral law. If there is no moral law, there is no good. If there is no good, there is no evil, so I am not sure what your question is!"
>
> *Student:* "Neither am I, can you please tell me what I should be asking you?"[28]

You don't need God in order to try to live according to what you think is right or wrong, good or evil. But no rational basis for good or evil can exist without God. Without God, right and wrong become a matter of emotions (you do what you feel is right or wrong), intellect (you do what you think is right or wrong), or opinion (you do what others you respect say is right or wrong). No ultimate, final objective right and wrong can exist apart from God.

Richard Taylor, an atheist ethicist, says, "To say that something is wrong because…it is forbidden by God, is perfectly understandable to anyone who believes in a law-giving God. But to say that something is wrong or forbid it…even though no God exists, is not understandable."[29]

If life has no meaning, then there isn't a right that is always right and a wrong that is always wrong. There can be no morality in life. But there *is* an evil to shun and a good to embrace. There *is* a hell to lose and a heaven to gain.

God Gives a Mandate for Justice

Solomon closes Ecclesiastes by saying,

> For God will bring every deed into judgment,
> including every hidden thing,
> whether it is good or evil.
> (12:14 NIV)

Without God there is no justice for evil. Without God, Adolf Hitler, Mao Ze-dong, and Joseph Stalin get away with killing over 150 million people combined. Jack the Ripper gets away with one of the most famous unsolved crimes ever. Without God, every unsolved murder remains not just unsolved but unpunished.

If God does not exist, then it doesn't matter whether you are good or bad. It doesn't matter if you are honest or you lie, whether you give or you take, whether you defend the life of the unborn or you take the life of the unborn. If no one rewards you for good or punishes you for evil, then what does it matter?

Richard Wurmbrand, a Christian who was tortured in communist prisons, observed,

> The cruelty of those who do not believe in God is hard to believe. When man has no faith in the reward of good or the punishment of evil, there is no reason to be human. There is no restraint from the depths of evil, which is in man. My communist torturers often said, "There is no God, no hereafter, no punishment for evil. We can do what we wish."[30]

When you don't believe in God, you will ignore the judgment of God. When you ignore the judgment of God, you will disregard the fear of God. Only God gives a mandate for justice.

God Gives a Message of Hope

The wisest man who ever lived, who did his best to live life without God, concluded,

> Now all has been heard;
> here is the conclusion of the matter:

Fear God and keep his commandments,
for this is the duty of all mankind.
(Ecclesiastes 12:13 NIV)

Only God can make the matter of life matter.

If God came to earth in Jesus, who died on the cross that he might deliver us from evil and came back from the dead that he might deliver us from death, then hope springs eternal, and he is the difference maker.

You might believe in God, but does he make a difference in your life? Are you only moderately interested in him? That is not belief. If God does exist, then our ultimate concern ought to be how to know that God, obey that God, worship that God, and love that God supremely. An equal concern should be how many others we can get to know, love, worship, serve, and obey that God as well.

When Anne Sullivan was twenty years old, she came to Tuscumbia, Alabama, to tutor a girl named Helen Keller, who was blind, deaf, and mute. With tremendous patience and perseverance, she was able to communicate with Helen through the use of her hands. She poured water over Helen's hands and then with her finger spelled *water* in Helen's palm. All of a sudden, the miracle of communication was planted in Helen Keller's heart.

When she later came to understand the spelling and the concept of G-O-D, Helen Keller said to her teacher, "I always knew he was there, I just didn't know his name." Billions of Helen Kellers in the world know he is there, but they need to hear his name, which is above every name.

There is a God who is there. His name is Jesus. He is the ultimate difference maker, both in this world and in your life. When you come to know him, what a difference he will make.

Prayer for This Week: *Heavenly Father, thank you for the difference you make in our lives. Give me a greater faith that I might have a greater hope that might inspire faith in others.*

Question for This Week: If an atheist friend were to ask you, "If God is real, what difference does it make?" how would you answer? Write out a response that reflects the difference God has made for you.

Section Four

Gone But Not Forgotten

Some of the greatest bearers of truth in history were God's prophets. In our day, when courage and conviction are lacking, these ancient prophetic messages are as fresh as daisies and still pulsate with practical principles and divine power. Read and be changed.

17

Seeing Clearly

Scriptures for This Week

- Exodus 34:4-7
- Isaiah 6:1-13
- 1 Peter 1:13-16
- 1 Corinthians 13:8-12
- Romans 10:9-15

A Blurry Picture

About half of Americans can't see clearly. We are nearsighted or far-sighted and we deal with astigmatism and cataracts. When we wake up, we struggle to make out the time. When we want to read on our tablets, we fumble for our glasses. There is pain involved in having imperfect vision.

Often there is pain in our faith journeys because we can't see. It's not because we haven't memorized enough Bible verses, or can't grasp deep concepts, or church doctrines are too complicated for us. It's because we don't see God clearly.

The single-most important concept of your life and mine is how we see God. Two sociologists from Baylor University surveyed almost four thousand adults and discovered that nine out of ten Americans believe in God. But the way they picture God determines their attitudes on everything, including economics, justice, morality, war, natural disasters, science, politics, and love.

How do you view God? Culture offers many options:

- the old man who's out to get us
- the buddy who hangs with us while we live our own lives
- the bellhop who gives us everything we need

Each of these is a functional image of God. Though we say we believe in a fuller picture of God, these are the default ways we relate to him in our daily lives. What is your picture of God? Do you draw a picture of him that you think is true, or do you allow him to show you what he's like?

A Brighter Picture

How do you react when someone misunderstands you? What goes through your heart when someone assumes your motives are skewed, your intentions are selfish, or your purpose is something other than what you know it to be? Do you feel disrespected and distanced?

Do we slight God in the same way with our incorrect pictures of him? And if so, what should our concept of God be?

The God who created the universe wants to have a personal, eternal relationship with you. Many people don't have a relationship with God because the God they claim to have a relationship with is not God, just a functional image. When our relationship is not based on reality, our rapport is ruptured.

If your view of God is wrong, then your view of life is wrong. Your view of success is wrong. Your view of what is important is wrong. Even your view of yourself is wrong. We must see God the way God sees himself because having a real relationship with the real God is paramount. It does no good to get up close and personal with a God who is not real.

We are going to look into an incident that took place in the life of a man named Isaiah over twenty-five hundred years ago. Isaiah gives us a better picture of God.

I See God the Way He Really Is

Where were you when the space shuttle exploded? When JFK was shot? When the twin towers fell? We are capable of mentally stamping such "big shift" experiences with detailed memories. We can retell the elements of important events because the event changed the way we went forward in life.

Isaiah 6:1 begins by telling us the exact year that this incident took place in his life; it was the year that King Uzziah died. Why would Isaiah remember that detail? Because in that moment, his vision changed. He saw something that changed everything.

Isaiah saw the Lord sitting upon a throne. For the first time in history, he saw God in a way no one had ever seen him. He saw the Creator of the universe, the King of all kings and the Lord of all lords, sitting on an eternal throne, "high and lifted up; and the train of his robe filled the temple." But that's not all.

> Above him stood the seraphim. Each had six wings: with two he covered his face, and with two he covered his feet, and with two he flew. And one called to another and said:
>
> "Holy, holy, holy is the LORD of hosts;
> the whole earth is full of his glory!"
>
> (Isaiah 6:2-3)

That is the single most important picture of God you will find in all of the Old Testament. God is not some man upstairs, not a good ol' boy god, not a homeboy god. This God is holy.

More often than any other attribute—mercy, grace, love, compassion, power, or knowledge—God is described throughout Scripture as *holy*. This is his chief attribute, separate from everything else. We cannot treat him like another human being, speak to him like a servant, and approach him with apathy. He cannot be compared with anyone else or anything else, because no one and nothing else is like him.

His glory doesn't fill just the temple, "the whole earth is full of his glory!" This is not a God who can fit in your box or mine. If you do not see God as holy, you have the wrong view of God. But how do you know when you have seen God the way God is?

I See Me the Way I Really Am

In Isaiah 6:4-5 we get to see Isaiah's next vision. He looked at God in all his holiness and noticed his own sinfulness. When you see the real God, you see the real you. You will never see yourself for what you are until you see God for who he is.

I visited an eighty-three-year-old man named John on his farm recently. As I told him about God, he told me about himself. I learned all the stories of his decent, noble, and righteous ways of living. At the end of our conversation, this man declared, "If my righteousness is not good enough for God, then he will just have to send me to hell." I could not help but look at him and say with a broken heart, "But John, it isn't and so you will send yourself."

Most of us live in two extremes. We are either full of God and empty of ourselves or we are full of ourselves and empty of God. When Isaiah saw who he was, he didn't like the picture. In verse 5 he mourned, "Woe is me! For I am lost; for I am a man of unclean lips."

When Isaiah saw God for who he was and then saw himself for who he was, he said, "All of my so-called goodness, integrity, and decency is nothing compared to God's holiness." When God is high and lifted up, we will be low and taken down.

When we get honest in our relationship to God, he gets merciful in his relationship to us. If we keep reading, we see that God deals with Isaiah's unclean lips, and in that life-shifting experience, Isaiah is relieved of his guilt and sin. Isaiah is cleansed and forgiven.

Want to have a relationship with this God? Then get real. See him for who he is and see yourself for who you are.

I See the World the Way It Really Is

Have you ever been so sold on a product that you couldn't wait to share it with your friends? When you've found something that makes you feel balanced, increases your rest, resolves anxiety, or saves you money, you want to proclaim it. When you're cured of a disease, you want to help someone find a fix for theirs.

This is what happens next in Isaiah 6:8-13. Right after his new vision of God, and a freeing experience of cleansing, Isaiah hears a conversation the triune God is having with himself. He hears God ask, "Whom shall I send, and who will go for us?"

I can picture Isaiah here. This man is filled to the brim and pouring over with gratitude and hope and praise. So he waves his hand wildly and shouts, "Here I am! Let me do it! People gotta know about this! People need this kind of relationship with this kind of a King, and I must go and tell them!"

This is true. Everyone needs this relationship. With his corrected vision, Isaiah could see the true picture of the people around him, and everyone had the same need. We can see it too, and when you perceive it, you'll have to pursue it even if other people won't.

God warned Isaiah about the people's imperfect vision. Their hearts would be dull, their ears heavy, and their eyes blind to the healing God offered. And no matter how much waste and destruction and desolation their distance from God caused them, they would not see God the way Isaiah did. But Isaiah kept using his new vision.

If you want to know if you're hitting on all cylinders in your relationship with God, this is how you know. Once you see God for who he is and experience the freedom he offers, you'll want to surrender everything you are to everything he is. The measure of the depth of your relationship to God is the extent of your surrender.

The single most important thing about you is not how much money you make, not what you look like, not how popular you are, or how prosperous you are. What matters in the end for every one of us is that we have a real relationship with a real God

Prayer for This Week: *Father, give me the eyes to see you for who you are, the courage to let you change me, and the excitement to tell others about the freedom they can find in you.*

Question for This Week: What are the details of your own image of God and where is your picture of God askew from his?

18

Breaking the Prayer Barrier

Scriptures for This Week

- Philippians 4:4-7
- 1 Thessalonians 5:16-18
- Jeremiah 33:1-3
- Romans 8:26-27
- Matthew 6:5-13

Breaking Through

In the fascinating world of aviation, the sound barrier was once considered unbreakable. For decades, pilots died trying to break through at Mach 1. You see, when a plane approaches the speed of sound, shock waves increase, causing pilots to lose control. There is increased air pressure and wave drag, which creates a recipe for a catastrophic nosedive.

On October 14, 1947, a B-29 took off from the California desert. Attached to the belly of the bomber was the Bell X-1 experimental plane piloted by Chuck Yeager. At twenty-five thousand feet, the X-1 dropped from the B-29, fired its own engines, and ascended to forty thousand feet. As the plane accelerated, it shook violently. At Mach .965, the speed indicator went haywire. Yeager's vision blurred and his stomach turned. Just as he thought he was about to die, a loud sonic boom was followed by a beautiful eerie silence. The unbreakable barrier had been broken and Yeager celebrated with the world.[31]

In the spiritual world there is—at some point for all of us—another barrier that seems to be unbreakable. I call it the "prayer barrier." I've never been satisfied with my prayer life. It's hard for me. If you are like me, you would like to know how to consistently and constantly break the prayer barrier, because if what we believe is true, then the greatest source of untapped power in your life, my life, and in the entire church is wrapped up in prayer.

Praying Through

Jeremiah was a prophet to the nation of Judah, a nation that formed following the death of King Solomon. Due to a revolt, Solomon's Israel split in two. The northern portion remained Israel and the southern became Judah. Because they had rebelled against God, Israel had been taken into captivity by the Assyrians and now Judah was about to fall to the Babylonians.

Despair is everywhere as we pick up our story and find the prophet Jeremiah in prison. His nation didn't believe his warnings. They no longer feared God, and in order to silence Jeremiah's voice, they shut him up. Now they were about to suffer the consequences of their disobedience. At this point, God says to Jeremiah, "Call to me and I will answer you, and will tell you great and hidden things that you have not known" (Jeremiah 33:3).

"Call to me and I will answer you." What if you had a special phone that was connected to God? Every time you picked up this phone, God would answer right away, you could talk as long as you wanted, and the call would be free. That phone would be priceless. You would take it everywhere and talk on it all the time.

God's telling us that when we pray, he is closer than a phone call. If despair is everywhere for you right now, if you feel locked up and silenced, you're sitting behind a barrier. If you want to break it, God tells you how to do it. He says, "Call to me." This is a command in the Hebrew language. God is not asking us to pray; he is demanding that we pray. To interpret tragedy, to know his will, to be more like Jesus, and to understand who we're to be, we must pray to break the barrier.

Talking to a God Who Hears Prayer

Jeremiah 33:3 begins with, "Call to me and I will answer you..." This tells us that there are two parts to prayer—our part is to call and God's part is to answer. God would never ask us to call to him if he were not going to listen to us.

You may remember that about thirty years ago we launched the spacecraft *Voyager 2*. The purpose of that flight was to travel to the planet Neptune to take pictures and send them back to planet Earth. It took *Voyager 2* ten years to travel 4.4 billion miles. Consider that it took only four hours and six minutes for signals traveling at the speed of light to make it to us from Neptune. It took thirty-eight giant radio antennas on four continents to catch the data and to see the pictures from that spacecraft, but we received its weak signal.

Prayer has no lag time. It's like this app on my phone that allows me to dictate messages. It is voice activated. When I speak, it records. When I stop, it stops. Your prayers are voice activated too. Every time you pray—God hears. What's more, when you pray you talk *to God*, not his assistant, an angel, or someone who's deceased. You're connected, immediately in his presence. God instantaneously hears us because he's not at the other end of the universe. He's truly "God with us." Talk to God. He hears prayer.

Trusting a God Who Heeds Prayer

Maybe your big question is, "Does God always answer prayer?" The answer is yes. The only prayer that God doesn't answer is the prayer that is never prayed. Baptist evangelist F.B. Meyer once wrote, "The great tragedy of life is not unanswered prayer: it is unoffered prayer."

Maybe the real question on your mind is, "*How* does God answer prayer?"

Sometimes God's answer is direct. This is God's "Yes." He'll often say it pretty quickly. When we scouted the property for our current church facility, I prayed that the land would be given to us. I prayed for only two days, and on the second day the owners called me and told me they were doing just that. We all wish every prayer was answered just like that—that we get what we want when we want it. But God doesn't always work that way.

Sometimes God's answer is delayed. This is God's "Yes, but not now." Answer delays are not necessarily denials. God not only wants to give us what is best for us, but he wants to give it *when* it is best for us. I remember asking my dad when I was about nine years old for a shotgun, but he wouldn't give it to me. When I was eleven, he gave me a BB gun, and from there I graduated to a rifle. Several years later, when I was proven trustworthy, he finally let me shoot his shotgun. God will never make the mistake of giving you too much or giving it to you too soon.

Sometimes God's answer is to deny our request. This is God's "No." Garth Brooks may call God's "No" unanswered prayer, but "No" is God's answer sometimes. God won't give us everything we want. If he did, we'd get a lot of the wrong things for the wrong reason at the wrong time. We should trust him and thank him for the no's. If God had answered some of my prayers with a yes, I probably never would have traveled the world and seen what I have seen. I wouldn't be a pastor or an author, and I would have missed out on marrying the greatest wife in the world.

Sometimes God's answer is different. This is God's "Sort of." When I was pastoring in Mississippi, I desperately wanted to pastor a church in Atlanta. I thought I would get a good shot at it because I once served in that church, but my phone stayed silent. They never even talked to me. Just months later, a far better opportunity opened and allowed me to pastor a wonderful church for eighteen years. It looked like a no, but it was just a different yes.

God answers every prayer. He may not always answer it when we want him to or the way we want him to, but he always answers.

Thanking a God Who Honors Prayer

The second half of Jeremiah 33:3 says, "I will tell you great and hidden things that you have not known." Prayer is not meant to be a one-way conversation like a monologue. It is meant to be a dialogue. When we pray, God will show us things that are inaccessible to human intelligence or even human investigation.

God uses prayer to show us things and tell us things we cannot learn any other way, things we never would have guessed, but he has to have our ear. This means that sometimes we need to just listen and sometimes we need to listen for a long time. We may never know when God will speak, what he will say, or when he will say it. That's why prayer needs to be a regular practice. It makes prayer like a time capsule.

My godly grandmother died six years before I was born. As she raised my mother, she would get up every morning and knead dough for breakfast biscuits. As she got those biscuits ready for the oven, she would pray out loud, and many times she said, "God, would you so favor me and so favor my family that you would call somebody out of my family to be a preacher of the gospel?"

The week before I was to graduate from college and go to law school, God called me into the ministry. When I called my mother to tell her that, she wept and told me this whole story about Grandma's time-capsule prayer. You see, in 1946 God heard my grandmother's prayer, but twenty-eight years later in a dorm room at Stetson University, God heeded her prayer. Every Sunday and throughout the week as I shepherd and teach, God continues to honor my grandmother's prayer. I am where I am, what I am, and who I am today because my grandmother broke the prayer barrier. And you can too.

Prayer for This Week: *Father, I thank you for this moment in your presence when I am assured you are listening. Teach me to pray in such a way that I will now hear, heed, and honor you.*

Question for This Week: What did God say to you when you prayed this week?

19

The Devil Is in the Details

Scriptures for This Week

- Romans 8:5-9
- Ezekiel 28:11-19
- Luke 8:9-15
- 1 Peter 5:8-9
- Matthew 5:33-37

Devil May Care

We have no trouble believing in villains. The fictitious ones fascinate us and we delight in their black masks and evil schemes. The factual ones, like Adolf Hitler or Osama bin Laden, terrify us. One other real villain goes by all sorts of names, such as the evil one, the adversary, the prince of darkness, the father of lies, Lucifer, and Satan, but he has one name that he answers to in every language—diabolos, el diablo, the devil.

I realize that in the twenty-first century many people will roll their eyes in utter disbelief at this. You might assume I'm talking about a figure with horns on his head who dons a red suit and carries a pitchfork, trying to stick you every chance he gets. If you don't believe in a real being called the devil, you are not alone. Most adults in the US don't.[32]

Yet some do believe in the devil. The Bible makes it plain that the devil is just as real as you and I. So why did God make the devil? He didn't. God created a holy angel whose original name was Lucifer, which means "Star of the Morning." Lucifer was once the top dog. He was one of a group of angels that God created to worship him and to carry out his purposes. God gave this angel the power of choice, just like he gives human beings. And just like humans, Lucifer chose to rebel.

Making the Devil Do It

The story of the devil is found in Ezekiel 28:11-19. You can refer to it as I walk you through this event. When you first begin reading, you think it's about a man called "the king of Tyre," but as this king is described further, it doesn't take long to realize that he is an illustration of a higher being and a greater power.

This higher being was "in Eden" the Garden of God and was "a model of perfection, full of wisdom and perfect in beauty." This can't be referring to Adam and Eve, and the only other party in the Garden of Eden was Satan himself. When Ezekiel says he was on "the holy mountain of God," this refers to a time when he was in God's presence in God's throne room.

Then something terrible happened. This angelic being decided to execute a coup d'état. He was not satisfied with being the highest of the angels. He wanted to be the highest of the *Highest*. So he led a revolt against God himself, and in that war, this angelic being fell. The prophet Isaiah described it this way:

> "How you have fallen from heaven,
> O star of the morning, son of the dawn!
> You have been cut down to the earth,
> You who have weakened the nations!"
>
> (Isaiah 14:12 NASB)

Lucifer, the son of the morning, became Satan, the father of the night. Satan fell and other angels, now known as demons, followed him. So we learn of two spiritual beings in the Bible, one good and one evil, but they are not equal opposites. God can do anything, knows everything, and is everywhere. The devil is *none* of the above, but he does have great power and worldwide influence. He is your number one enemy and he wants to destroy you mentally, emotionally, spiritually, and even physically if you will allow him to do so.

The Devil to Pay

You can ask any army general or head coach, "What is the greatest key to victory?" and both of them will tell you that the key is to know your opponent.

We know our opponents well, don't we? We know thieves are more likely to strike at night, so we lock our windows and install motion-sensor lights. We know that germs are the culprits of disease, and if we don't kill them first, they'll kill us. We know not to leave our purses in grocery carts, meet strangers in private places, or accept rides from strangers. We are well versed in the ways and means of our everyday potential villains, and we live in defensive ways to protect ourselves.

How much more should we know an opponent who is out to ruin our lives, victimize our kids, and keep us away from God? Be assured that this is Satan's agenda, one he achieves by making sin look attractive. As the world's greatest salesman, he wants you to think he's leading you to safe places that will bring you happiness. We need to beware.

I was fascinated to find out how an Eskimo kills a wolf. He coats his knife blade with blood and lets it freeze. Then he adds another coat of blood and then another coat until that blade is hidden deep within a thick coat of frozen blood. Then he buries the knife—blade up—in that hard frozen ground. The wolf smells this blood, goes over to this knife, and begins to lick it. He licks it more and more and harder and harder until the blade is exposed, but he just keeps on licking and because of the cold he never notices the pain of the blade. He never notices that he is tasting his own blood until he bleeds to death swallowing his own life.

That is the way the devil works on us. He does everything he can to make sin attractive, making us think all the time that what we are doing is bringing us pleasure, when all we are doing is bringing ourselves pain and hurt and heartache and even death.

The Devil's Workshop

The devil tries to infiltrate your life in four specific ways. If you are practicing any of these four things, you are doing what the devil wants you to do.

First, Satan tempts you to rebel against authority. The first sin ever committed was Satan's rebellion in heaven against God. The second sin was Adam and Eve's rebellion in the Garden of Eden. The first sin we commit as children is rebellion against our parents. When the devil wanted to be the number one authority and couldn't, he rebelled against all authority, and ever since Adam and Eve's rebellion, we too find it difficult to get under authority. You are never more like the devil than when you rebel against the authority over you.

Second, he tempts you to repudiate truth. The first lie that was ever told was told by the devil. He questioned whether God had told Adam and Eve they could not eat of a certain tree, and then he told them that they wouldn't die even though God had said they would. John 8:44 tells us that whenever the devil speaks a lie, "he speaks out of his own character, for he is a liar and the father of lies." If you didn't know that verse, then it might be because you're falling right into his hands. He will do everything he can to keep you from reading, hearing, and obeying the word of God. It makes it easier to repudiate truth when you're not always in it.

Third, he tempts you to reject God's forgiveness. One of Satan's greatest tools, in both the believer and the unbeliever, is guilt. He will try to make you believe that your sins are too great to forgive or that they're not great enough to need forgiveness. He will even try to make you feel guilty over sins that have already been forgiven, which will feel a lot like he's kicking you in the shins and then blaming you for limping.

Finally, Satan tempts you to refuse to forgive. Ephesians 4:26-27 (NASB) says, "Be angry, and yet do not sin; do not let the sun go down on your anger, and do not give the devil an opportunity." The devil does not want you to be forgiven and he does not want you to be forgiving.

If any of these things I have just mentioned are true about you, then you can mark this down—the devil is alive and well in your life whether you want to admit it or not.

Shame the Devil

The devil is shrewd and crafty, so how can we oppose him?

Receive the defeater. Even though the devil is not all powerful, he is still more powerful than you. Even the finest follower of Christ cannot defeat the devil in his or her own power. Jesus is the only one more powerful, and if you don't have him on your team, you have no shot at defeating the devil. The first step to victory is receiving the only one who has already fought him and won. Jesus won over the devil when he defeated death itself.

Resist the devil. When you say no to the devil and mean it, it is just like kryptonite to Superman. Contrary to the popular saying, the devil can't make you do anything.

Resign the decision. James 4:7 (NASB) says, "Submit therefore to God. Resist the devil and he will flee from you." Satan is always going to try to get you to surrender some area of your life to him. When you do, he'll take that area and use it as a stronghold to beat you down. Concede the decision to God; the devil cannot take from you what you have already surrendered to God.

The more often you resist Satan the weaker his temptations will become and the easier victory is obtained. A villain is roaming out there. The devil is in the details, but your God is greater.

Prayer for This Week: *God, my defender, guide, and refuge, reveal to me the ways that I am falling into the devil's plan and falling farther away from yours. Give me your strength to defeat his advances in all that I do today.*

Question for This Week: In which of the four ways is the devil trying to infiltrate your life? How can you resist him and surrender that weakness to God?

20

A Line in the Sand

Scriptures for This Week

- Psalm 20
- Daniel 1:1-21
- Proverbs 3:5-6
- Hebrews 3:12-14
- John 5:16-18

Resist the Giant Obstacle

At the end of my junior year in college, I was as discouraged as I had ever been. I was going to be $2000 short of being able to pay tuition for the coming year and I was out of options. I didn't have a rich uncle, a Hilton-sized trust fund, and my dad made only $100 a week. I had taken out all the student loans that were available and had no way to make that amount of money with a summer job. I thought I would have to quit school and go to work before my senior year.

Few feelings are worse than being convinced you are out of options. People are in prison today because they believed this, so they embezzled from their employer or they robbed a convenience store or worse. When we feel like we're out of options, we give up on marriages, friends, and even on life itself. We need to learn a valuable lesson before things get desperate for us and that is that with God, there are always options.

In my case, my accounting professor called me in before summer vacation and told me he had awarded me the Winn-Dixie scholarship, which would meet my financial need almost to the dollar. Yes, with God there are *always* options.

Reset a Genuine Loyalty

One of the promises God made to the nation of Israel was to bless them if they obeyed him and punish them if they rebelled. A host of prophets warned the rebellious nation, but they didn't repent. Thus, Jerusalem was conquered by the pagan nation of Babylon, which was ruled by a famous king named Nebuchadnezzar.

The Babylonians practiced some ruthless intimidation tactics. From taking away a country's idols, thus making them feel powerless, to brainwashing the best and the brightest of the conquered nation's young men, these warriors were clever and calculated. It could make you feel helpless and hopeless, as if you were out of options.

One young man didn't just look for options; he created them. Daniel was one of the young Hebrew men who was given a full scholarship to the University of Babylon. He was given a Babylonian name and Babylonian clothes. He learned the language, read the books, and was offered the buffets. The goal was to make him think, act, and live like a Babylonian.

But Daniel did something unexpected, something we all must do if we are going to follow God and not the world. He drew a line in the sand. When Daniel was asked to eat the king's food and drink the king's wine, a trip wire was crossed that alerted Daniel to a line he should not cross.

> But Daniel resolved that he would not defile himself with the king's food, or with the wine that he drank. Therefore he asked the chief of the eunuchs to allow him not to defile himself (Daniel 1:8).

In that Middle Eastern culture when you sat down to eat a meal, particularly with a ruler or a king, it was a sign of a covenant commitment. You were pledging loyalty to the king, to submit to and share his life. But the only one Daniel was going to submit to was God, and he wanted to make that clear. Never cross a line that God has drawn. The world will tempt you, but when you stay on the God side, you will stay on the good side. To do that, follow Daniel's footsteps.

Resolve to Guard Your Boundaries

A lot was at stake. Though Daniel was being trained for a position of honor and power, being promised all the benefits of that finer life, he was still a slave. All he had to do was just go along with the regimen, take what he was given, keep his mouth shut and his head down.

Why did Daniel choose not to go along? Nobody back home would ever know about it. He was one of probably hundreds of Jewish teens there and everybody else was going to eat the king's food. I don't know what the menu was, but it would be hard for me to turn down steak, twice-baked potato, and some cabernet. But this was not a matter of diet but of dedication. One of the most beloved college basketball coaches, John Wooden, once said, "There is a choice you have to make in everything you do. You must always keep in mind the choice you make makes you."

Keep in mind that although Daniel is a young man (Daniel 1:4), his life up until now had prepared him for this moment. He likely grew up in a home where he was taught to love God with all of his heart, soul, mind, and strength. You could change Daniel's home, his name, or his knowledge, but you couldn't change his heart, his nature, or his wisdom. A God-shaped boundary surrounded Daniel's life.

Daniel had already drawn this line in his life before he got to this point. If you wait until you are tempted to determine your boundary, it's too late. It's too late to decide what your ethical standards are going to be when you are filling out your first income tax return. It's too late to decide what your sexual boundaries are in the heat of the moment or what your alcohol limits are when you're already at the party. Build your boundaries early. Build them now and resolve to guard them.

Rely on Guidance from Heaven

Everyone has beliefs. Beliefs are what we know to be true. But convictions are a deeper level of belief that inspire us to act. A belief is what you have in your head; a conviction is what you hold in your heart. A belief says, "I am convinced of this truth." A conviction says, "I am committed to it." People will argue for their beliefs, but they will die for their convictions. Beliefs are negotiable; convictions are not.

Conviction is a word we use for God-given boundaries. Not everyone listens to God and so not everyone has them. This means that without God-given boundaries, we run out of options pretty quickly. Daniel and his three friends decided to exercise their option to rely on divine guidance. "And God gave Daniel favor and compassion in the sight of the chief of the eunuchs" (Daniel 1:9).

When you are determined to follow God's path for your life, God will direct you to the right path. Remember our chapter on Proverbs 3:5-6? Maybe it's worth rereading. When you think you are out of options, there is always an option with God. This doesn't mean that God is optional. He guides us through all our options and makes the right way clear.

Daniel's survival wasn't guaranteed. Daniel, just like this Babylonian official, had to wait on God for the results of the new diet Daniel proposed. At the end of the ten-day trial, he didn't know how he would look in the eyes of the king. But all that mattered to Daniel was how he would look in the eyes of God.

Remember that God Is Working

One word repeated three times in this chapter is the key to the entire book:

> "And the Lord *gave* Jehoiakim king of Judah into his hand" (1:2).
>
> "And God *gave* Daniel favor and compassion in the sight of the chief of the eunuchs" (1:9).
>
> "As for these four youths, God *gave* them learning and skill in all literature and wisdom" (1:17).

God gave. It was God who gave Israel to the Babylonians, gave Daniel favor, and gave Daniel and his friends wisdom and understanding that made him the king's right-hand man.

God is always working for good. Daniel's home was destroyed and he was snatched away from his family and his friends. Daniel was shipped off to a foreign land with foreign gods, language, and customs. Do you think Daniel believed that in all those things God was working? I *know* he did because he *acted* on his conviction. We also know that God was working because we see the end of the story.

We see that through all of Daniel's story, God was still *giving.* He was giving Daniel seventy years to climb to the highest positions in the courts of both Babylon and Persia. In the last years of his life, God *gave* Daniel more power than any other member of the Jewish race has ever known. He was *given* the privilege of leading his nation back to God, preparing them for their return to their homeland. God had a plan greater for Daniel than Daniel could have ever had for himself, and Daniel got to see it because he first saw God's line in the sand and he refused to cross it.

Every day of your life you will come across lines in the sand. The world will tell you to cross them and to indulge in the promise of money, sex, or power. You may be convinced you are in a place where there's no way out. All options leading out of your dilemma feel exhausted. You're one step away from doing what everybody else would do and deciding the way everybody else would choose. But you can still exercise your God-given boundaries, stay on God's side of the line, and find out what God's best is for your life.

Prayer for This Week: *Holy God, I want to follow your way. Give me the discernment to know the way you're leading me and the courage I need to trust you.*

Question for This Week: Consider the dead end you face today. What would happen if you traded in all your options and decided to act with integrity and devotion to God?

21

Take the Heat

Scriptures for This Week

- Philippians 4:8-9
- Mark 12:24-27
- Daniel 3:8-30
- Hebrews 10:32-39
- Deuteronomy 6:13-19

Concede the Options of God

Wagner Dodge was a smokejumper, someone who parachutes into a remote area to battle wildfires. In 1949, Dodge and his crew of fifteen jumped from a plane to fight a fire at Mann Gulch in Montana. As he got within one hundred feet of the fire, he discovered the conditions were windier than he'd thought, and the fire was cutting off their escape route and advancing rapidly up the gulch he and his men were in.

Within a minute or two, he and his men would be engulfed in the fire. Smoke was as thick as fog. The superheated sap was exploding whole trees like bombs. Embers were falling like snow. Escape was impossible. They had about sixty seconds to live, and Dodge thought, *I'm out of options.*[33]

We've all been surrounded by the fires of circumstances where there is no apparent option except to cheat on our taxes, on an exam, or on a spouse. The heat and pressure make it seem right to embezzle from our company, pad our expense account, or compromise our convictions. What do we do when there's nothing to do except to give in?

Depend on the Certainty of God

One of the most famous stories in all the Bible is relevant to where we all are today, and it's a continuation of Daniel's story. In the previous chapter we saw how Daniel drew a line in the sand, guarded his boundaries, and trusted that when all the options looked dire, God's option would be best. Daniel was brave to resist joining the king's table, but now his friends are going to resist worshiping the king's god.

When the Babylonians took Israel captive, King Nebuchadnezzar ruled over more people and property than any king before or since. He was not only commander-in-chief of the most powerful army on earth, he was the high priest of political correctness. He wanted to make sure *everyone* bowed down to the same god. No exceptions.

Keep in mind when you read stories in the Bible that you are not just reading what God has said, you are reading what God is saying. You are reading how God wanted his people to live then and how God wants his people to live now. So when we read about Daniel, we read about us, and we can watch Daniel's steps to learn how to stay true to our God as we face difficulties in our homes and in our nation.

Take Courage from God

Nebuchadnezzar raised a ninety-foot golden image of his pagan god. It must have been a tremendous sight. Everybody who was a somebody had gathered to join the cult of conformity. He had established a new religious obligation, and at the appointed time he wanted everyone to bow down and worship this new image.

Then the wind of this demonic commandment collides with the wall of a divine courage. Three young Hebrew men—Shadrach, Meshach, and Abednego—stood up when everybody else bowed down, and their actions were reported to the king. They were courageous rather than compromising.

You've heard it before and maybe you've *said* it before:

"Well, I don't believe I ought to let my beliefs interfere with my politics."

"When in Babylon do what the Babylonians do."

"I don't believe I ought to impose my morality on someone else."

"I'll bow down on the outside. I just won't bow down on the inside."

"It is legal so I guess it must be right."

These three men show us what real faith is. Warren Wiersbe says, "Real faith means obeying God regardless of the feelings within us, the circumstances around us, or the consequences before us."[34]

One of the greatest lessons a parent will ever teach their child is to have the courage to stand for what is right even when they stand alone. The only place you will find this courage is in God. When you stand for what is right, you never stand alone. God always stands with you.

Keep Confidence in God

Nebuchadnezzar hears about the disobedience of these men, and he can't believe their audacity. How dare they defy him. He screams, "If you do not worship, you shall immediately be cast into a burning fiery furnace. And who is the god who will deliver you out of my hands?" (Daniel 3:15).

That is the question you will always be asked when you are being tempted to compromise, to give in, to go along to get along, to take the bait, to get in line. Do you really trust God? Do you believe in a God who delivers?

But these guys don't fear or flinch. They look this king square in the eye and say, "The time for talk is over. It is not up for debate or discussion. Read our lips—we may burn, but we won't bend, bow, or budge."

In a storm, the tallest tree in the forest is most likely to draw the lightning. If you decide to stand tall for what is right and for God, you will draw the fire and you will face the heat.

At this point they were out of options. What do they say? "If this be so, our God whom we serve is able to deliver us from the burning fiery furnace, and he will deliver us out of your hand, O king" (Daniel 3:17).

What they say next is one of the all-time great statements of faith in God in the entire Bible: "But if not, be it known to you, O king, that we will not serve your gods or worship the golden image that you have set up" (3:18).

They knew that God could deliver them from the fiery furnace, but they didn't know that he would. Whether he would deliver them from it or through it, they were going to stand with God and for God, live or die.

Real faith is not the confidence that God will work things out the way you want. It is the confidence that God will work things out the way he wants. If you face the fire and you take the heat, remember that his eye is on the thermometer, his hand is on the thermostat, and we can take the heat when it comes.

Honor Commitment to God

The contract of their commitment had no small print. Whether they lived or died, they had made a commitment to God and they were going to honor it. Nebuchadnezzar had made an equally strong commitment to his god. If they were willing to take the heat, he was willing to give it.

He heats up the furnace seven times hotter than usual. Shadrach, Meshach, and Abednego are tied up and thrown into the fire, but Nebuchadnezzar sees a fourth man in there (Daniel 3:25). Scholars debate whether this was *the* Son of God or *a* son of God (an angel), though this seems to me like an Old Testament appearance of Jesus. Regardless, Nebuchadnezzar now realizes these guys are being protected by a powerful God. He waves the white flag and lets them out.

Verse 26 tells us that three men came out of the fire. Where does that leave the fourth man? He is still in the fire. When you take the heat for God, he is waiting to take the heat with you.

It turns out the smokejumpers weren't out of options. Wagner Dodge took out a match, lit it, and threw it into the shoulder-high grass in front of him. In an instant, the grass was ablaze in a widening circle, leaving a charred safety zone in the middle. As the ring of this new fire spread, he jumped to the charred center, and called for his men to join him.[35]

The tragedy is that thirteen of his fifteen men thought their best option was to make a run for it. Only the men who realized that fire does not go where fire has already been were saved. Only the men who were willing to take the heat lived. Jesus walked into a fiery furnace in the shape of a cross. He took the heat of God's wrath against our sin so we could be forgiven and redeemed from the fire of death. We ought to take heat for him because he took the greatest heat for us.

Prayer for This Week: *God, I want to trust you in the fire and not just after it. Help me to experience your presence, enjoy your power, and be enveloped by your protection.*

Question for This Week: Where do you need to demonstrate divine courage right now? Pause to envision Jesus waiting in the middle of it to take the heat with you. How does this change your options?

22

The Fugitive

Scriptures for This Week

- Matthew 12:39-42
- Jonah 1:1-17
- Jonah 2:1-10
- Jude 20-23
- Ephesians 2:1-10

Running Hard

In 1974, I was a fugitive on the run. Not from the government but from God. God had already called me to the ministry, and I was accepted to go to seminary, but I ran for four months. As my summer as a student minister ended, I reconsidered what I was about to do. I thought about all the weekends I would lose, all the money I could make, all the demands that would be made of me. I went to multiple interviews and enlisted two headhunters in order to find a different job. You could say that I was *resistant* to following God's will.

I wasn't saying, "I am not going to do this," but I was saying, "I don't want to do this." I was running like a fugitive. Maybe you are too. Maybe you're running from a difficult marriage, a make-or-break conversation, or your own hard calling.

The Old Testament tells of a fugitive named Jonah. Sometimes people get hung up on what was going on inside the fish in the story, but a better story is what was going on inside of Jonah. However, we can step back a little further and see that the book is about the one who is mentioned the most—God. In this great story of God, we want to focus on his persistent and unending mercy.

Running Away

We learn three things about God in Jonah's story.

1. God's will is commanding.

God told Jonah, "Go to the great city of Nineveh and preach against it" (Jonah 1:1-2 NIV). God never makes requests or suggestions in the Bible; every time he speaks, he commands. Yet, we don't resist him because he's commanding. We resist him because he tells us to do things we don't want to do. God was telling Jonah to go to a rebellious, wicked nation and an enemy of Israel and preach God's mercy. It was the equivalent of asking a Jew in 1942 to go to Germany to tell Hitler that God loved him and had a wonderful plan for his life. When we don't tell our friends, family, and neighbors about God's mercy, our silence is our way of running. Whenever we avoid doing what God says, we're escaping.

2. God's will is composed.

God commands but he does not force. He is patient with us as long as we are in the valley of decision. He understands when we are afraid. He shows us mercy when we are arrogant. He loves us enough to give us the freedom to make our own decisions and guides us in whatever way we go. Saying yes to his will provides personal peace. Saying no promotes pain. But both will get us where God thinks we need to be. Jonah could have gone five hundred miles to Nineveh, but he chose Tarshish twenty-five hundred miles the other way. Saying no always takes us out of our way, but God still gets us to Nineveh even if it takes a storm to get us there.

3. God's will is consequential.

Jonah 1:3 (NIV) says he got on that boat "to flee from the LORD." It wasn't an extravagant excursion but an expensive escape. Disobedience will take you farther than you want to go, keep you longer than you want to stay, and cost you more than you want to pay.

> Then the LORD sent a great wind on the sea, and such a violent storm arose that the ship threatened to break up. All the sailors were afraid and each cried out to his own god. And they threw the cargo into the sea to lighten the ship (Jonah 1:4-5a NIV).

The hard consequence of Jonah's disobedience affected not only him but also the livelihood and the peaceful vocation of the sailors. Fugitives always hurt others. Family and friends will be hurt by the shrapnel of your life when you are running from God.

Running on Fumes

Jonah's story goes on to tell us that everybody else on that ship tried praying to his god and it didn't work. So they asked Jonah to pray to his God, hoping they all might be saved. But Jonah was ignoring God, so the sailors cast lots to determine who was responsible for their dilemma, and the lot revealed Jonah's guilt. Even then he remained stubborn, determined to disobey God, and said, "Throw me into the sea."

In those months that I ran from God, I lost all the money I had saved for my first semester in seminary. I wasted a lot of time looking for dead-end jobs. I spent a lot of nights tossing and turning when I could have slept in perfect peace in the will of God. I was playing my last cards and running on fumes.

One Sunday I went to a little country church in order to avoid my own and to hear an older friend of mine preach. The title of his sermon was "Little Is Much If God Is in It." All he talked about was the blessing that will come when we do God's will. My tears hit the floor as I made that final surrender to God's will for my life. I walked out of that church with a skip in my step and joy in my heart, because the God I had been running from was waiting for me the whole time.

Running Scared

Those tough times you are navigating are not signs that God is absent. He doesn't allow tough times to happen in order to *pay* you back but to *bring* you back. You play a role in how it all pans out when you do these three things:

1. Look up.

Jonah has been swallowed by a great fish and now, engulfed in total darkness and smelling the stench, he is alert to God. The belly of that fish was a rock-bottom experience, and when you are at the bottom, up is the only way you can look. For Jonah, a prophet, he looked "toward the temple," the place where he knew he would find God. If you are at a point where you don't know where to turn, you can always turn to God. You can always look up, and when you do, you will find God was there all the time.

2. Speak up.

At the start of Jonah's story, the pouting prophet never said a word to God. However, now he says,

> "In my distress I called to the LORD,
> and he answered me.
> From deep in the realm of the dead I called for help,
> and you listened to my cry."
>
> (Jonah 2:2 NIV)

When we are determined to shut up, God has a way of making us speak up. When we do, we acknowledge where we are, how we got there, admit our fault, and throw ourselves on God's mercy. In our distress, we call out to the Lord and he is there to listen.

3. Give up.

Jonah closes his prayer with thanksgiving.

> "Those who cling to worthless idols
> turn away from God's love for them.
> But I, with shouts of grateful praise,
> will sacrifice to you.
> What I have vowed I will make good.
> I will say, 'Salvation comes from the LORD.'"
>
> (Jonah 2:8-9 NIV)

He is thankful. How could this be? God hasn't delivered him from the fish, and Jonah didn't know if he ever would. Jonah was thankful because he knew God was present and able. With these words, Jonah surrendered his flight and let God have his way. Whether your problem is guilt or grief, the only solution to either one comes in the grace of giving up.

Running Free

Every day that you run from God is a wasted day. Don't waste any more. Look up, speak up, and give up; he will pick you up, not because you deserve it, but to teach you that he is a second-chance God.

My nephew is living proof of that truth. With his permission, I share his story.

My nephew is an alcoholic, and he has lived a heartbreaking story that began with drinking. He went through job after job, was discharged from the Air Force, and began to collect DUIs. He was married and had two beautiful children, but his drinking continued. Then in June 2002, while on his way to an AA meeting, he changed lanes on the expressway and hit an SUV, causing it to flip out of control. A fourteen-year-old boy was ejected from the SUV and died. My nephew panicked, left the scene, stopped at a convenience store, drank some more, and was arrested.

He has been incarcerated for over seven years now. He's sitting in his own belly of the fish, and he wrote to me, "I have never felt freer in my life." You see, being shut in that jail was the moment he realized he was powerless over his problem. He never owned a gun, and yet he had just killed someone. He broke down and wept with overwhelming grief. That was the moment he gave up and surrendered to God. "Immediately," he told me, "I felt an overwhelming sense of true peace...a peace I had never known before."

My nephew discovered how to stop being a fugitive. Though he was given a fifteen-year sentence, he found true freedom in his imprisonment. In his lowest moment, he looked up and saw God. He spoke up and God heard. He gave up and God poured out his grace. God is a second-chance God for fugitives, sailors, and pagan Ninevites. God's mercy on each person in this story is the same mercy he will show to you.

Prayer for This Week: *Father, in my distress I'm calling out to you because you hear me. Show me how to be thankful for my storm and to trust that your mercy is my only salvation.*

Question for This Week: Where are you ignoring the command of God? How would your life be different if you obeyed it?

23

For Goodness' Sake

Scriptures for This Week

- Micah 6:6-8
- Galatians 5:22-26
- Proverbs 31:8-9
- Deuteronomy 10:14-22
- Philippians 2:1-11

The God-ness of Goodness

In June 1783, an unbelievable military upset took place when a fledgling coalition of thirteen American colonies banded together to defeat the most powerful armed forces in the world at that time. The leader of that victory was General George Washington. On June 14, when he sent a circular to the colonies to advise them on how to become a strong nation, he wrote the words of a retiring successful war general and closed it with a prayer:

> I now make it my earnest prayer that God…would most graciously be pleased to dispose us all, to do Justice, to love mercy, and to demean ourselves with that Charity, humility, and pacific temper of mind, which were the Characteristics of the Divine Author of our blessed Religion and without an humble imitation of whose example in these things, we can never hope to be a happy Nation.

The heart of his prayer is this powerful verse from the prophet Micah:

> He has shown you, O mortal, what is good.
>   And what does the LORD require of you?
> To act justly and to love mercy

and to walk humbly with your God.

(Micah 6:8 NIV)

General Washington was telling the nation, "If you want to be a happy nation, then be a good nation." And the ultimate example of goodness is "the Divine Author of our blessed Religion." Jesus is the one who took our punishment so God could execute justice. He offers us mercy, withholds the punishment we deserve, and through grace gives us what we don't deserve. You can't talk about goodness without talking about God.

Goodness Is an Accomplishment of the Spirit

You may not know that the word *good* comes from an old Anglo-Saxon word that had the same connotation as *God. Good-bye* is an abbreviation of the saying, "God be with you." *Good* means "to be like God."

So it isn't surprising to see that *good* is listed as a trait of those who live according to the Holy Spirit. Galatians 5:22-23 lists these traits or "fruit" for us: "But the fruit of the Spirit is love, joy, peace, patience, kindness, *goodness*, faithfulness, gentleness, self-control; against such things there is no law" (Galatians 5:22-23). In The Message, Eugene Peterson describes *goodness* as "a conviction that a basic holiness permeates things and people." That sounds a lot like God.

As Christians, we believe that the Holy Spirit takes up residence in the lives of believers. The inclusion of goodness as a fruit of the Spirit tells us that God gives it. We cannot manufacture goodness.

Apart from God, no true goodness exists and no one does good. Romans 3:12 says, "no one does good, not even one." But our potential for goodness is animated by the Spirit who lives in us, and with this fruit, he wants you and me to live in such a way that our lives will taste good to others.

What does it mean to be good? In the verse that General Washington quoted, God tells us what goodness is. He leaves us no doubt. God says goodness is loving the right things and living the right way. You can take this definition of goodness and measure just how good you are.

Goodness Is an Action That Helps

What is good and what does the Lord require of you? First, "to act justly." The word *justice* or *justly* is found over two hundred times in the Old Testament. It means to treat people equitably. Israel was to have the same law for everybody whether they were an Israelite or not. Justice was to be blind to race and to class.

Justice is comprised of punishing wrongdoers and giving all people their rights. Justice is giving people what they are due whether it is punishment or protection.

Several specific classes of people arise when the Bible speaks of justice: widows, orphans, immigrants, and the poor. These people had no social power, political influence, or financial strength. Today, we would expand that list to include refugees, the homeless, many single parents, and the elderly.[36]

This wasn't the norm in ancient cultures. The powerful did not connect with the outcast but with the elites—the people in political power, the generals, the kings, and the wealthy. The God of Israel was different. He identified with the orphan, the alien, the widow, and the poor. Unlike every god that pagans worshiped, this big God of Israel, our God, was and is on the side of the powerless, and we should be like him.[37]

In my church, Cross Pointe, caring for orphans is a high priority. In Georgia alone there are fifteen hundred children in foster care who are available for adoption. In 2010, we began developing an orphan-care ministry and later launched a ministry called One.27 (James 1:27). We've hosted a Discover Adoption event for our community, a foster family Christmas party, and have done orphan-care mission trips.

The goodness of a church, an individual, or a nation can be measured by the justice it metes out to these groups of people. Goodness is godliness in action.

Goodness Is an Affection That Cares

The second part of being good is "to love mercy." Justice and mercy go together. Justice is what we do, but mercy is why we do it. Justice is giving people what they deserve. Mercy is not giving people what they deserve.

The word *mercy* refers to God's unconditional grace and compassion. It is often translated from the word *hesed,* which means "lovingkindness."

Micah doesn't say that if you are good you will be merciful. He says if you are good you will *love mercy.* When you love mercy you will live mercy. There is something liberating about being merciful and treating the lowest, the littlest, and the least with kindness and grace. Augustine once said, "He that is good is free though he be a slave; he that is evil is a slave though he be a king." There would be a lot less bitterness and conflict in this world, our nation, our homes, and our neighborhoods if we would fall in love with mercy.

Lightning is an example of how we experience the goodness and mercy of God. While lightning can terrify and destroy, it also keeps us alive. It starts with nitrogen in our atmosphere, something our bodies need but that we can't absorb through our lungs. Mercifully, God's electrical charges in lightning separate the nitrogen from the atmosphere. In his goodness, he brings it down to earth with the rain, bacteria transforms the nitrate into a nitrite, which plants can then absorb. We eat the plant (or the animal that ate the plant), receive the nitrogen, and live. The only way that nitrogen is manufactured in a form that we can absorb it is through a bolt of blessing called lightning. The next time lightning flashes through the sky, thank God for his goodness and mercy.

Goodness Is an Attitude That Inspires

The last requirement of goodness is to "walk humbly with your God." This is the real source and secret of goodness. If we leave God out, then we don't have good. The good person will walk with God because goodness is the work of God. God is telling us that being good comes before doing good.

There are at least two myths associated with goodness.

Myth 1: Goodness is a matter of the head. People say if you know what is good, then you will do what is good. That is not true. Education does not make people good. You can educate a thief, but all you will wind up with is a brilliant bandit. Paul wrote the truth in Romans 7:19, "For I do not do the good I want to do, but the evil I do not want to do—this I keep on doing" (NIV).

Myth 2: Goodness is a matter of the hands. People say goodness is treating others well. If you do good to others, then you must be a good person. That is not true either. The San Bernardino terrorists were described as happily married and had a six-month-old daughter they responsibly dropped off with family before they went on their killing spree in December 2015.[38] They were good to their daughter, but we would not say they were good.

Goodness is a matter of the heart. It comes from walking with God. Jesus said, "A good man brings good things out of the good stored up in him, and an evil man brings evil things out of the evil stored up in him" (Matthew 12:35 NIV). Goodness is not a matter of what you know or what you do; it is a matter of what you are.

Consider Billy Graham, who has ministered in orphanages, hospitals, and in the streets around the world. He would be at the top of many lists of good people. From the beginning of his ministry, he insisted that his crusades and the leadership in his organization be open to all races. Throughout his public life, he has shown nothing but mercy to even his most vocal and vociferous critics. How did this great man manage to be so good?

He was once invited to a meeting with the president and other political officials. He arrived early and was told to go up to the platform and take a seat from backstage. As he walked on stage to sit down, the hundreds of reporters gathered for the event gave him a standing ovation. Graham turned around to see who they were standing for. Only when he noticed that he was the only one on the platform did he realize they were standing for him.

Do justice. Love mercy. Walk humbly with your God.

Prayer for This Week: *God, you are the only one who is good. Change my heart so that I love mercy. Empower my hands so that I can live justly and transform my mind so that I can be renewed as I walk with you.*

Question for This Week: Do you love mercy? Who do you know that, even though they may not deserve it, needs your lovingkindness?

24

On the Ropes

Scriptures for This Week

- Job 13:13-19
- Habakkuk 3:1-19
- Romans 8:18-21
- Psalm 145:3-13
- Psalm 100

Fear That Leads to Death

Alan Gardiner set sail in 1851 with five other missionaries. He had felt the call of God to take the gospel to an unreached tribe in one of the remotest parts of the world. Unfortunately, they shipwrecked on an island off the tip of South Africa with no way of ever leaving. One by one they starved to death. Alan Gardiner was the last one left alive. When searchers found the bodies, Alan's journal was lying by his side. The last words he wrote were Psalm 34:10 (KJV), "The young lions do lack, and suffer hunger: but they that seek the LORD shall not want any good thing." And then he added, "I am overwhelmed by the sense of the goodness of God."

Can you imagine giving your life for the sake of taking the gospel to an unreached tribe? And then not only dying of starvation, but dying without ever getting to share the good news with even one person? In the last moments of your life, of all the questions you could demand an answer to, to say instead, "I am overwhelmed by the sense of the goodness of God," is a defense of God's faithfulness that remains unmatched. Had it been me, my journal would have indicated how my faith was up against the ropes.

If you have come to a true knowledge of God and developed a serious relationship with him, if you've determined to walk with God, you aren't out of the woods of distrust. There will be times when your faith is on the ropes and times when your relationship with God consists of questions:

- What is God up to?
- When is God going to do something?
- Why doesn't God do something now?
- Where is God in the middle of my storm?

A Fate Worse Than Death

Habakkuk was a prophet called by God who knew God but wrestled with God. He lived in the nation of Judah in a time of rebellion, idolatry, drunkenness, and wickedness. He had been praying and praying for God to bring repentance to his people and revival to his country. He never heard anything in response. Confused and frustrated, he confronted God: "You are supposed to be holy and righteous. Why don't you do something to punish your wicked people? Why don't you answer my prayer? What are you up to? Where are you right now?"

Then God answers: "I *am* going to do something. I am going to send the most wicked nation on the planet to crush my people." Habakkuk couldn't believe his ears. "This is your solution? No matter how wicked my people are, they are not as bad as the Babylonians. How could you, a holy and righteous God, do this?" To which God replies, "I know what I am doing and I will do what is right. Trust me."

Then the Lord told Habakkuk to write down one of the greatest statements in all the Bible. It is a statement that sparked the Protestant Reformation. It is a statement that transformed the church: "But the righteous shall live by his faith" (Habakkuk 2:4).

When we face tough times, we will take one of two paths: the path of fear or the path of faith. If you are living in fear over anything that could end up in a bad way for your family, your finances, or your future, Habakkuk will show you that fear is defeated by focused faith.

Focused Faith Desires the Will of God

Throughout this short book, Habakkuk moves from doubting God to debating God to defending God. In the final chapter he takes his eyes off his circumstances, forgets about what he thinks is best, and puts his focus back where it belongs—on God's plan, God's purpose, and God's priorities. He is no longer doubting God's method of restoration. He is now defending God's ways and wants God's will.

Like Alan Gardiner, when you're facing what looks like the end, your whole perspective changes. Habakkuk no longer wants what he wants. He wants what God wants in whatever way fits God's plan. This is the way Jesus told us to pray. We are to say to God, "Your kingdom come. Your will be done."

There are two things you can do to get to this point:

1. "Stand in awe of [his] deeds" (Habakkuk 3:2 NIV). In the middle of tough times and dark days, remember who God is, what God has done, and what God can do. Then you will also remember that God can always be trusted.

2. Keep eternity in view. God "marches on forever" (3:6 NIV), but your circumstance will change. Our ways are earthly, flawed, faulty, and failing. His ways are eternal, constant, consistent, and confirmed.

Habakkuk makes a standout request: "In wrath remember mercy" (3:2 NIV). Thank God that he does just that. In his justice he had to punish sin, but in his mercy he provided for forgiveness. Seventy years after Babylon destroyed this nation, the people were restored to their land, the temple was rebuilt, Jerusalem's walls were reconstructed, and a nation came alive again.

Focused Faith Remembers the Works of God

What do your doubts sound like right now?

"Is God involved in my life?"

"Has God fallen asleep at the wheel?"

"Is God even listening to my prayers?"

You can stop driving yourself crazy with questions by looking back and seeing how God took care of things yesterday. That is what Habakkuk does—he recalls a litany of great things God had done in the past:

- In 3:3, Habakkuk refers to that time when God raised

Moses up to deliver his people out of bondage in Egypt. He reminds himself of how God was working even when the people of Israel didn't know it.

- In 3:8-9, he recounts the great miracles when God parted both the Red Sea and the Jordan River so that the people of Israel could pass through.
- In 3:11, Habakkuk acknowledges that God's powerful intervention extends to the cosmos when he recalls Joshua's prayer for the sun to stand still so that Israel could complete its victory over its enemies (Joshua 10).
- In 3:13, Habakkuk makes an incredible statement that's about Jesus, the anointed one of God. He didn't know it, but we can look back to what Habakkuk was looking forward to: the cross of Jesus Christ. If nothing else reminds me that the God of yesterday is the God who can take care of today, it ought to be the cross.

Habakkuk teaches that the God who has been faithful to us in the past will be faithful to us in the present. What about you? If you were to sit down and think, you could write down page after page after page of the way God came through for you in the past or the way you could see God working in your life—his protective hand, his precious provision, and his powerful prompts. "Our God is a God who saves" (Psalm 68:20 NIV). When you are going through tough times look back and remember the works of God.

Focused Faith Continues the Worship of God

I will be the first to admit that all of this sounds good in theory, but what about those who still don't have a job, are still battling cancer, are still going through a divorce, still have unpaid bills? Habakkuk would say, "I know how you feel." The English in 3:16 says "my body trembles," but that is cleaned up. In the Hebrew it says "my bowels tremble!"

The Babylonians were coming. Habakkuk's nation was going to be destroyed and his friends were going to be taken into captivity if they were left alive. His greatest fear was coming to pass. In verse 17 we see that Habakkuk also feared *complete devastation* because the whole economy of Judah—figs, grapes, olives, sheep, goats, and cattle—would be destroyed.

Fear sees all the difficulties. Fear sees all the problems. Fear sees all the disappointments. But faith continues to see the strong hand of the promises of God, the provision of God, and the plan of God. To the job loss, the cancer diagnosis, and the painful loss, you can also say as Habakkuk, "Yet I will wait patiently" (3:16 NIV). To the mysterious disease, absent spouse, crashed retirement, and suffering child, you can also say, "I will rejoice in the LORD, I will be joyful in God my Savior" (3:18 NIV). When the worst things that could happen to you happen, they will bring out the best things that are in you. Even though you lose everything, yet you can worship him, praise him, and love him. Courage is not the absence of fear. Courage is faith in the face of it.

If your number one desire is to be wealthy, healthy, prosperous, and full of people you love, then when those things don't happen, you won't be able to praise God. If your goal is to stay close to God, to be in the center of his will, and to glorify him no matter what, then you can praise God in every circumstance, knowing that every circumstance can bring you closer to him.

If God never did another thing for us for the rest of our lives other than send his Son to die for our sins and raise him from the dead so that we could live with him forever, we would have more than enough to praise God for, more than enough to love God for, and more than enough to worship God for.

Prayer for This Week: *Holy Father, when I am anxious in my sufferings and the cares of my heart are many, I know I can cast them all on you because you care for me.*

Question for This Week: If this moment were your last, what rejoicing would you write out in your journal?

25

On the Money

Scriptures for This Week

- Acts 20:32-35
- Psalm 50:7-15
- Malachi 3:6-10
- 1 Corinthians 9:7-14
- 2 Corinthians 9:6-15

Money Matters

The first time I understood how important money could be was when I got my first paycheck. I was a teenager when I got my first real job, which was at a dime store. These stores sold inexpensive items and paid their workers inexpensive salaries.

I was making the grand total of a dollar and ten cents an hour. I thought I was rich. As I looked at that check with my name on it, I realized for the first time in my life, *This money belongs to me.* This money mattered because it made me ask, *What am I going to do with this?*

Money is an important part of my life, just as it is yours. I think about it, read about it, talk about it, and, today, I write about it. I like to tell people that money is not the most important thing in life, but it is close to oxygen. You do need money to function and to survive. So it shouldn't be any surprise to know that it is also important to God.

Jesus talked more about money than he talked about heaven and hell put together. Five times more is said in the Bible about money than is said about prayer. There are five hundred verses on faith and over two thousand verses about some aspect of finances. God has a lot to say to you about your money, because your money says a lot about you.

Be Thoughtful in How You Make Money

As I looked down at that first paycheck, I kept thinking, *This is my money. It is not my dad's money nor my mom's money. Nobody gave it to me. I earned it. It belongs to me*. But I was dead wrong.

You may think you earn your money by the good job that you have or the good work that you do. However, what I understood years later was that *work was the way God puts money into my hands, but the money is still his.*

It is God who gives life and health so you can work. Being able to work doesn't ensure you a job, so it is God who gives you the opportunity to have a job and earn that paycheck. Everything that is represented by that paycheck comes from God: the ability, the knowledge, the health, the job, and the money.

King David desired to build a temple for the Lord. He took up an offering from the people to do so and they gave generously. They rejoiced and praised God for the financial victory. David prayed a beautiful prayer before these people and said, "But who am I, and who are my people, that we should be able to give as generously as this? Everything comes from you, and we have given you only what comes from your hand" (1 Chronicles 29:14 NIV).

Up until I got that job in that dime store, every time I bought presents for my parents, I bought them with the allowance they gave me. For a long time my parents were buying their own presents because what I gave to them came from them. David said the same thing: "What we put into one of your hands, God, we took from the other."

The first key to learning how to handle money is to remember, *It's not your money. It is God's.*

Be Careful That You Master Money

The last book of the Old Testament was written by a prophet named Malachi. As we unfold what Malachi had to say to the nation of Israel, we are going to learn some ancient truths that are as relevant in the twenty-first century as ever.

One of the biggest problems that God had with Israel was that they had allowed their money to master them. They had gotten away from

God and didn't even know it. When God made them a most merciful offer, "Return to me, and I will return to you" (Malachi 3:7), they played dumb and pretended they were innocent. "How shall we return?" they asked. God's answer gives them the shock of their lives. He doesn't talk about their morals, their manners, or their methods. He talks about their money and accuses them of robbery.

How were they robbing God? There are only two ways you can rob somebody. You either take something that doesn't belong to you or you keep something that belongs to somebody else. They were doing both by not giving God his tithe. They had forgotten that it wasn't their money. They had forgotten that all of their money was God's, and he had a right not just to part of it but to all of it. When they refused to give any of it, they were robbing God.

Something Jesus said makes so much sense here: "No one can serve two masters. Either he will hate the one and love the other, or he will be devoted to the one and despise the other. You cannot serve God and money" (Matthew 6:24). This nation was full of people serving their money rather than having their money serve them. They were independent, but they weren't free.

Be Purposeful in How You Minister Money

Several telltale signs reveal that money is your master rather than your slave:

- You are far more excited about getting money than you are about giving money.
- You place normal daily expenditures on credit cards because you don't have the cash.
- You continue to borrow money to buy luxury and depreciating items.
- You are consistently late paying your bills.
- Your thoughts are dominated by get-rich-quick schemes.
- You are dishonest in your financial dealings.
- You find it difficult to give to God's work.

- You hate chapters like this one.

You are not qualified to get anything from Neiman Marcus until you give something to Neiman Marcus. If you shop there and see a shirt or a dress that you like, you pay whatever the price of that item is, and then you receive the item. You are not qualified to receive anything until you give something to that store, otherwise you are robbing them.

Many people go to church every week and are introduced to a life with Jesus through the church's ministry. Their marriages might be restored, their children are taught to love God, their teenagers are encouraged to be obedient, pure, and godly, they receive leadership training, service skills, compassion in their grief, and companionship in their struggles. But they don't do anything financially to keep the ministry going. The draw to "spiritual shoplifting" is likely greater than it ever is to steal that belt from the department store. So what's the solution for this tendency to rob God?

Be Successful in How You Manage Money

God has a one-sentence formula on how to be successful with your money. The way to manage money is to tithe a part and to trust God with the rest. If all your money is God's money, then every spending decision is a spiritual decision. The first and the best decision you will ever make in this area is to do what God says in his word.

> "Bring the whole tithe into the storehouse, that there may be food in my house. Test me in this," says the Lord Almighty, "and see if I will not throw open the floodgates of heaven and pour out so much blessing that you will not have room enough to store it" (Malachi 3:10 NIV).

Tithing has several positive effects:

It provides the best investment for your money. Jesus said, "Do not store up for yourselves treasures on earth, where moths and vermin destroy, and where thieves break in and steal. But store up for yourselves treasures in heaven, where moths and vermin do not destroy, and where thieves do not break in and steal" (Matthew 6:19-20 NIV).

It puts God where he belongs. "The purpose of tithing is to teach you always to put God first in your lives" (Deuteronomy 14:23 TLB).

It positions you for God's favor.

> Honor the LORD with your wealth,
> with the firstfruits of all your crops;
> then your barns will be filled to overflowing,
> and your vats will brim over with new wine.
> (Proverbs 3:9-10 NIV)

Tithing isn't an investment for a return. It's not a savings plan and it's not a spiritual tax. Tithing is, above all else, an act of worship that says, "God, all of it came from you, and if it weren't for you, I wouldn't have it to begin with. I am going to give the first portion back to you and trust you with the rest." In return God says, "I will meet every need you have in this life and reward you far more than you ever gave in the life to come." So, giving generously and giving sacrificially should be both easy and logical.

God doesn't need your money. He gave it to you to begin with. God wants what your money represents: your heart. He wants you unattached to any other idol. If he is not first in your finances, priorities, time management, or any other area, then something else is in his place. Tithing releases us from the tyranny of a master we'll never appease and releases us to join the Master we can always adore.

Prayer for This Week: *Father, you are abundant in your kindness and boundless in your generosity. Show me where I lack trust in you and guide me as I steward the money you've provided for me.*

Question for This Week: What role does selfishness play in the way you spend, save, and give your money? What role does worship play?

Section Five

One Solitary Life

The most important character in the book that changed everything is the one who changed everything—Jesus. His life is written in four Gospels that cover his last three years and is the major source of what we know about the most influential person by far who has ever lived. They explain why he should be trusted and worshiped.[39] Read and be changed.

26

Gospel Truth

Scriptures for This Week

- John 2:18-22
- Luke 1:1-4
- Jeremiah 31:31-34
- Revelation 21:1-7
- 2 Timothy 3:14-17

It All Comes Down to Jesus

The three major world religions have core differences. The Muslim religion boils down to belief in and obedience to Allah. The Jewish religion boils down to belief in and obedience to God. The Christian religion boils down to receiving life from and with Jesus. No other faith is so dependent on one human. If you're a Christian, how can you trust all you know about Jesus to be true?

Our faith is based on Jesus. If Jesus was not the Son of God, and if he did not die on the cross for our sins and come back from the dead, it doesn't matter whether he was a real historical figure. The entire Christian faith collapses like a house of cards. Most everything we know about Jesus comes from four books called the Gospels—Matthew, Mark, Luke, and John. The Gospels are the biographies of Jesus Christ and help us to make up our mind about Jesus.

The Gospels tell the story not just about Jesus but about what God did *through* him. In his Gospel, Luke explains the *why* of his writing, beginning in verse 1: "Inasmuch as many have undertaken to compile a narrative of the things that have been accomplished among us..." The word *accomplished* means "the complete fulfillment of something." That fulfillment is of a Savior whom God promised long ago when sin first entered the world through Adam and Eve's disobedience.

Luke digs deep, like an archeologist in search of evidence, and his shovel hits the same rock that ours should hit, the rock of a true and trustworthy resurrected Jesus.

Presenting the Proof

I can't prove to you a man named George Washington was the first president of the United States. I can't prove that Henry Ford built the first Ford automobile. I can't prove that this world was created. What I can do is present evidence, and when I look at the evidence, all of those things seem more probable than not. The trustworthiness of a historical document or event is always based on evidence, not proof.

Luke is a master of working with evidence, and he claims that the Gospel he wrote is a serious literary and historical volume. He invites serious scholars to analyze and study its literary and historical value. Luke tells us how the events, the sayings, the teachings, the miracles, the life, death, and resurrection of Jesus ended up in a book to begin with.

The first four verses are a prologue that makes his work stand out with the other well-respected writings of Greek and Roman historians. In the Greek language, these four verses are one long sentence of the most excellent Koine Greek found anywhere in the ancient world.

> Inasmuch as many have undertaken to compile a narrative of the things that have been accomplished among us, just as those who from the beginning were eyewitnesses and ministers of the word have delivered them to us, it seemed good to me also, having followed all things closely for some time past, to write an orderly account for you, most excellent Theophilus, that you may have certainty concerning the things you have been taught (Luke 1:1-4).

The Gospels are a genre of historical writing called *narrative* (not myth, fiction, or fable). Luke makes it plain he is writing a historical account about real people, real places, and real events. His story of Jesus doesn't take place in some mythical Neverland. He provides geographical detail about places you can still visit today, such as Bethlehem, Nazareth, and Jerusalem. A wedding in Cana and a well in Samaria. Jesus doesn't just walk on water; he walks on the Sea of Galilee. He is not just baptized, but is baptized in the Jordan River.

Luke is my favorite Gospel. It's the longest and most complete, and when combined with Acts, his second book, it spans sixty years. Of his 1151 verses, 568 are the words of Jesus. If you want to know what Jesus said, read Luke's Gospel. He does what a great lawyer would do and shows us the steps in testing truth.

Investigating the Evidence

I did my doctoral dissertation on the book of Luke, and one of the things that makes a dissertation worthy of a doctoral degree is research that consults every available original source. Ancient historians, too, let their readers know they had done their homework and had searched out any other account that had been written before theirs. Luke is no different.

He was not the first person to attempt to write about Jesus. Scholars are sure that Luke pulled from the Gospel of Mark and the Gospel of Matthew, because both had already been written. Personal sources also informed Luke. He had been a companion of Paul and traveled with him on many of his missionary journeys. He also met Mark, who had accompanied Paul as well. While traveling in Jerusalem, he likely met Matthew, so it is not farfetched to say they compared notes.

Luke wants us to know he has done meticulous research. He has pored over every source he can find on the life of Jesus. That's why he goes on to say that he has "followed all things closely for some time past, to write an orderly account for you" (1:3). Luke has turned over every rock and opened every door. He doesn't include anything in his Gospel he can't trace back to a reliable source. He did what all of us should do when we are trying to uncover the truth—he investigated the evidence.

Interrogating the Witnesses

There are two basic ways you can be convinced that something is true: you can witness something or you can listen to an eyewitness of something. Luke consults eyewitnesses to the life of Jesus: "just as those who from the beginning were eyewitnesses and ministers of the word have delivered them to us" (1:2). These eyewitnesses were with Jesus from the beginning of his ministry, probably his baptism.

In that culture, experiences were passed on through oral tradition. Because illiteracy was around 95 percent, the only record of what happened in the Gospels was spoken, which might seem like that leaves room for inaccurate reporting. However, in first-century Palestine, the ability to memorize and retain lengthy oral tradition and information was a prized and developed skill. From the earliest age, children were taught to memorize many, many Scriptures.

Furthermore, these stories were not whispered in private places. They were spoken out loud in front of many others who were also familiar with the tradition and could corroborate the accuracy of what was told. Third, the sayings of Jesus were memorable and phrased in a way that facilitated memorization. The parables that Jesus told were short, relevant, and committed to memory. Luke was a thorough investigator, a great detective, and now we'll look at his reporting.

Inscripturating the Results

It is now about thirty years since Jesus ascended to heaven, eyewitnesses are starting to die off, and because Jesus was a story for all time, Luke, having gathered all his facts, wrote so that Theophilus and others—like you—could trust it.

How do we know that the document we have today is what Luke wrote down? We can make a comparison. Of all the ancient documents, the New Testament has the most and the oldest manuscripts to support it by far than any other ancient writing. We have over fifty-seven hundred manuscripts, original copies, of the New Testament, two thousand of which contain all or part of the Gospels. The number of Gospel manuscripts is twenty times larger than the average number of manuscripts of comparable writing, such as Julius Caesar's *Commentaries on the Gallic War* (there are only ten) and Plato's writings (there are only seven).

Furthermore, the oldest fragment of John's Gospel dates to thirty-five years after the New Testament was completed.[40] Julius Caesar's earliest copy is dated a thousand years after he lived. Plato's earliest manuscript is dated twelve hundred years after he wrote. All of that is to say the text of the New Testament that we have today, including the Gospel of Luke, is almost the same as it was written and is about 99 percent established.

Luke was writing for Theophilus, who was evidently a new convert to Christianity and was beginning to have doubts. Luke wanted him to know that he had a firm foundation to believe what he had been taught and to have certainty of the historical reality of Jesus. More than a philosophical system, faith in Jesus is built on the historical Jesus dying a historical death and experiencing a historical resurrection. More than historical reliability, it is historical reality. Verified time and time again by the archeological spade, Luke's Gospel continues to win over its harshest critics.

For Luke, the Christian faith is not a leap into the dark and a hope for the best. It is a rigorous faith that rests on the solid foundation of the most reliable facts. It initiates hope, instills trust, and inspires faith both in Luke's day and in ours.

Prayer for This Week: *God, I am in awe at the great lengths you went to get this story into my hands. Help me to be a faithful storyteller of your marvelous works so that I may add certainty to an uncertain world.*

Question for This Week: What is it about Jesus that is easiest for you to believe and how can you use it to encourage someone who is doubting?

27

Don't Touch That Dial!

Scriptures for This Week

- Isaiah 44:6-8
- 1 Peter 1:10-12
- Matthew 1:18-25
- Psalm 62:5-8
- Isaiah 55:8-11

Tuning In

The greatest inventions and technological advances in history have taken place from the end of the nineteenth century up until the present day. Perhaps no invention has had a greater impact than radio. The radio was the first device that allowed for mass communication. People who lived thousands of miles away could be affected by the words of one person speaking into a microphone. Words that were spoken into the air could now be transmitted through the air.

Even with the advent of television, the Internet, and the computer, radio is bigger than ever. In the twenty-first century, the radio has reached its greatest heights primarily because it is now expanded into the Internet and satellite markets. Sirius XM Radio alone has twenty-nine million subscribers.[41] Your cellphone also uses radio technology.

Some important announcements have been made via radio: the Hindenburg disaster, the election victory of President Warren G. Harding, and the attack on Pearl Harbor are a few. These announcements gave the news immediacy and set the listeners into the story. Had there been radio two thousand years ago, there might have been a program on titled "Christmas on the Air," because the birth of Jesus was announced "on the air" and "in the air." And the listeners were changed forever.

We Are Proud to Announce

Of the major characters in the Christmas story, the angels are pivotal to the entire drama. An angel first announced the birth of Jesus to Mary, the birth of Jesus to Joseph, and the birth of Jesus to the shepherds. Angels express the significance of the birth of this baby born in Bethlehem. A remarkable birth gets a remarkable birth announcement.

Angels announced Christmas on the air. If you turn on your radio at Christmastime, you will hear about angels and their roles over and over with songs like these:

- "Angels from the Realms of Glory"
- "It Came Upon a Midnight Clear"
- "Angels We Have Heard on High"
- "The First Noel"
- "While Shepherds Watched Their Flocks"
- "Hark! the Herald Angels Sing"

The first time we hear angels on the air is in the first chapter of the Gospel of Matthew. As we gather around and listen to this Christmas broadcast, I want you to see why it is so important that you always stay tuned to what God may be doing or saying in your life. While angels come and go, God is always on the air.

While the angels play an exciting role, it's just a supporting one. We want to consider a specific interaction that the angels had with a man named Joseph. He would have made a terrible radio actor in the Golden Age because he's silent. If you go to any Christmas play and watch Joseph, all he will ever do is stand by Mary. He never talks in the Gospels. Yet, one of the greatest men in the Bible by far is this Joseph because he was adept at listening and obeying.

God Acts in Unusual Ways

"Now the birth of Jesus Christ took place in this way. When his mother Mary had been betrothed to Joseph, before they came together she was found to be with child from the Holy Spirit" (Matthew 1:18).

This verse and the ones that follow it can confuse us about Joseph's marital status. This verse tells us that Joseph was "betrothed" to Mary, in the next verse we see he's thinking about "divorcing" her, and then in verse 20 she is called "his wife." This may have made sense to a Jew two thousand years ago, but it leaves us scratching our heads.

In the Jewish mindset, marriage wasn't an event but a process. First, there was the engagement. Your parents would choose whom you would marry, and at that point, you were contractually bound to the other person.

The second stage was the betrothal. That is what we read about in verse 18. This was equivalent to *our* engagement period. Betrothal typically lasted about a year and was a binding contract that could be dissolved only by divorce. Even though the couple was bound together morally and legally, they were not to have sexual relations until they were married. Verse 18 makes it clear that Joseph and Mary had not "come together."

The final stage was the wedding, which lasted for about a week before the relationship was consummated to begin a lifelong marriage. God introduced a pregnancy into step two of the process for Joseph and Mary, although couples were not to be involved sexually until the end of step three. Joseph was trying to do right, but God was making it seem all wrong. After discovering Mary's pregnancy, Joseph fell asleep considering his options: "And her husband Joseph, being a just man and unwilling to put her to shame, resolved to divorce her quietly" (Matthew 1:19).

Joseph was likely a faithful Jew, even a serious student of the law. He could have had Mary stoned because the Jewish penalty for adultery was death. He could have forced her to admit that the baby was not his and shame her. Instead, Joseph just wanted to tear up the contract and walk away. He wanted to change the channel on his life, but God said, "Don't Touch That Dial!" Joseph is learning, as we need to learn, that God acts in unusual ways.

God Speaks at Unusual Times

"But as he considered these things, behold, an angel of the Lord appeared to him in a dream, saying, 'Joseph, son of David, do not fear to take Mary as your wife, for that which is conceived in her is from the Holy Spirit'" (Matthew 1:20).

God spoke to Joseph in an unusual space. God doesn't speak to Joseph while he is awake. He speaks to Joseph while he is asleep. God also spoke to Joseph in an unusual state. Joseph is in the midst of making a tough, life-altering decision. There's no way he fell asleep easily that night. From the moment that Joseph noticed Mary's pregnancy, he must have wondered, "Who's the father?" Here in his dream, God gives Joseph an answer that would shake the world: "I am." God doesn't always speak to us when life is humming along as normal. When we're struggling during a test of faith, we need to pay attention and be ready to obey.

When I was considering planting my current church, I struggled. Did I want to leave a church where I had been for almost twenty years, with a thriving ministry, staff, and facilities? Did I want to put a television ministry I had spent ten years building on the line knowing I might lose it?

These thoughts were racing through my mind as I was sitting in a doctor's office. As I was going back and forward as to what I should do, the thought came to me, *You could stay right where you are and coast the rest of your life*. I picked up a copy of *Forbes* and saw a little quote on the side of the page: "Remember, when you are coasting it is all downhill." I almost looked around to see if God was sitting right beside me speaking into my ear. But I knew God had spoken and I knew God expected me to listen to what he told me and to obey what I heard. I had come close to forgetting the whole thing when God said, "Don't touch that dial!"

God Accomplishes Unusual Things

When God told Joseph what was about to happen, he also told Joseph what to name the baby. The human name for this boy would be *Jesus*, which is the Greek form of the Hebrew *Yeshua,* which is the Hebrew form of the English name *Joshua*. It means "God saves." That one name tells us who Jesus is (God) and what Jesus does (saves).

For centuries the Jewish nation had been awaiting the Messiah, someone who would save them from the Egyptians, then the Babylonians, and then the Romans. But Joseph realized something unusual; this Messiah, this Jesus, would save his people not from a sovereign but from their sins. We've heard that Jesus was this kind of Savior all of our lives, but two thousand years ago, that is not the Savior the Jewish people were expecting. The single cause of every problem we have on this planet is sin. God's angel had just announced to this Jewish father-to-be that God had sent the one solution to that problem—a Savior.

When Joseph wakes up, his only response is to do what God had told him to do. If Joseph had changed the dial of his life, he would not have witnessed the greatest, most momentous, life-changing birth in the history of the world.

When life is hard, times are tough, and you are thinking about giving up on the church, giving up on your marriage, giving up on truth, giving up on prayer, giving up on God, and giving up on yourself, don't touch that dial. God still acts in unusual ways. He still speaks in unusual times and still accomplishes unusual things to those who will stay tuned to him.

Prayer for This Week: *Holy God, when my struggles are great and I want to doubt your programming, give me the courage to listen and obey.*

Question for This Week: What keeps you tossing and turning at night? What would it look like for you to stick with God *through* the mess?

28

Demons: The Bad Guys

Scriptures for This Week

- Colossians 1:15-20
- Mark 1:21-28
- Mark 5:1-20
- Acts 8:4-8
- 1 John 4:1-6

Demons Are Villains

Almost every sport has a team called the Angels or the Devils or the Demons. In movies, demonic forces played major roles in *Rosemary's Baby, Angel Heart, The Devil's Advocate,* and *Ghost Rider.* Deep down, we all recognize that this world is populated with spiritual beings. The Bible affirms this as well and tells us some serious stories of demons.

When God created the world, "God saw everything that he had made, and behold, it was *very good*" (Genesis 1:31, emphasis mine). Angels had also been created. Since everything was good, there could not be evil angels or demons. However, in the third chapter of Genesis, Satan, in the form of a serpent, tempted Adam and Eve to disobey God. So, as we discussed in chapter 19, somewhere between Genesis 1:31 and Genesis 3:1 there was a rebellion in the angelic world.

Demons are evil angels who rebelled against God and now work evil in the world.[42] We tend to sit at the extremes when we think about demons: either we ignore them or we grow obsessed with them. Most of us assume we have never encountered a demon, but most of us have encountered demon-influenced people or the results of demonic work. As we go along, you'll start to see how this is true.

Demons Are Viable

One of the greatest dangers facing both the church and the world today is not the existence of demons but our disbelief in them. German theologian Rudolph Bultmann expresses the opinion of many today: "It is impossible to use electric light and the wireless and to avail ourselves of modern medical and surgical discoveries and at the same time believe in the New Testament world of demons and spirits."[43] I disagree. Demons are real and there are several reliable stories that demonstrate their presence.

One of the major emphases of the entire Gospel of Mark is the power demons exercise over people. The first miracle that Mark records is at the beginning of the ministry of Jesus:

> The people were amazed at his teaching, because he taught them as one who had authority, not as the teachers of the law. Just then a man in their synagogue who was possessed by an impure spirit cried out, "What do you want with us, Jesus of Nazareth? Have you come to destroy us? I know who you are—the Holy One of God!"
>
> "Be quiet!" said Jesus sternly. "Come out of him!" The impure spirit shook the man violently and came out of him with a shriek.
>
> The people were all so amazed that they asked each other, "What is this? A new teaching—and with authority! He even gives orders to impure spirits and they obey him" (Mark 1:22-27 NIV).

The second miracle Mark talks about is found just a few verses later:

> That evening after sunset the people brought to Jesus all the sick and demon-possessed. The whole town gathered at the door, and Jesus healed many who had various diseases. He also drove out many demons, but he would not let the demons speak because they knew who he was (Mark 1:32-34 NIV).

Mark says in 1:39 that *everywhere Jesus went he encountered demons.* God himself not only believes in demons, but he encountered and commanded them. The demons, in turn, believe in God. James 2:19 (NIV) says, "You believe that there is one God. Good! Even the demons believe that—and shudder." Demons have more sense than atheists do, and just because you might not believe in demons doesn't mean that they don't believe in the power of God in you.

Demons Are Vicious

Not all sin is caused by Satan or demons. But demonic activity is a factor in much of our sin. It is behind the violence, the terrorism, the sexual perversion, and the hostility toward Christ and Christianity that we find in our world today. The Bible gives us examples of this.

The story of the Geresene demoniac in Mark 5 shows us that not only did the Lord Jesus believe in demonic forces, he wasn't afraid to address them even though they are *impure* (NIV). Here *impure* means "vicious" or "degenerate," and the fact that the demoniac "cut himself with stones" shows us that demons love to cause physical pain. Demons are also bloodthirsty. Psalm 106:37 says that people "sacrificed their sons and their daughters to the demons." Child sacrifice—whether the child is born yet or not—is evidence of demonic activity. God is in the life-giving business. Satan and his demons are in the life-taking business.

In Matthew 10:1, demons are also described as *unclean spirits*. The word *unclean* means "morally filthy." The pervasiveness of pornography and the worship of sex is due in no small part to the activity of demons.

Finally, in Matthew 12:45 (NIV), demons are referred to as *wicked spirits*. The spiritual work of demons is to encourage worship of false gods. The devil and his demons are behind false religions. Paul said in 1 Corinthians 10:20 (NIV), "The sacrifices of pagans are offered to demons, not to God, and I do not want you to be participants with demons." The number one desire of every demon is to keep people from coming to the true God, hearing the true gospel, and placing their faith in Jesus Christ.

Demons Are Vanquished

I don't want to underestimate *or* overestimate the power of demons. Demons do have great power. They give human beings great power. I am often asked, "Is it possible for a Christian to be demon-possessed?" The answer is no. No demon is more powerful than the Holy Spirit. Once the Holy Spirit takes control of a Christian's life, all the demons in hell cannot force him to move out. However, followers of Christ can be demon-*influenced*. That is why we need to keep our spiritual guard up, stay in the word, continue to pray, and not allow ourselves to fall into temptation.

Three verses give us some keys when it comes to understanding the limited power of the devil and his demons.

> Submit yourselves, then, to God. Resist the devil, and he will flee from you (James 4:7 NIV).
>
> You, dear children, are from God and have overcome them, because the one who is in you is greater than the one who is in the world (1 John 4:4 NIV).
>
> And having disarmed the powers and authorities, he made a public spectacle of them, triumphing over them by the cross (Colossians 2:15 NIV).

If you do not follow Jesus and do not have his Holy Spirit living within you, then you are defeated before you have even started. But the moment you come to the cross of Jesus Christ and trust him as your Lord and Savior, you will battle demons, but you will never be possessed or defeated by them.

Demons Are Visible

We may not be able to see them with our eyes, but demons are visible in the lives of people. We can see the *destruction of* their influence and the *deliverance from* their influence all around us. Adolf Hitler was responsible for the deaths of approximately twelve million people.[44] What you may not know is that Hitler was initiated into Satanism by a man named Dietrich Eckart, one of the seven founders of the Nazi Party. They formed an inner circle known as the Federal Commissary for Occultism. This was a group of Satanists who practiced black magic to achieve communication with demons. Hitler has often been called "evil personified."

Sometimes we see the *deliverance* from the influence of demons in a graphic way. A friend of mine served ten years in a Georgia prison and saw how demonic powers can oppress and even possess people. Another inmate, a friend named Alonso, attended chapel one night and sought help from God for the sin in his life. My friend tells this story:

> Shortly after Alonso started to pray, he began to scream out in agony, making startling, animal-like noises. Some shocked inmates tried to pray over him, but nothing would loosen him from the power that controlled him, and he returned to his cell exhausted.
>
> The next day a small group of us met to seek God in prayer and discuss what to do. We agreed to fast for three days and then pray over Alonso for his deliverance. Then we met at the chaplain's office to pray over Alonso as he asked God for forgiveness of his sins and gave his heart to the Lord.
>
> Immediately, he was taken back into the same kind of convulsions. This time we were prepared, and the entire group of us began to call on the name of Jesus for Alonso's deliverance. Within a minute, the screaming and convulsions ceased. Alonso stood up, and the look of complete peace and serenity on his face is still ingrained in my mind to this day. I remember thinking, *This can't be the same person*, but it was. God had provided a miracle, and Alonso stood before us delivered.

The Bible teaches that demons will become more active and their influence will be felt more and more as time goes along. Paul said, "The Spirit clearly says that in later times some will abandon the faith and follow deceiving spirits and things taught by demons" (1 Timothy 4:1 NIV). We cannot ignore demons, but we don't need to fear them either.

Prayer for This Week: *Lord, show me the power in Christ and the power in the cross so that I might face the devil and all of his demons and win every time.*

Question for This Week: Who do you know that is bound by the spirit of rebellion against God? How can you pray and present the gospel to them for their freedom?

29

Angels: The Good Guys

Scripts for This Week

- Psalm 8
- Luke 2:8-15
- Nehemiah 9:5-6
- Psalm 91:9-16
- Revelation 5:11-14

Angel Attraction

When I was in the first grade, our class was chosen to put on a Christmas play for the entire school. Everybody was wondering which part they would get to play. I was excited to get out of class, but I was more excited about the possibility of being an angel. I thought it would be cool to wear wings. I've always wanted to fly. I wasn't chosen for that part, and to this day I still regret not being able to wear one of those angel costumes.

Angels and demons are two fascinating spiritual beings, and Jesus encountered both of them during his life. Even today, angels continue to be hot topics among believers and nonbelievers alike. With angel books, catalogs, seminars, pins, paintings, and even newsletters, angels are big business.

Even in the most technologically advanced time in history, surveys show public belief in angels is still strong. A Harris Interactive Poll found that nearly 7 in 10 Americans believe in angels; 68 percent of American adults believe in angels compared to 74 percent of teens.[45] As Billy Graham said,

> I am convinced that these heavenly beings exist and they provide unseen aid on our behalf. I do not believe in angels,

> because someone has told me about a dramatic visitation from an angel impressive as such rare testimonies may be...I do not believe in angels because of the sudden world-wide emphasis on the reality of Satan and demons. I do not believe in angels, because I have ever seen one—because I haven't. I believe in angels because the Bible says there are angels and I believe the Bible to be the true Word of God.[46]

While there is a huge fascination with angels, not a lot of good information about them exists. Let's fix that.

Angelology

Max Lucado describes the study of angels as biblical whale watching. "Angels surface just long enough to grant a glimpse and raise a question, but then disappear before we have a full view."[47] Angels have always been and continue to be mysterious. But they don't have to be.

Angels are not eternal. They are created beings with a beginning, but they will live eternally. Angels do not have bodies like humans, so they cannot die. They are 100 percent pure, immortal spiritual beings. Even though in Scripture they are always portrayed as male when they take on human form, angels have no gender. And though angels take on human form, humans do not take on angelic form; people don't become angels when they die.

Angels rank below God, but they are above humans in some ways. They are not omnipotent like God, but they are stronger than humans. They are not omniscient but have greater knowledge than humans, and though they are not omnipresent, they can travel more easily and quickly than humans.[48]

Angels are messengers. The word *angel* or its derivatives occurs in the Bible almost three hundred times. The most common term means "messenger." The most famous picture of angels in all the Bible is probably in Luke 2. In the Christmas story we see angels appearing to Mary, to Joseph (twice), and to the shepherds. A whole choir of them announce the birth of Jesus:

"Glory to God in the highest,
and on earth peace among those with whom he is pleased!"
(Luke 2:14)

This isn't the last place we see them, however, nor is it the first. Why are they here and what purpose do they serve?

Angels Worship for God's Glory

When God and Job talked, God informs Job that when he created the heavens and the earth, the angels were singing and shouting for joy (Job 38:4-7)! Angels were worshiping at the incarnation when Jesus came into this world. Listen to Hebrews 1:6: "And again, when [God] brings the firstborn into the world, he says, 'Let all God's angels worship him.'" They worshiped then and they worship now.

The angels' worship of God never ends:

> All the angels were standing around the throne and around the elders and the four living creatures. They fell down on their faces before the throne and worshiped God, saying,
> "Amen!
> Praise and glory
> and wisdom and thanks and honor
> and power and strength
> be to our God for ever and ever.
> Amen!"
> (Revelation 7:11-12 NIV)

So, angels worship, but what may be even more fascinating is that we worship with angels today and they worship with us. The author of Hebrews said, "But you have come to Mount Zion, to the city of the living God, the heavenly Jerusalem. You have come to thousands upon thousands of angels in joyful assembly, to the church of the firstborn, whose names are written in heaven" (Hebrews 12:22-23 NIV).

From everything we can find in Scripture, angels worshiped God from the time they were created. At almost every great event in the Bible, you will find angels worshiping God. If angels who cannot be saved worship God, how much more should we who have been saved and can have a personal relationship with Christ, worship him in spirit and in truth?

Angels Work for God's Pleasure

We've seen that angels are messengers and worshipers, but is that all they do? Contrary to popular belief, angels don't just sit on clouds playing harps all day. They have work to do. Psalm 103:20 (NIV) says they "do his bidding" and "obey his word." This paints a picture of angels standing at attention, waiting on an order from God to do whatever he wants them to do.

Their major work, believe it or not, is to take care of us and to look after our needs. Hebrews 1:14 says they are "ministering spirits sent out to serve for the sake of those who are to inherit salvation." In two words, they *provide* and *protect*. Angels provided food for Jesus after he had been fasting for forty days in the wilderness. They provided food for Elijah, who was alone in the wilderness without anything to eat or drink. And more than a few of us have been provided for by others that we thought were people but may have been angels.

We have all heard of guardian angels. I hate to burst a bubble, but the Bible doesn't teach that everyone has a guardian angel. Angels guard and protect with one condition: Angelic protection is limited only to those who know God, love God, and trust God. Psalm 34:7 says, "The angel of the LORD encamps around those who fear him, and delivers them." The most powerful and wealthy people in this world don't enjoy the protection that God's servants have.

On President Obama's first trip overseas, he flew in Air Force One, the most technologically advanced aircraft in the world. When he landed he got into the $300,000 presidential limousine made of reinforced steel, aluminum, titanium, and ceramic with an armor-plated body. With a sealed interior, night-vision camera, an armored fuel tank, pump-action shotguns, tear-gas cannons, oxygen tanks, and a supply of the president's blood, it's an impressive fortress of protection. If you are a follower of Jesus, you have better protection than that.

If God opened our eyes, sometimes we would see angels escorting our kids to school, encircling the aircraft we are flying in, monitoring the moves of the surgeon operating on us, and watching over us as we sleep. Psalm 91:11 says, "For he will command his angels concerning you to guard you in all your ways." We can be grateful that angels are working for God's pleasure.

Angels War for God's Victory

Contemporary portrayals of angels don't match up with the biblical picture. Often we see angels like fairies with see-through wings—meek and mild-mannered. But they are mighty in power.

At the moment of Jesus's arrest, Peter drew a sword and cut off the ear of the high priest's servant. Jesus chastised him and said, "Do you think that I cannot appeal to my Father, and he will at once send me more than twelve legions of angels?" (Matthew 26:53). One legion was equal to six thousand soldiers so you do the math. At least seventy-two thousand angels were ready to rescue their Master.

These angels are also mighty angels. Second Thessalonians 1:7 calls them his "mighty angels." It took only one angel to kill every firstborn child in the entire nation of Egypt, to close the mouths of the lions to protect Daniel, or to wipe out an entire army. God's angels are powerful.

The war that was fought in heaven between the angels and demons would make every other war fought on earth look like a picnic. "Then war broke out in heaven. Michael and his angels fought against the dragon, and the dragon and his angels fought back. But he was not strong enough, and they lost their place in heaven" (Revelation 12:7-8 NIV).

As powerful as the devil and his demons are, they are no match for God's angels. The angels are on the side of Jesus Christ. They worshiped him when he came into this world, they worked for him after he left this world, and they will war for him when he comes back to this world.

Prayer for This Week: *Holy God, thank you for your salvation and the loving care you offer me through your angels. May I join them in worship, work, and battle for your name.*

Question for This Week: When have you experienced God's supernatural protection? What does this say about his great love for you?

30

There's More to Life

Scriptures for This Week

- Romans 5:15-17
- Isaiah 58:9-12
- John 10:1-10
- Psalm 37:25-26
- Acts 20:22-24

Two Kinds of Life

One of the greatest movies ever made is *Braveheart*. Some of the greatest thoughts ever uttered on the silver screen appear in that film, such as this from William Wallace: "Every man dies, but not every man lives."

Existing and living are not the same. The ancient Greeks understood this in a way that we don't. In English, we have one word for *life*, but the Greeks had two words. *Bios* refers to bone-and-flesh existence—the same life we share with animals. *Zoe* is life that is qualitative, spiritual, and inward, not physical or outward.

The ancient Greeks understood there is more to life than life. It has been said that man's greatest problem is not to add years to his life (*bios*) but life to his years (*zoe*). Jesus came to die for us and to give us eternal life, not just life after death. Jesus came that we might live abundantly, right now. He didn't come just to give us a permanent extension of life. He came to give a purposeful intention to life.

Experience the Life of Jesus

In John 10:10, Jesus said "The thief does not come except to steal, and to kill, and to destroy. I have come that they may have life, and that they may have it more abundantly" (John 10:10 NKJV). The word Jesus uses here for life isn't *bios* but *zoe*. Jesus said, "I didn't come just to give you quantitative life. I came to give you qualitative life. There is more to life than life and I have come to give you that more."

As we get older we get more concerned about the quality of our life than the quantity of our life. When we are young, our goal is to have a *long* life. As we get older, we realize the goal should be a *good* life. As someone once said, "If I'd known I was going to live this long, I would have taken better care of myself."

Life is not all about possessions or financial security. When Jesus called the disciples to follow him, every one of them left everything behind. Neither did he guarantee a long or peaceable life; tradition tells us that the disciples died by swords, crucifixion, fire, beheading, or beating.

Because Jesus was God, the life he gives is God-made. It is abundant. It is an overflowing life with surplus and plenty. In Jesus, all our needs are satisfied.

I dated quite a bit before I met Teresa, but from the moment I met her, I didn't want any more women. I found more than what I was looking for in her. I was confident I had found the one woman for me and I had contentment in my heart that she was all I would ever want. When you are looking for more and you find that more, you don't want any more. There is more to life than life and that more is found in Jesus.

Enjoy the Presence of Jesus

What is it about having a personal relationship with Jesus that brings contentment, satisfaction, and joy? The key is found in the context of John 10, the picture of the shepherd and his sheep.

Sheep who have a good shepherd live content and satisfied. For three years, Jesus gave his disciples what a good shepherd gives to sheep. They enjoyed his presence, walked with him, talked with him, and lay beside him at night. They sat at his feet during the day, listened to his teachings, and learned from his actions. Is there anything greater in life than knowing you can get personal with your caring God who is going to speak to you, guide you, and listen for you? This is what gives life *more.*

We can experience God's presence every day of every year until we leave this life and experience our full eternal life in the full presence of God forever. Jesus said to his disciples and to us, "I am with you always, to the end of the age" (Matthew 28:20). You have God's undivided attention. He is always there. One ancient Greek said, "Touching his human nature, Jesus is no longer present with us; touching his divine nature, He is never absent from us."[49]

Though we always have the presence of God, we do not always have the awareness of his presence. My favorite season is autumn when the trees fill with colors, exploding into a quilt of red, yellow, and orange. It reminds me of the presence of God in my life because those colors are in the leaves *all year*. They are hidden by the abundant green chlorophyll until the sunlight decreases, the chlorophyll breaks down, and the green disappears. Then one morning, we wake up and those hidden fall colors start appearing. They were there all along, but we just didn't see them.

Sheep have poor eyesight. They can't always see the shepherd, but the shepherd is always there whether they can see him or not. There is more to life than life, and it is found in enjoying the presence of Jesus.

Expect the Provision of Jesus

Every disciple left everything to follow Jesus. Yet, we never read of them missing a meal or needing a place to sleep or something to wear. Every one of their needs was met. All they had was the calling of Jesus on their life, and wherever Jesus leads, he meets the needs. Wherever Jesus guides, he provides.

I am not promising anyone that Jesus will always give you everything you want, only what you need. I had this proved to me in the greatest way when I was a seminary student. Teresa and I arrived at the school with about $100 in our bank account, and I was still recovering from back surgery. Under doctor's orders, I could not do anything for the first three months. She, however, worked as a legal secretary and was making just enough for our bills and groceries. When I was cleared to work, I was called to pastor a church about ninety miles from the seminary. My grand salary was $100 a week.

Then the famous "Blizzard of '77" hit. It snowed so much we didn't see our car for almost two months, and for three months we were cut off from our little church. We didn't know what we were going to do because Teresa's salary wasn't enough. That first Friday I went to check my mailbox and found a check for $100 from this country church. And for the next twelve Fridays, I got a check for $100 even though I could not fulfill my pastoral duties.

I will always be grateful to that little church for keeping food on our table and heat in our apartment. I realize looking back that this is part of the abundant life—knowing that Jesus is more aware of your needs than you are and will meet all your needs according to his riches.

Embrace the Purpose of Jesus

Tom Brady, the quarterback for the New England Patriots, is one of the greatest quarterbacks who has ever played in the NFL. By the age of twenty-eight, he won three Super Bowls. But his personal life hasn't quite matched his professional life. In an interview on *60 Minutes*, he wondered aloud, "Why do I have three Super Bowl rings and still think there is something greater out there for me?...I think 'God, it's got to be more than this.' I mean this isn't, can't be what it is all cracked up to be."[50]

Even probable NFL Hall of Famers say, "There's got to be more to life than this." Maybe Tom needs to learn to be a sheep. Sheep don't exist just to eat some grass, drink some water, and eventually die. Sheep exist for the benefit of the shepherd. They give food and clothing. They are productive for the shepherd rather than for themselves.

Though the disciples experienced violent deaths, we are sitting here today talking about them because they experienced the *more* of life. They fulfilled the purpose God had for them, and the only thing that gives life value is a purpose that will outlive your life. The apostle Paul said in effect in Acts 20:24, "If I don't fulfill the purpose God put me here for, my life counts as nothing."

In that *60 Minutes* interview, Steve Croft asked Brady, "What's the answer?" Brady said, "I wish I knew. I wish I knew."

We live for the One who gave his life so that we might have life and give it to others. Life begins when we give the life that will end in order to have the life that will never end. Yes, there is more to life than life and that more is found in Jesus.

Prayer for This Week: *Great Shepherd, let me follow you as you lead me to abundance, holding loosely to all that I believe is mine so that you may have all that is yours.*

Question for This Week: How can you let Jesus guide you freely and fill you fully?

31

Towel Off

Scriptures for This Week

- Luke 12:35-40
- John 13:1-17
- Romans 12:3-8
- Hebrews 3:1-6
- Luke 1:46-55

When Rulers Serve

In 1981, President Ronald Reagan was recovering from the gunshot wound that almost took his life. Just days after his surgery, one of his aides walked into his room to discover him on his hands and knees wiping up water from the floor. When the aide rushed over to him to ask what he was doing, President Reagan said, "I was worried that my nurse might get in trouble."[51]

Imagine that scene for a moment. The leader of the free world, the most powerful person on the planet, while recovering from an assassination attempt climbs out of his hospital bed in order to clean up some spilled water to protect his recovery nurse from a scolding.

John 13:1-20 tells us another story about a powerful leader who was facing some fierce wounds of his own. On the night before Good Friday, Jesus knew he would be crucified in less than twenty-four hours. The smell of betrayal hung in the air. The shadow of death hovered over his head. He was going to be betrayed, arrested, tried, mocked, scourged, and crucified. Yet with the weight of the world on his shoulders, he does not think about himself. He thinks about dirty feet.

This story illustrates one of the greatest lessons you will ever learn, not only about what it means to follow the leader, but the blessing that comes when you do. The lower you go, the greater you become. If you are going to touch people the way Jesus did and make an eternal difference in the lives of others, you've got to do what Jesus did.

Surrender Your Power

Verse 3 says, "Jesus knew that the Father had put all things under his power, and that he had come from God and was returning to God" (John 13:3 NIV). God had put everything under his power. He could have said, "I am not doing this." He could have stopped the arrest, the trial, and even the crucifixion. He could have come down off the cross any time because he was in charge and had all the power.

He answered to no one—except his heavenly Father. "So he got up from the meal, took off his outer clothing, and wrapped a towel around his waist. After that, he poured water into a basin and began to wash his disciples' feet, drying them with the towel that was wrapped around him" (John 13:4-5 NIV).

Back in that dusty, dirty day of bare feet and sandals, foot washing was a common practice at public baths and upon entering a home. It was the job of a slave, not a self-respecting Jew. In this case, the disciples had rented an upper room and no slave was present.

To make it clear that he was taking on the role of a slave, Jesus took off his outer clothing, robes that slaves didn't have, and wrapped a towel around his waist just like a slave. Jesus was sending this unmistakable message to his disciples: "Though you know I have all the power, I am surrendering my power and becoming your slave." The One who was higher than the heavens stooped low. The Sovereign of the universe became a servant to his disciples.

When nobody else will take up the towel, a follower of Jesus will. A follower of Jesus will do things other people won't, stand up when others sit, remain silent when others speak, serve when no one else will. As a mom or dad, CEO or manager, captain, teacher, or chief, whatever power, authority, and influence you have, God did not give it to you so you could use it for your benefit. He gave it to you for the benefit of others. A follower of Jesus surrenders his power for the good of others.

Serve Other People

These disciples were waiting on each other to do what Jesus did for a hidden reason. Luke tells us about an argument they were having that evening:

> A dispute also arose among them as to which of them was considered to be greatest. Jesus said to them, "The kings of the Gentiles lord it over them; and those who exercise authority over them call themselves Benefactors. But you are not to be like that. Instead, the greatest among you should be like the youngest, and the one who rules like the one who serves. For who is greater, the one who is at the table or the one who serves? Is it not the one who is at the table? But I am among you as one who serves" (Luke 22:24-27 NIV).

They weren't interested in serving but in ruling. They weren't looking for service but for servants. While the basin of water sits in the corner and the towel hangs on a rack, they are arguing over who ought to be number one in the kingdom. Jesus does for them what they are not willing to do.

Two thousand years later, not much has changed. We still don't ask the same questions Jesus asked. We ask, "How much money do you make?" Jesus asks, "How much money do you give?" We ask, "How high have you climbed?" Jesus asks, "How low have you gone?" We count all the people that report to us. Jesus wants to count all the people that we serve.

Serving requires our humility. We lower ourselves in order to raise up others, even those we know don't like us. Remember verse 2? "The evening meal was in progress, and the devil had already prompted Judas, the son of Simon Iscariot, to betray Jesus" (John 13:2 NIV). Here was a disciple whose feet were caked with the dirt of disloyalty, and Jesus washed his feet just the same.

Part of following the leader means taking the high road, and the high road is when we are willing to treat others better than they treat us. We should willingly do for others what others are not willing to do for us.

Shift Your Perception

Why did Jesus do this? "Having loved his own who were in the world, he loved them to the end" (John 13:1 NIV).

For three years, Jesus had loved these men as they had never been loved before and had modeled love for them unlike any they had ever seen. School is about out and Jesus is saving some of his strongest lessons for last. They now know if you are going to love others, the towel has to come off the rack and into your hands, and you must use it to serve others.

Now we can grasp what Jesus said, "I have set you an example that you should do as I have done for you" (John 13:15 NIV). Jesus was not telling us that we ought to establish a new ritual in the church of washing feet. He was saying, "Think the same way." Always see how you can serve others and don't worry about how others can serve you. Shift your thinking. Switch your perceptions, and then you'll be able to do the next thing.

Share Your Passion

Most of us carry around in our pocket a picture of someone who lived this out. George Washington is still to this day known as the greatest American of all. He led the Revolutionary Army, defeated the most powerful nation, and served as the first president of our country. However, he is famous because he spent all of his life surrendering his power, serving other people, shifting his perception, and showing his passion.

When he was asked to command the Revolutionary Army, he did so only after guaranteeing that after the war was over he would resign his commission. When he was elected president, he refused to let people make him the king. He refused a third term and set a precedent that every president followed up until Franklin Roosevelt.

When King George III asked American painter Benjamin West what Washington was going to do now that the war was over, West replied, "From what I have heard, he is going to return to his farm." With a gasp, King George said, "If he does that he will be the greatest man in the world."

George Washington was a great man, but the greatest man who has ever lived showed us all the way to greatness. Jesus didn't just take up the towel. He took up a cross and washed the dirt of sin off our hearts by his own blood. When you follow the leader, you will want to follow the passion of the leader.

You serve others in order to share your passion for them. This sheds light on one other part of this story.

> He came to Simon Peter, who said to him, "Lord, are you going to wash my feet?"
>
> Jesus replied, "You do not realize now what I am doing, but later you will understand."
>
> "No," said Peter, "you shall never wash my feet" (John 13:6-8 NIV).

Even though Peter said, "You'll never wash my feet," he did not go on to say, "But I'll be more than glad to wash yours." If we are honest, Peter's response reveals a lot about us; we don't serve because we don't share Jesus's passion. Jesus was doing for Peter what Peter should have been doing for Jesus. Peter wasn't willing to wash the feet of Jesus because he still didn't love Jesus, or his fellow disciples, the way he needed to. To love people is to serve people. When you serve people, you show people you love them. Go low, get dirty, take up the towel, and give your life in the service of others.

Prayer for This Week: *Father, thank you for showing me the way to greatness. Teach me to take off my pride and put on humility as I serve others today.*

Question for This Week: How can you make love your greatest responsibility and service your first job in every role you fill in life?

32

The Warrior Rises

Scriptures for This Week

- 1 Corinthians 1:18-25
- Matthew 27:15-26
- Hebrews 10:1-4
- Galatians 3:10-14
- Romans 3:21-26

Fallen Heroes

What would you do if you were the president of the United States? If I had the chance, I would order Starbucks to give out free coffee every Monday. I would change the national symbol from an eagle to a football. And I would order that in all movies the hero never dies.

Nothing ruins a movie for me more than when the hero dies. A dying hero seems unjust regardless of how noble or how great the cause he or she died for.

One hero died for the noblest of causes—to rescue a world that had been created pure and perfect but turned profane and polluted when the serpent tempted the first man and woman to disobey and rebel against God. The human race was plunged into a war with sin that it could not win against an enemy, Satan, it could not beat.

All looked lost until God promised to send someone to restore the relationship that the first humans had with God. That promise is found in Genesis 3:15.

> "And I will put enmity
> Between you and the woman,
> And between your seed and her Seed;
> He shall bruise your head,

And you shall bruise His heel."

(Genesis 3:15 NKJV)

From that single prophecy the picture of a warrior forms in the minds and hearts of rabbis and Old Testament scholars down through the ages. When would this warrior come? How would he arrive? How big would his army be? How long would the war to rescue this world take?

Surprise Savior

The people expected this warrior to take over this world and usher in a kingdom where Israel would be restored to her rightful, premier place on the planet. This warrior was the bruiser. No one could touch him because he was God's Son. God sent him to finish a war he didn't start, but rather than fighting, he would win by dying.

When you understand why Jesus died on the cross and what happened after his death, then you understand why only he could give every one of us the ability to win our war. Our two greatest enemies are sin and death, and Jesus is the only warrior capable of defeating both.

When he showed up, he seemed anything but a warrior. He was from a little town and a carpenter by trade. He neither looked nor acted like a warrior. Still many believed he must be the one. He had a power to perform unbelievable miracles and a presence that made you feel as if you were talking to God himself. This had to be him.

To those who had convinced themselves the warrior had arrived, it must have been hard to watch when "[Pilate] had Jesus flogged, and handed him over to be crucified" (Matthew 27:26 NIV).

How could this be? Surely this warrior had not come to die without wielding a sword or slaying even one of those blasted Roman soldiers. He went off to the cross without a whimper. But this death, this cross, turned out to be his greatest weapon. When you understand why Jesus died, you understand why only he could have been this warrior.

Jesus Sacrificed His Life for Me

Most of us know where Jesus died (outside of Jerusalem). Most of us know when he died (around AD 30). Most of us know how he died (by crucifixion). But too many of us don't understand *why* he died.

Passover enlightens us as to why Jesus died. After Israel had spent four hundred years in captivity in Egypt, God raised up a man named Moses to lead them to freedom. On the night of their release, a death angel was poised to visit every home in Egypt, killing each firstborn. To be saved, the Israelites were instructed to kill a lamb and paint its blood on the doorposts of their homes. As the angel proceeded throughout the country, when he saw the blood, he "passed over" that house peacefully. To this day, Jews still celebrate Passover.

After this, God instituted a system of animal sacrifice to continue that principle of blood covering sin. For hundreds of years the Israelites could go to the tabernacle and then later to the temple to slaughter a lamb as a sacrifice for their sins. This was always meant to be a temporary arrangement as a reminder of sin, not a final remedy.

Teresa and I like to celebrate our wedding anniversary by going to a nice restaurant. We enjoy a delicious meal, and then I pay for it with a credit card. When we walk out, the meal hasn't been paid for, but the credit card gives me the privilege of having something immediate for the promise of future payment. All those animal sacrifices that you read about in the Old Testament were, in effect, putting the debt of sin on credit, and the credit kept piling up. Nothing was paid through them.

God required the offering of sacrifices in order to let the people know how serious sin is. It's a formidable opponent we cannot beat. The war against sin was too great for anybody to win—that is, until the warrior came. The warrior used the only weapon that could defeat sin and death and bruise the devil who caused it all. That weapon was not a sword or a spear but a cross. This warrior did the greatest thing any soldier can do in a war. He gave his life for the spiritual freedom of others.

Jesus Substituted His Death for Me

Legally, Jesus was crucified because another man's life was spared. His name was Barabbas, and he was a murderer and a rebel. He was probably public enemy numero uno. He was supposed to die on the middle cross between those two thieves, who were probably his buddies. Had it been any other day or had there been any other person to choose than Jesus, Barabbas would have been the one to die.

After Barabbas was chosen to go free, perhaps he wandered over to that place where he was supposed to be crucified. Maybe he even stood at the foot of the cross and said to this Jesus he had never met, "I don't know who you are, but I know you are dying in my place."

Why do you think Barabbas is even in this story? Because you are Barabbas. I am Barabbas. We are all Barabbas. Jesus was not only his substitute, but he was *our* substitute. He died not only in Barabbas's place, but he died in *our* place. The Lord Jesus Christ "died for us" (1 Thessalonians 5:10). He died for us because he is the only warrior who had the power to win the battle.

That God allowed his own Son to be that warrior and lay down his life for us tells us that we are in a war we can't win. We are in a battle with sin that we can only lose. We face an enemy called "death" that will kill us for all eternity if we do not put our faith and our trust in the warrior.

Jesus Satisfied God's Justice for Me

Later in the New Testament, the apostle Paul wrote in Romans 3 about the animal sacrifices. He said that they weren't payment but a symbolic way of letting everyone know payment was coming. He said that Jesus was crucified to demonstrate the justice of God. God's justice had to be satisfied.

All debt must be paid. The justice of God demands that sin is fully and finally paid for. It isn't ever overlooked. To make sure that no one would question his justice, God sent his Son to be that warrior who would make that final and full payment for sin.

Before you and I were even born and this world was created, God's Son agreed to become the warrior who would take the sin of the human race upon himself. He would take our punishment, pay the bill, fight the battle, and win the war. It was the way that God could forgive us and still be justified in doing so. Our payment for sin was deferred by God's mercy, demanded by God's justice, but delivered by God's grace.

How do we know he was the warrior promised thousands of years ago in that garden? Because the warrior rises. Many warriors have fought, many warriors have bled, and many warriors have died, but this is the warrior who rises.

You need this warrior. If you try to defeat sin in your own power, you will lose. If you die without this warrior, death wins. Come to the cross and surrender your life to him so that the warrior who rose from the dead will come into your life, fight your battles, and give you victory over sin and life after death.

Prayer for This Week: *Father, thank you for revealing the breadth of my sin and for delivering me through your victorious Son. Help me surrender the battle of sin to you.*

Question for This Week: Is there a sin that you think the cross cannot cover? How can you let Jesus fight that battle for you?

Section Six

Church Matters

Jesus promised he would build his church, and beginning in the book of Acts, almost all of the New Testament focuses on its birth, explosive growth, its growing pains, and some of the greatest truths ever penned by human hand. Read and be changed.

33

Set on Fire!

Scriptures for This Week

- Hebrews 12:28-29
- Matthew 3:7-12
- 1 Thessalonians 1:4-10
- Acts 1–2
- Luke 12:49-53

Rebuild the Fire

One of my favorite stories about Billy Graham recalls a time he was doing a crusade in a certain city. Some critics didn't care for his style and methods. Calling a press conference, they said, "If we let that man come to our city and preach his message, he will set the church back fifty years." That got back to Dr. Graham, who smiled and said, "I don't want to set the church back fifty years. I want to set the church back two thousand years."

What was so appealing about the church two thousand years ago? Three thousand people were saved in one day. People shared what they had with others. Ordinary shepherds, farmers, and fishermen were bearing witness about Jesus to anybody who would listen. The early church did what they did without buildings, budgets, or bands. Financially, they had no money. Politically, they had no influence and were just a tiny fraction of the world's population. But what they started is alive and well two thousand years later.

There are 2.1 billion people on this planet who claim Christianity as their faith; that's one out of every three people. Today, we have the same mission and the same message and the same might that can set this world ablaze. Because Jesus is alive and because the Holy Spirit is with us, we ought to be ignited and excited to fulfill this mission of taking this message to the entire world.

Light the Fire

Acts is a spellbinding story of how a ragtag band of believers became a spiritual juggernaut that turned their world upside down for Christ. The book of Acts talks more about the Holy Spirit than any other book in the New Testament. The Spirit is mentioned over fifty times in this one book alone. The major symbol for the Holy Spirit is fire, and because the early church was made up of people who were ignited by God's Spirit, Christianity spread like a fire from one place to another.

Is your Christian faith a raging fire or a dull habit? Someone said, "We are not going to move this world by criticism of it, nor conformity to it, but by the combustion within it of lives ignited by the Spirit of God."[52]

Because Jesus is alive, we should be ignited and excited to share him with the world. We have everything we need to be set on fire for God. We have everything the early church had to be everything the early church was.

We Have a Mission to Fulfill

At the beginning of Acts, the disciples are still wrapping their heads around the risen Jesus and what the resurrection meant. But Jesus sidesteps some of their questions and instead makes a shocking promise: "But you will receive power when the Holy Spirit has come upon you, and you will be my witnesses in Jerusalem and in all Judea and Samaria, and to the end of the earth" (Acts 1:8).

At a time when the disciples had been trembling in fear behind locked doors, Jesus was moving his mission forward, confident in its success. He didn't say, "You *might* be my witnesses" or "You *could* be my witnesses" or "You *should* be my witnesses." He said, "You *will* be my witnesses." This is our mission. So what does it mean?

You can experience something and not bear witness to it—refuse to testify as it were. But you cannot bear witness to something you have not experienced. Are you a witness for Jesus Christ? If not, it's because either you refuse to testify to the Jesus you have experienced or you have never experienced Jesus.

Jesus's witnesses weren't to stay put either. When the Spirit came, they would go to family, friends, and neighbors, then go out into counties and states. Further, they would extend to other countries and cultures. The mission, the fire, the Spirit wasn't going to quit in Jerusalem.

Was Jesus's vision too big? Was his mission unreachable? No. In the twentieth century, Christianity became a global faith and is now practiced in large numbers on every continent of the world, particularly Africa, Asia, and South America. Whereas in the early church Christianity was a minority even in Israel, today 90 percent of all Christians live in countries where they are the majority. If we want to be a church ignited by the Holy Spirit, we have a mission to fulfill.

We Have a Might to Use

Jesus has given the disciples their marching orders. They know what they are to do. They know where they are to do it. But Jesus tells them to wait. For ten days they wait. Then, we come to Acts 2 where the disciples are about to receive the power to carry out the mission.

In the first century, only kings possessed power. Nobody rose to power by earning it or running for office. You were either born into it or you took it at the point of a spear or a sword. But Jesus was not talking about political power or military power but a supernatural power. This kingdom was to be spread by witnesses, not by soldiers, through a gospel of peace, not a declaration of war, by the work of the Holy Spirit, not by the force of bullets or bombs.[53]

In the past, the Holy Spirit would come upon someone for a specific task or a specific purpose. But in Acts 2 he took up permanent residence in the followers of the Lord Jesus Christ. He didn't come into existence now for the first time, but he came in presence for all time. This was "God with us." And this was the birth of the church.

Something amazing happened on the church's birthday: everyone who was speaking was talking about the same thing, "the mighty works of God" (Acts 2:11). Everybody was witnessing because everyone was tapped into the might of God. They were letting the power of the Holy Spirit speak through them.

There are 6,909 languages in the world today. God wants Jesus to be proclaimed in every one of them. This is the promise of Pentecost. If you are in Christ, then the Spirit is in you and Jesus will come out of you.

When the spark of the Holy Spirit meets the kindling of a heart for God, it will ignite a fire for Jesus Christ.

We Have a Message to Share

In verse 14, Peter begins to preach the first sermon in the history of the church, and the same message Peter preached is the unchanging message we are to preach today. Peter tells the whole story about the incarnation, the crucifixion, and the resurrection. The resurrection makes his main point, one that to those Jewish listeners must have been a mind-blowing conclusion: "Let all the house of Israel therefore know for certain that God has made him both Lord and Christ, this Jesus whom you crucified" (Acts 2:36). The resurrection is the crowning proof that Jesus was God's Son.

Peter and all of these witnesses were ignited and excited that Jesus has been raised from the dead. This isn't just something you hear and walk away from. This is something you respond to, and the crowd asks Peter, "What shall we do?" to which Peter answers, "Repent and be baptized every one of you in the name of Jesus Christ for the forgiveness of your sins, and you will receive the gift of the Holy Spirit" (Acts 2:38).

He tells the people to change their mind about Jesus Christ, to turn away from their sin, and to turn their hearts toward him as the risen Lord. Three thousand people did just that. As a result, they received forgiveness of their sins and the gift of the Holy Spirit. When you receive the risen Lord into your heart, you will get freedom from what you used to be and the power to be what you ought to be.

Christianity is a historical faith built around a historical figure named Jesus Christ and substantiated on a historical fact—that he is no longer in the tomb. He is risen. Take it to the world.

Prayer for This Week: *Lord, set us on fire and let our light shine as bright and our faith burn as hot today as it did two thousand years ago.*

Question for This Week: Either you refuse to testify to the Jesus you have experienced or you have never experienced Jesus. What is quenching your fire to share the story of Jesus?

34

Be Sure

Scriptures for This Week

- Mark 1:16-20
- Romans 3:23-24
- Romans 6:5-10
- Acts 2:38-39
- Romans 10:5-13

Attractive Assurance

There are about thirty thousand different kinds of fish, yet most of them share two similarities beyond just living in water and breathing through gills. First, they don't see well except up close. Second, they don't have eyelids, so they can't close their eyes. As spiritual ichthyologists we can apply those two traits to fishing for people. People will see their need for salvation when someone gets close to them and demonstrates what a real Christian is. Likewise, they always have their eyes open, watching to see if our faith is genuine and worthy of their attention.

What does a person need to know and what does a person need to do to become a Christian? The apostle John was one of the earliest followers of Jesus Christ. In 1 John 5:13 (MSG) he says, "My purpose in writing is simply this: that you who believe in God's Son will know beyond the shadow of a doubt that you have eternal life, the reality and not the illusion." John says that we can be sure we have eternal life. My goal is to help you be sure of it, and I'm going to use the letters *s-u-r-e* to make it easy.

See

Libraries are filled with books trying to explain what is wrong with this world. The answer is the world is wrong with the world. We must lovingly speak of sin to people without Christ or else they will never see their need for Christ.

We need to see that we—you, me, your nice neighbor—are sinners in God's eyes and we are separated from him. The Bible says, "For everyone has sinned; we all fall short of God's glorious standard" (Romans 3:23 NLT). You will never see God correctly through your eyes until you understand how God sees you through his eyes. Do you wonder if you too are a sinner? If you are not perfect, you qualify.

We live in a day when instead of admitting our sinfulness, we insist on how good we are. Many of the moral controversies of our day, such as abortion, homosexual marriage, and sex outside of marriage, are attempts to define away sin. Defending our sin doesn't help us destroy our sin.

Understand

"It is this Good News that saves you if you continue to believe the message I told you...Christ died for our sins, just as the Scriptures said. He was buried, and he was raised from the dead on the third day, just as the Scriptures said" (1 Corinthians 15:2-4 NLT). This is the gospel in a nutshell, and understanding that Jesus died for our sins and, as God, came back from the dead is a key to our faith.

Contrary to popular assertions, not all religions can and do lead to heaven. If you bypass Christ and you bypass the cross, you bypass heaven. You will never enter heaven. You won't see anything about it. Jesus said, "I am the way, and the truth, and the life. No one comes to the Father except through me" (John 14:6).

The cross is both a bridge and a wall. It is a bridge to heaven for those who take it and a wall over heaven for those who reject it. If you are going to become a Christian and be sure that you have eternal life, you must understand that Christ, the only sinless man and Son of God, died for your sins and came back from the dead.

Receive

If the world had needed knowledge, God would have sent a teacher. If the world had needed money, God would have sent a philanthropist.

If the world had needed technology, God would have sent a scientist. If the world had needed peace, God would have sent a diplomat. But the world needed forgiveness, so God sent a Savior. Forgiveness is the remedy for sin, and when the Savior offers it, we need to receive it. We need to receive *him.*

Romans 3:22 (TLB) says, "Now God says he will accept us and acquit us—declare us 'not guilty'—if we trust Jesus Christ to take away our sins. And we all can be saved in this same way, by coming to Christ, no matter who we are or what we have been like." If you believe sin exists and see that you are a sinner, then you understand the only remedy for sin is forgiveness. And the Savior provides it in abundance.

Forgiveness is a financial word and sin is like a debt. There are only two things you can do with a debt: pay it or declare bankruptcy. These days, the most famous chapter in the book of life is Chapter 11, and we are all in Chapter 11 with God. Spiritually bankrupt and unable to pay, we try all kinds of ways to pay off that debt. We might go to church, try to live a good life, give money to charity, or work for a good cause, but that is all like trying to pay off a debt with counterfeit money.

Jesus, the Savior, came to earth to pay off a debt he didn't owe, providing God's forgiveness for our sins. That is what a savior does. Following after him is not about taking on punishment but about getting out of the punishment we deserve. It's about gathering up all that proof of our debt and handing it over to him, knowing he'll stamp his ledger with "Paid in full." But at that point we don't walk away happy; we walk *with* him happy because as 1 John 1:7 (NLV) says, "And the blood of Jesus Christ, His Son, makes our lives clean from all sin."

Express

Jesus wants to do more than cancel your sin. He wants to control your life. He also wants to do more than promise you a future. He wants to walk with you in your present. So eternal life isn't just about the promise of living forever somewhere. Eternal life is life that is right with God and spent with God for now and all eternity.

To become a Christian, you have to know that you are a sinner in God's eyes and that Jesus died for your sins and came back from the dead.

Becoming a Christian means receiving God's forgiveness for your sins by trusting Christ. These aren't works you're doing on your own, but they're works you're agreeing with God to do *for* you.

Expressing our desire for Christ to be the Lord of our lives is the moment when Jesus's fishing business is successful. Romans 10: 9 (NLV) says, "If you say with your mouth that Jesus is Lord, and believe in your heart that God raised him from the dead, you will be saved from the punishment of sin." Together, let's take the bait of the gospel out to the sea of humanity and bring others into his kingdom.

Prayer for This Week: *Loving Father, thank you for opening my eyes to sin. Open my eyes so that I might see where my life doesn't please you and draw me near to you, assured of Jesus's love and grace.*

Question for This Week: Expressing our desire for Jesus to be Lord of our life isn't just a one-time act. How can you make this a daily practice that draws you to God's bait instead of the world's?

35

You Can Know Everything Will Work Out

Scriptures for This Week

- Colossians 3:15-17
- Romans 8:28-30
- Job 10:8-12
- Isaiah 38:15-19
- Hebrews 12:7-13

When Bad Days Happen

No matter what you do, how hard you work, or how clean you live, sometimes the wheels just come off. The ship develops a leak. The engine on the plane quits. There are times when life is just a mess. But in those times, we can be certain that everything works toward God's glory and our good. That is not wishful thinking. God himself has given his word and you can take it to the bank.

When you wake up facedown on life's pavement, you need hope. You need encouragement. The Bible is a repository of both.

If I were to compile a list of the ten most comforting verses in the Bible, Romans 8:28 would make the cut: "And we know that God causes all things to work together for good to those who love God, to those who are called according to his purpose" (NASB).

The "we" in the first part of the verse refers to those who "love God." This promise is only for those who love God. But this same verse says that these people have been "called according to his purpose." These are the people who have responded to God's call by surrendering to Christ and becoming a child of God. This promise is not for everybody.

I Must Believe God's Word to Me

What this verse does *not* say is that you will always like or understand what is happening in your life, or that what is happening in your life is always good at the moment. It doesn't say that all things *are* good but that God causes all things to work together *for good*. God *is* good and he will make every piece in the puzzle of your life fit perfectly. God doesn't work all things out for our good most of the time or some of the time. God works all things out together for our good all the time.

You may not always see how things work together for your good. There are a lot of things that I have never seen but know exist. George W. Bush has a ranch in Crawford, Texas, but I've never seen it. Bill Gates is worth $48 billion, but I've never seen a dime of it. If I believe God's word for me, then I can know everything will work out.

It is not just that everything mysteriously settles itself out, but that God works to make it so. Behind every promise of God is the providence of God. Things don't work out coincidentally, things don't work out accidentally, but things work out providentially. *Providence* means to "see before." God sees every event before it occurs and has already provided for it to advance good.

I Must Receive God's Working for Me

We have all had things happen to us that we thought at the time were bad, but looking back were for our good. We lost a job, an investment, a friend, or worse. Yet, things that may seem bad turn out good in the end. Ruth Graham, Billy Graham's wife, once said, "I almost married the wrong man three times."

Have you ever been bitter or angry toward God because of something you think he caused? That he did not give you something you thought you should have? Because he didn't prevent something horrible? Are you resentful about your God-given physical appearance or about a situation that didn't turn out the way you wanted?

God always acts in your best interests. It may be hard to believe in light of the hurt and loss you have experienced, but your bad days are his materials for building good. As we saw in the story of Joseph, sometimes you get a raw deal. Yet Joseph was still able to say, "As for you, you meant evil against me, but God meant it for good" (Genesis 50:20 NASB).

This is a tough phrase to declare in tough times. When we are in the heat of difficulty and life seems rotten, how can we declare God's intention to make the sour taste sweet? Somehow Joseph found a way, and if we understand what the Bible says here, we can too. Every child of God can proclaim that they serve One who turns sour grapes into sweet, life-giving wine.

I Will Achieve God's Will for Me

The last two words of Romans 8:28 are a real key to understanding why God works things out for us. Those two words are "his purpose." God's purpose is not to make us healthy, wealthy, happy, or famous. In the next verse, we find out what God's purpose is. He wants us "to become conformed to the image of His Son" (Romans 8:29 NASB). God works everything in your life to make you become just like Jesus. That is what God has called you for and that is what God has created you for.

God uses our life on earth to prepare us for a life in eternity. When we get into a bad situation, we want God to change the circumstances, but God is more concerned about changing our character. He wants to change what happens *in* us more than what happens *to* us.

If you give your heart and your life to Jesus Christ and become a part of God's family, every day is going to be a good day. I am not going to tell you that God will always make every day pleasant. But without apology I will say that God makes promises he doesn't break. To all of us who surrender to him and trust him, we can know that everything will work for our good because he purposes it.

All Things Mean All

In 1971, Hien Pham was a young, devoted Christian Vietnamese who was a translator with the American military. During a long jail term for aiding the American cause, he was restricted to reading only communist propaganda and doubted the existence of God. One morning, as he completed the dreaded job of cleaning the latrines, he found a paper in the putrid waste. It was a page in English from Romans that an officer had used for toilet paper. He washed it off and slipped it into his hip pocket.

Late at night he read these words: "We know that all things work together for the good of those who love God, to those who are called according to his purpose." He cried out to God asking him for forgiveness and promised that he would never turn his back on his Christian faith.

When Hien Pham was released, he made plans to build a secret boat and escape from the country. Fifty-three other people were planning to escape with him. Everything was well until, just before they were to depart, four Viet Cong knocked on his door. When he opened it, they said they had heard he was trying to escape. Rather than try to control his own destiny, he relied on God to "work all things together for my good." He told the men the truth.

After a pause, he asked, "Are you going to imprison me again?" They leaned forward and whispered, "No, we want to escape with you!" In an incredible escape plan, all fifty-eight of them found themselves on the high seas fleeing Vietnam. They weren't on the water long before they were engulfed by a violent storm.

Hien Pham fell on his face before the Lord, crying out, "Did you just bring us here to die?" At that point those four Viet Cong looked at him and said, "Didn't you know that we were sailors?" If it had not been for the sailing ability of those four Viet Cong, he would have never made it.[54]

Life has a final act. We are going to pass through a lot of difficult, stormy times in this first act, but God makes a promise that everything will work out together for our good. In the final act, we'll see just how he did it and praise the God who loves us.

Prayer for This Week: *Lord God, don't waste the storms I face. Open me to receive your work, knowing that you'll use these bad days to make me more and more into the image of Jesus, my Savior.*

Question for This Week: Where in your life do you need to shift from believing that your struggles are "from God" and instead are "for you"?

36

The Message That Could Change Your Life

Scriptures for This Week

- Mark 8:34-38
- 1 Corinthians 15:1-8
- Acts 13:26-33
- Isaiah 53:7-9
- Romans 1:16-17

Get the Gospel Right

Have you ever said something that came out all wrong? Yogi Berra of the New York Yankees was waiting to be honored, along with his teammates, for winning another World Series. Next to him sat the mayor of New York City and his wife. She looked over at Yogi and said, "Yogi, you look real cool today." Yogi looked over at her and said, "You don't look so hot yourself!"

It's important to say what you mean and mean what you say or you'll never communicate what people need to hear or what you want them to know. If someone gives you wrong directions, you can figure out how to adjust and make it to your destination. Yet if some directions are miscommunicated or not communicated at all, it can be the difference between life and death. If a doctor prescribes a drug but the pharmacist delivers a different one, a patient could die. If you are driving down a dark country road and someone has torn down the warning sign, "Bridge out," you are in for some trouble.

There is a message that will save your life, and whether or not you hear it, believe it, and respond to it in the appropriate way will determine your eternal destiny. We call that message *the gospel.*

Identify and Clarify the Gospel

Even where I live, in the buckle of the Bible belt, there are a growing number of people who have never heard the gospel. But just as concerning are the many, many people who have never *understood* the gospel.

When I went to the dictionary and looked up the word *gospel,* I understood why confusion reigns. These were the various definitions I read:

1. The teachings of Jesus and the Apostles.
2. One of the first four books of the New Testament.
3. A selection from any of the gospels included as a part of a religious service.
4. A teaching or doctrine of a religious teacher.
5. Something as an idea or principle accepted as true.

We're not alone in our confusion about the meaning of *gospel.* Paul says to the church at Corinth, "Now brothers, I want to clarify for you the gospel I proclaimed to you" (1 Corinthians 15:1 HCSB). Even the early church needed to clarify what the gospel was. The gospel needs to be heard and understood, and people should have a chance to respond to it.

Prioritize the Message of the Gospel

Paul says the gospel is *how you are saved.* "You are also saved by it, if you hold to the message I proclaimed to you" (1 Corinthians 15:2 HCSB). You cannot come to know God through faith in Jesus unless you hear and respond to the gospel. Paul calls it "of first importance" (15:3), so we need to prioritize its message.

First Corinthians is one of the most fascinating books in all the New Testament. It reads like a Christian soap opera. This church was in the middle of a bunch of fights: incest, speaking in tongues, lawsuits, and drunken Lord's Suppers. Paul had to teach them about sex, marriage, the single life, and temptation as well. Wouldn't you say that those are all important topics? And yet, he says here the most important subject is the gospel of Jesus Christ.

The church is unique in that its mission is determined by its message. Practically every other organization in the world determines its message by its mission. For example, Delta Air Lines has a mission. Their mission is to fly people from one place to another. Their message is, "We love to fly and it shows." The church is just the opposite. The message is the gospel and the mission is to spread it.

When I visit other churches, I always ask myself, "If I walked in here as a lost person without a relationship with Jesus, after the service was over, would I know how to stop being lost? Did I hear the gospel and did I have a chance to respond to it?"

Recognize the Meaning of the Gospel

In order to clarify the gospel, Paul tells the Corinthians:

> Christ died for our sins in accordance with the Scriptures (15:3).

Jesus's death stands out above every other death in history because he died *for* our sins. He did not die as a martyr. He did not die as an example. He died as a Savior.

Harry Rimmer was a great Christian and a great scientist in the early to mid-twentieth century. After one of Dr. Rimmer's lectures, a young man raised his hand, identified himself as Jewish, and asked, "What did Jesus do that no one else ever did?" Dr. Rimmer replied, "Son, since you are a Jew, I take it that you know the early history of your people and that Titus and Pilate and the old Roman emperors crucified some thirty thousand young Jews?" The young man gave an affirmative. Dr. Rimmer said, "I will name one of those Jews and then you name one. I name Jesus Christ. Now who of the other thirty thousand can you name?" The young man stammered for a moment and couldn't name another. Dr. Rimmer said, "Do you know why out of thirty thousand Jews that were crucified, you can name only one? Because Jesus was the only one who died for your sins and was raised from the dead."

> He was buried (15:4).

Only dead men are buried, and Paul wanted to reaffirm that Jesus did die. People were going to, and do, deny the resurrection of Jesus.

Muslims do not believe that Jesus died and so they do not believe in his resurrection. If you are going to deny the resurrection, you must either deny that he was raised or deny that he was dead.

Some have formulated what is known as the "swoon theory," which claims that Jesus didn't die. He just went into shock. His pulse rate got low and faint and he was at the point of death, but he didn't die. After being laid in that cool tomb, his vital signs returned, his strength came back, and somehow he wiggled out from behind that rock and was free. People will go to great lengths to deny Jesus's death, but the Bible goes to great lengths to affirm it.

> He was raised on the third day in accordance with the Scriptures (15:4).

The other two parts of the gospel don't matter if this third part is not true. This part confirms that he didn't die just like any other man, but he died *for our sins* and God was pleased by it. The resurrection is the proof. Romans 1:4 (NLT) says, "he was shown to be the Son of God when he was raised from the dead by the power of the Holy Spirit. He is Jesus Christ our Lord."

The crowning point of the gospel is the resurrection of Jesus, but it is not the whole gospel. If you preach the death of Jesus alone or his burial alone or his resurrection alone, you've not preached the gospel. The resurrection demonstrates the power and pleasure of God. You must turn a deaf ear to the truth if you deny the powerful evidence of the resurrection of Jesus Christ.

Emphasize the Might of the Gospel

The gospel is the most important message you'll ever hear because it's the only one that can and will save your life. The gospel is the only message that has the power to take a person from sin to salvation, from hell to heaven, from deadness to life, and from darkness to light.

One of my favorite verses in the Bible is Romans 1:16 where Paul said, "For I am not ashamed of the gospel, for it is the power of God for salvation to everyone who believes, to the Jew first and also to the Greek."

Paul got the gospel right, and he went on to say that when you call upon the name of the Lord, if you do it in sincerity and surrender to Jesus Christ, the Holy God *will* save you. Let this verse spark your heart to read through the Bible and understand the gospel. If the gospel is not true, nothing else matters. If true, it is the thing that matters most.

Prayer for This Week: *Father, thank you for the good news, which is Jesus himself. Help me to share his story with others with grace and truth.*

Question for This Week: Consider someone you know who might need to hear the gospel. How can telling the story of Jesus be good news to them?

37

No Small Comfort

Scriptures for This Week

- Isaiah 66:12-13
- 2 Thessalonians 2:16-17
- 2 Corinthians 1:3-7
- Psalm 23
- 2 Corinthians 7:8-16

Comforters on Call

In my second pastorate in a small country church in Kentucky, I faced one of the most difficult parts of my calling. On Good Friday a great servant of our church called me with devastating news. His beautiful daughter, Beth, a freshman at Western Kentucky University was on her way home for Easter and was killed by a drunk driver just a mile from home.

I rushed over to their home, and for the first time in my short ministry, I didn't have a clue what to say. I am usually ready with a quick answer, but I was speechless. I had no idea what they felt or what would help. I had no idea what they were going through because I had never been through it.

Three months later, one of my finest young deacons was driving home from Louisville in the rain. His nine-year-old boy, John, and his six-year-old daughter, Amy, were in the backseat. A teenager, speeding in the oncoming lane, hydroplaned over the line, and in the ensuing crash, John suffered a severe head injury.

Once again, I rushed to the hospital. Once again, all I could do was sit and hear the anguished cries of a mother. The next day her phone call was quiet, "John is brain dead." When I joined her at his bedside, she and her injured husband were confronted with turning off their son's support. The answer to their tearful question, "What should we do?" caught in my throat.

In that eerily quiet room, God brought someone to my mind who could look at this family and say, "We know how you feel. We have been through this and we can walk with you." That was Beth's family. When your heart is breaking, when tragedy has left you emotionally devastated, you need a comforter.

We Are Not Immune to Pain

One of the things I've learned as a pastor is if you talk to anybody long enough and dig deep enough, you discover they have experienced heartache. Each of you reading this sits with a broken heart and broken hopes. Or you know someone who does.

No matter how much you love Jesus and no matter how much you trust God and no matter how faithful you are to his church, you are not immune to horrors and heartaches. The storm of suffering rains on all houses. The wind of hurt blows against all doors.

God never wastes anything. When God created the universe there were no leftover stars or planets. There wasn't too much water in the oceans or too much land on the earth. Everything fit perfectly. He will not waste any experience either. When that tragedy strikes, when that heartache comes, when life gives you its worst sucker punch, God's divine counsel is found in his Scriptures.

See God's Care

The apostle Paul was well acquainted with sorrow and suffering, pain and problems, hurt and heartache. In his second letter to the Corinthians, he shares out of his personal experience where to turn during those times.

In 2 Corinthians 1:3, Paul calls God something unique: "God of all comfort." *Comfort* is the same word that is used to describe the Holy Spirit and it means "called alongside to help." Paul talks more about comfort than anyone else in the Bible because he knows that God has cornered the market on comfort. Only one type of comfort is strong enough to penetrate the inner chambers of the heart. Only one comfort can give you the strength to make it through, and that is the comfort of God.

Paul is saying that no matter what you go through, you never go through it alone; God is always right beside you to help, strengthen, and comfort you.

God is the source of all true comfort. My heart breaks for people who try to find comfort through alcohol, addictions, and abuse—anywhere but God. You can drink yourself, drug yourself, or entertain yourself into a comfortable state, but that comfort won't last. The comfort of God sticks. The comfort of God stands. God himself stays.

Seek God's Comfort

When it comes to pain, people who know God, love God, serve God, trust God, believe God, and obey God are just like people who don't. We all have heart attacks, miscarriages, and misunderstandings. We all lose jobs, friends, and money. The difference is every follower of Christ has the comfort of God available to him or her.

Paul goes on to tell us that God "comforts us in all our affliction" (2 Corinthians 1:4). This verse does not say, "the God of all comfort, who *keeps* us from all affliction." We all wish it did. But even for his own children, God doesn't keep affliction away. We don't always expect trouble and we can't always escape trouble, because we know there are times we must endure it.

The most famous psalm in the entire Bible is Psalm 23. The psalmist talks about how the shepherd leads the sheep to green pastures and still waters. He is out in front. When is the shepherd right *beside* the sheep? "When I walk through the valley of the shadow of death you are with me." When you look back on your life, you will find the times that you were closest to Jesus were those times when everything was going the worst.

You don't find out who your friends are in the good times; you find out who your friends are in the bad times. You will never know just how much God cares about you and how much he loves you until you go through trials and tribulations and find he is standing right beside you to comfort and strengthen you.

Troubles often come our way because God wants to force us to look up. God wants us to seek his comfort. That is why he says, "You will seek me and find me, when you seek me with all your heart" (Jeremiah 29:13). When things are going good we often forget God, but troubles can snag our attention.

Share God's Compassion

When we feel strong and confident, we assume that God has given us abilities and spiritual gifts so that we can be a blessing to others. But our brokenness provides us with equally prized abilities to be a comfort to others. He comforts us in our troubles so that we can comfort others in theirs. Paul says in 2 Corinthians 1:4, "who comforts us in all our affliction, so that we may be able to comfort those who are in any affliction, with the comfort with which we ourselves are comforted by God."

God does not comfort us to make us comfortable but to make us comforters. God wants to take the heartache in your life and transform it into a balm of comfort in someone else's life. He wants to turn your river of tears into a fountain of comfort. The comfort of God is always the calling of God to share that comfort with someone else, the way that Beth's family did for young John's.

When we do this, we live into the life that Jesus lived. Jesus experienced the same heartache and hurt that we do. He knows what it is like to see loved ones die, to be treated unfairly, and to be rejected by the people you thought loved you the most. No matter where you are right now, he has been there. That Jesus who hung on a cross, rejected by his friends and despised by his enemies, says to us every day of his risen life, "I know how you feel. I've been where you are. Together, we will not just get through it, but we will help others get through it as well."

Whenever you go through tough times, don't become a cistern of self-pity but become a channel of blessing. We block up the channel when we retreat into a shell, shut ourselves off, lock the door, close the curtains, and focus on ourselves. In this, all that suffering and heartache becomes meaningless. Warren Wiersbe once wrote, "You cannot cure your sorrow by nursing it, but you can cure it by nursing another sorrow."[55] When you focus on yourself, you magnify your misery. But with God's help, when you focus on others, you multiply your ministry.

If you live in the valley of despair and wake up on the mountain of misery, see God's care for you, seek his comfort, and share his compassion. He is always right beside you showing you how.

Prayer for This Week: *Father, you can make all things new. Please don't waste the pain in my life. Show me how you want to redeem it.*

Question for This Week: Reflect on a difficult experience in your past. What form did God's comfort and compassion take for you during that time?

38

Dying to Live

Scriptures for This Week

- Galatians 2:19-21
- Galatians 5:22-26
- Philippians 1:20-26
- Romans 8:12-17
- Luke 9:23-26

Dying 101

Would you agree with this: "I'm trying to live the Christian life the best way I know how"? Over three billion people have become Christians in the last two thousand years. But Jesus is the only person who has truly lived the Christian life. Even with all the teaching and mentoring we have available to us, the average Christian knows far more about how to become one than how to be one. Do you desire a life that shows Christ to those who don't know him? Those who don't know Christ need to see him in his followers.

One verse in the Bible gives us a comprehensive, compact, complete description of the Christian life: "I have been crucified with Christ. It is no longer I who live, but Christ who lives in me. And the life I now live in the flesh I live by faith in the Son of God, who loved me and gave himself for me" (Galatians 2:20).

You cannot live until you die. And this death won't just turn your life around; it will turn it upside down. That's the way God runs his kingdom.

Host Your Own Funeral

Two people must die in order for you to become a Christian. Jesus was first, but you go second. Thinking about the self dying goes against the grain of our human nature, ambition, and desire. Putting self ahead of God is common. The greatest idol in the world today is self. The real American idol is self. Actress Shirley MacLaine expresses the natural tendency we are all born with:

> The most pleasurable journey you take is through yourself... the only sustaining love involvement is with yourself... When you look back on your life and try to figure out where you've been and where you're going, when you look at your work, your love affairs, your marriages, your children, your pain, your happiness—when you examine all that closely, what you really find out is that the only person you really go to bed with is yourself... The only thing you have is working to the consummation of your own identity, and that is what I've been trying to do all of my life.[56]

The first step to *becoming* a Christian is accepting Jesus's death for you. But the first step to *being* a Christian is experiencing your own death. The Christian life is a crucified life that then becomes a resurrected life.

The entire Christian life is a paradox. The way to get is to give, the way to be first is to be last, and the way to be over is to be under. In the same way, to live Jesus's life is to both die and live at the same time.

I Must Die to Me

The apostle Paul talks about three different kinds of death in the Christian life. First, he talks about our death to sin, which happens when we accept Jesus Christ. The second death is to self—dying to what we want, desire, and will. The third death is to safety, when we are called to take up the cross knowing that we might suffer for the Lord Jesus Christ.

So we must start every day with our own funeral. Bill Bright, the founder of Campus Crusade for Christ (now called Cru), once said, "In every man's life there is a throne. When self is on the throne, Christ is on the cross; but when Christ is on the throne, self is on the cross."

This crucifixion is not a feeling but a fact. Just as Jesus died for you, when you come to him you die with him. Paul describes what happens in Romans 6:6, "We know that our old self was crucified with him in order that the body of sin might be brought to nothing, so that we would no longer be enslaved to sin."

A Christian should be different because the old you dies and the new you is born. The new you is not just a clone of the old you, a new version put together with the same tired parts. It's all brand new. Second Corinthians 5:17 says, "Therefore, if anyone is in Christ, he is a new creation. The old has passed away; behold, the new has come."

When people die to self, allowing their desires, preferences, and wants to be crucified and put to death, arguments stop, marriages last, and people start majoring on the majors and forget about the minors.

Christ Must Live in Me

Galatians 2:20 goes on to say, "It is no longer I who live, but Christ lives in me." You have been crucified with Christ, but the new you has been raised with Christ. So being a Christian means dying to live. These four words tell us what the Christian life is: "Christ lives in me."

I cannot live the Christian life, Christ lives it in me. Think of the word *Christian* as a combination of *Christ* plus *in*. The Christian life is not you living for Jesus; it is Jesus living in you. It is not your responsibility; it is your response to his ability.

Martin Luther once said, "When someone knocks at the door of my heart, I open it and they say, 'Who lives here?' I answer, 'Jesus Christ lives here.' Inevitably they will say, 'I thought Martin Luther lived here,' to which I say, 'Martin Luther used to live here, but he died. Jesus Christ lives here now.'"

A Christian is not the old man trying to live his best for Jesus. The Christian is someone who allows the old man to be crucified so that Jesus can live through the new man. That's why you must "live and let die." Let self die to you so the Savior can live within.

Faith Must Work for Me

Paul finishes Galatians 2:20 by saying, "and the life I now live in the flesh I live by faith in the Son of God, who loved me and gave himself for me." The Bible says you and I are to live a crucified life, yet we cannot crucify ourselves. God through his Holy Spirit will both put our old self to death and live his powerful life through us.

The world not only lives in the flesh, it lives by and for the flesh. The world says, like Shirley MacLaine above, "Look out for number one; eat, drink, and be merry; grab all the gusto you can; if it feels good do it; I did it my way." But the Christian lives by faith. We must live *in* the flesh, in our human body, but we don't have to live *by* the flesh. The Christian lives by *faith*, which is the work of the Spirit of God. You were saved by faith, you stand by faith, you serve by faith, and you see by faith.

Faith alone doesn't make a difference. People exercise faith all the time by getting on airplanes, taking medicines, or sending kids to school. Everyone exercises faith every day. The difference is that our faith must be rooted "in the Son of God who loved me and gave himself for me." The Muslim cannot place his faith in a Muhammad who loved him and gave himself for him; the Buddhist cannot place his faith in a Buddha who loved him and gave himself for him; the Hindu cannot place his faith in a god who loved him and gave himself for him. But you and I "live by faith in the Son of God who loved me and gave himself for me."

A surgeon was called to an emergency surgery one morning. When he returned home, his young son asked, "Dad, did you have to cut the man open to see what was inside of him?"

"Yes, son, I did."

"Could you see his lungs and his stomach and his heart?"

"Yes, son, I could."

The surgeon's four-year-old daughter looked at him with wide-eyed amazement and said, "Dad, did you see Jesus in his heart?"

That's what Christianity is—when the old you dies, and Jesus comes into your heart, and everybody can see him living in you. You can become and remain a Christ follower because he loved you and gave himself for you. Jesus gave his life for you in order to take your life from you so that he could live his life in you.

Prayer for This Week: *Living God, thank you for seeing the possibilities in me in spite of my sin and my selfishness. Call out the old me so that you can grow greater and greater within.*

Question for This Week: What characteristics do you *not* share with Jesus Christ? Why do you still tolerate them in your life?

39

The Shadow

Scriptures for This Week

- Philippians 3:7-11
- Galatians 6:13-16
- 2 Corinthians 5:14-15
- 1 Corinthians 4:18-21
- Luke 9:22-26

Life in the Shadow

Some of the most sobering events in history cast a shadow forever. One of those occurred in Alamogordo, New Mexico, on July 16, 1945, when the first atomic bomb was detonated. That one day has affected our foreign policy, government spending, and military unlike any other event in history. No matter what we do, where we go, or what we say, we cannot get out from under that shadow.

This world lives under another shadow every day—the shadow of the cross. From the time that Jesus was born, he also lived in that shadow. The cross was never absent from his mind and never far from his soul. Ever since his resurrection, we live in the shadow of the cross, and if we are Christ followers, we can do this joyfully.

The apostle Paul made a statement that captures how the cross should affect our lives every single moment: "May I never boast except in the cross of our Lord Jesus Christ, through which the world has been crucified to me, and I to the world" (Galatians 6:14 NIV).

Paul had much to brag about. He was the greatest preacher in the world, the greatest missionary in the church, the greatest teacher of the faith, the greatest theologian, and the greatest religious author. He wrote almost half of the New Testament. Yet, Paul said, "There is only one thing that I will ever show pride in: the cross of our Lord Jesus Christ."

The three major cultures of that day did not see the cross as something to brag about. To the Romans, the cross was despicable and offensive. To the Jews, crucifixion was a curse. To the Greeks, the cross was absolute nonsense. Nevertheless, Paul said, "My life is lived in the shadow of the cross." You are going to live your life in the shadow of something. Maybe it is in the shadow of money, work, depression, or guilt. What would it mean for you to live in the shadow of the cross?

I Will Live a Life of Praise

Listen again to these words, "May I never boast except in the cross of our Lord Jesus Christ." The cross doesn't make Jesus special; Jesus makes the cross special. Crucifixion was common in Bible days; over thirty thousand Jews were put to death by crucifixion in the Roman Empire. Jesus experienced a death that thousands of others experienced. But Jesus makes the cross unique because we can live a life every day praising God as a result of it.

The Lord Jesus is God, the Messiah, and the Savior of the world. When you realize who was crucified on that cross and why he was crucified on that cross, then you will live a life of praise.

Thousands of Jews died on a cross for themselves and themselves alone. Jesus died on that cross, not for himself, but for you and for me. That should tell me that no matter what the circumstances may be in my life—maybe I am unemployed, maybe I am battling a difficult disease, maybe I am going through a rough spot in some of my relationships—but living in the shadow of the cross, I should praise God every day that the Lord Christ died on that cross for me.

I Will Live a Life of Purpose

Through the cross of Jesus Christ, God proved once and for all his love for the world. He defined what real love is all about. We don't have to look at the sinful world and wonder where God's love is. It's hanging on the cross. It's rising from the dead. The cross is the shadow and the symbol that reminds you that God loves you.

Every religion and ideology has a visual symbol that illustrates the significant beliefs.

- In Buddhism it's the lotus flower depicting the cycle of reincarnation.
- In modern Judaism it's the Star of David, which speaks of a Messiah promised to David's line by God.
- In Islam it's the crescent, which in ancient times was a symbol of sovereignty and power.
- In Communism it's the hammer and sickle, representing industry and agriculture.
- In the Nazi regime it was the swastika, a symbol for their overarching control in all of life.

The cross is not just a symbol of the Christian faith but the secret of the Christian life. If the cross tells me anything, it tells me that everything has a purpose. God had a purpose for the cross and the cross has a purpose for me. Acts 2:23 (NIV) says this about the crucifixion of Jesus: "This man was handed over to you by God's deliberate plan and foreknowledge." Yes, God had some specific purposes in mind when he sent Jesus to die on the cross.

Romans 5:8 (NIV) says, "But God demonstrates his own love for us in this: While we were still sinners, Christ died for us." The only explanation for the cross is the love of God, and any definition of divine love must include the cross.

The purpose of your life, as you live it in the shadow of the cross, should be defined therefore by love. The two greatest commandments God has ever given revolve around love. Your number one purpose in life, above everything else, is to "love God with all of your heart, soul, mind and strength." Your number two purpose in life is to "love your neighbor as you love yourself." If you live in the shadow of the cross, your life will be lived for the purpose of love.

I Will Live a Life of Power

Living in the shadow of the cross is powerful, as we find in the next statement in Galatians 6:14: "May I never boast except in the cross of our Lord Jesus Christ, through which the world has been crucified to me."

When Jesus was crucified on the cross, so was the world. Where this world tries to drag us down morally and philosophically, all of that was crucified on the cross. Because of the cross, those who are followers of Jesus have the power to overcome our greatest problems.

If you are fighting a spiritual battle that you seem to be losing, take ten seconds and focus on Jesus dying on the cross. The cross both kills the thrill of temptation and gives life to the desire to be holy and righteous. That's what the shadow does. It deadens the power of sin and drives the power of life.

I Will Live a Life of Passion

The common definition of *passion* is, "A compelling emotion or desire that drives everything you do." We are willing to lay down our life for what we are passionate about. Why do we refer to the death of Jesus as "the Passion"? The cross tells us that God is passionate about spending eternity with us and forgiving our sins.

Paul says that through the cross of Christ, "the world has been crucified to me, and I to the world" (Galatians 6:14 NIV). Crucifixion is one form of death that you cannot inflict upon yourself. You can shoot yourself, drown yourself, hang yourself, stab yourself, or poison yourself, but you can't crucify yourself.

Crucifixion is something that must be done to you. You must surrender to the crucifixion and die to your ego, ambitions, wants, and beliefs. Surrender is the key to the whole Christian life, and we cannot do it without passion. It is in the shadow of the cross, where we submit to the God who loves us, the Christ who died for us, and the Spirit who wants to fill us, that we find our victory in life, and that is something we all ought to be passionate about.

When I met my beautiful, precious Teresa and we made our plans to get married, our whole outlook on life changed. We no longer talked about "mine" and "yours." We talked about "ours." From the moment that we decided to become one, every decision involved how to spend our time and money, how to plan, what activities to do. They are all governed by our passion for one another. Never again could we conceive of one without the other.

In the shadow of the cross, no sacrifice we make could be too great. No amount of suffering we endure could be too unbearable. No burden we carry could be too heavy. No assignment that God gives us could be too difficult. As you get under the shadow of the cross, remember that the One who created this universe would rather die for you than live without you. So brag about that.

Prayer for This Week: *Holy Savior, thank you for the evidence of your love. Let your love overshadow my life and compel me in all that I do.*

Question for This Week: What spiritual battle are you losing right now? Consider giving in to that sin, and then stop and take ten seconds to focus on Jesus.

40

The Prize Is Not for Sale

Scriptures for This Week

- Revelation 21:5-8
- 2 Peter 2:1-3
- Ephesians 2:8-10
- Galatians 2:11-16
- 2 Corinthians 3:4-6

No Sale

Have you ever been in a situation where you couldn't pay your bill? Maybe you came up short on cash at the grocery store and had to put items back. Maybe you had to work out a payment plan with the utility company for a season. These experiences make us feel a little beaten down and a little ashamed. When we can't purchase all that we want or need, we go without, and going without communicates inadequacy and imperfection.

Fending for ourselves gives us a sense of distinction, honor, and power—even when so much that brings us success is out of our hands. We feel vindicated when gas prices dip, genius when our investments rise, and remarkable when we find a good deal. Without even thinking about it, we measure our net worth by our net wealth. Our purchase power translates to our personal power.

But money can't buy everything and some things are not for sale. Good health, a strong marriage, well-adjusted children, treasured friendships, a good name—all the things that make life meaningful are not for sale.

But what about access to a life with God? Billions of people ascribe to a faith tradition, and the majority of them are trying to purchase their access to God. Of the forty-two hundred religions on this planet, all but one take the path of self-effort. But Christianity is where access to God is not being sold. It's being given.

The Open Market

In every continent on the globe, you'll hear the common threads of thought:

- I just try to be a good person every day.
- I try to follow the Golden Rule and keep the Ten Commandments.
- I follow the eightfold path of the Buddha.
- I follow the path that will end all suffering.
- I follow the five pillars of Islam.
- I follow my good impulses and repent when I fail.

These are the paths of good works and sincere religious practice. In some form or fashion, every religion except one is man's quest to earn God. It makes sense to us. After all, free lunches are myths. Everything has a price tag. Because you never get something for nothing, the logic goes, a relationship with God must work the same way.

If the Bible is true, it blows this path to pieces and changes everything. God relates to us through grace, and we relate to him through faith.

God Gives Salvation by Grace

God deals with people in three ways. God can deal with us according to *justice* by giving us what we deserve. God can deal with us according to *mercy* by not giving us what we do deserve. Or God can deal with us with *grace* by giving us what we do not deserve.

Paul tells us in Ephesians 2:8, "For by grace you have been saved." Is there a more beautiful word in the entire Bible than *grace*? Yet, we have the hardest time understanding, giving, and receiving it. Why do humans struggle so much with the idea that salvation and eternal life are free?

We think everything good, including heaven and God's presence and pleasure, must be merited. To think that blessing is something we can earn, deserve, or achieve by our goodness has been part of idol worship forever. But Paul assures us, "Salvation is not a reward for the good things we have done, so none of us can boast about it" (Ephesians 2:9 NLT). Grace is not only something we cannot earn, but it's given to people who would never, ever deserve it.

Grace is also hard for us because it messes up our systems and makes us vulnerable. We love the idea of winning a prize, but when we're given something by someone who knows us well, we balk a little. Accepting something that has already been bought and paid for takes all our effort out of the equation. If we receive God's way of salvation as a gift, then we have it. If we try to earn it by our goodness, we will never be able to take it.

Grasping grace is hard because we sometimes want to share the load with Jesus, as if we could climb up on the cross with him. We're treating his death like a down payment if we believe that though he *did* die for our sins, *we* must work to pay the installments. Do you go to church, give money, do good deeds, follow the rules, and somehow believe you're paying for your salvation? Your currency is no good with God.

We Receive Salvation Through Faith

Sometimes we act as if we're applying for a relationship with God, and we hand him our tax returns, baptismal certificates, degrees, medals, and commendations. If we think a relationship with God begins with our résumé of worthiness, we can shred that paper. He's looking for faith.

When the Bible talks about faith, it doesn't mean believing *in* something. It means believing *on* something. Children believe *in* the tooth fairy, but I believe *on* the Lord Jesus Christ. To believe *on* Jesus means to receive Jesus. When you receive Jesus, you receive what Jesus has, which is salvation by grace.

Your unbelief will keep you distant from God and out of heaven. If your good behaviors don't gain you access to God, then your unsavory behaviors won't keep you away. I used to pastor in Kentucky, which is a big tobacco-raising state. One day I went out with some of my members and helped them gather in tobacco to see what it was like. As we were putting the tobacco up, one of the men said to me, "Preacher, do you believe I can smoke and still get to heaven?" I said, "I not only believe that, but I believe if you keep smoking, you'll get there a lot sooner."

Grace is God's hand giving eternal life. Faith is your hand receiving it. Grace is his part and faith is your part. You can sum up everything God wants out of you and me in one word—*faith.*

We Demonstrate Salvation by Works

Some think that all they have to do is believe and receive, and then they can go and live any way they choose. But Ephesians 2:10 says, "For we are his workmanship, created in Christ Jesus for good works, which God prepared beforehand, that we should walk in them."

Yes, good works are related to salvation, but not the way most people think. Good works are not the price of salvation. They are the proof of salvation. Good works do not produce salvation. Salvation produces good works.

God is always working. When he offers you his salvation, by his grace, he is working for you. When you receive his salvation, through faith, he begins working in you. As you grow in him, he produces good works by working through you. That is the way works work. Real goodness is not what I do for God. Real goodness is what God does through me. A person does not have a relationship with God because he does good works. He does good works because he has a relationship with God.

Too many people are in the wrong business. They think they are in the saving business. They think they are their own savior. But I guarantee that soon enough, their business will be bankrupt. If that describes you, get out of the savior business, and with the faith God gives you, accept his grace and his salvation for free.

Prayer for This Week: *Father, give me the faith that I need to depend on you. Your grace is amazing. Let me accept it and reflect it back to you with my life.*

Question for This Week: What can you do to give someone else what they don't deserve? How will this be a reflection of your heavenly Father?

41

One Thing

Scriptures for This Week

- Proverbs 21:5
- Habakkuk 2:2-3
- Philippians 3:12-14
- Psalm 62:11-12
- Numbers 23:18-20

Ambition Attrition

In recent years it's become popular to choose one word that will inspire you for the entire year. Maybe you've done this and picked a word that represents for you a hope, a dream, or a goal. Or maybe you've set a few goals that help you to be productive and live a life pleasing to God. The longer you live, the more you realize just how fleeting these years are and just how important it is to maximize the potential of our days.

Setting goals can be exhilarating, but it can also be frustrating. According to USA.gov, the top ten resolutions Americans make every New Year's Day are:

1. Lose Weight
2. Manage Debt/Save Money
3. Get Physically Fit
4. Eat Healthy
5. Learn Something New
6. Drink Less Alcohol
7. Quit Smoking
8. Reduce Stress
9. Take a Trip Somewhere

10. Volunteer to Help Others

Though these are great resolutions, the four-out-of-five people who make them will break them.

A psychology professor at Florida State University did a study and gave two reasons why people fail to keep New Year's resolutions: Resolutions are too general, and people make too many. "Studies suggest that will-power is a limited resource," this professor said. "If you make too many resolutions, you won't have enough willpower reserves to stick to all of them. It is better to make one resolution and stick to it than make five."

No matter what time of year you're reading this, there is a biblical pathway to help get you to your goals.

Not There Yet

Paul wrote to the church at Philippi from a Roman prison. As far as he knew, each day could be his last. And he makes a candid admission that is the secret for how to make every day your best day. "Not that I have already obtained this or am already perfect, but I press on to make it my own, because Christ Jesus has made me his own" (Philippians 3:12).

Paul admits that he has not arrived. He doesn't have it all together. Though he has done a lot, more remains. Though he has been to a lot of places, there are still more places to go. Though he has reached a lot of his potential, he has not reached all of his potential. No matter our age, there are always more lessons to learn and more principles to apply and more room to grow.

Forget What Is Behind You

The only race I ever participated in was a 5K run for charity. A 5K is only about three miles, so if you are a runner that's nothing. To me, it was like a marathon. A buddy who ran with me said, "Just remember as you run, where you've been is not important. What is important is where you are and where you are headed."

In Philippians 3:13, Paul says, "Brothers, I do not consider that I have made it my own. But one thing I do: forgetting what lies behind and straining forward to what lies ahead..." You can't focus on where you are going until you forget where you've been. Paul must have loved athletics because he uses a lot of sports terminology. He is talking here about a race. He talks about straining forward, pressing on, going toward a goal, and reaching for a prize.

The word *forget* here doesn't mean "to fail to remember." You can never erase the past from your memory. The word *forget* means "to not be affected by." When God says, "I will remember your sins no more," it doesn't mean that God all of a sudden gets spiritual amnesia. It means he no longer allows your past to affect your relationship to him.

You cannot sail your ship into the seas of the future with joy and peace if your anchor is stuck in the mud of the past. You can't run forward if you are always looking backward. Think about your mistakes, your failures, the recent things you didn't do that you should have done and the things you did that you shouldn't have. What can you learn from those things and how can they make you a better person? Now move on.

You can know that you have forgotten what is behind you when you can talk about it. "Yes, I did fail here or I did make a mistake there, but this is what I learned from it. This is why I won't ever do it again. This is how God used it in my life."

Focus on What Is in Front of You

Two words in Paul's instruction make all the difference in the world: "Brothers, I do not consider that I have made it my own. But *one thing* I do..." (Philippians 3:13, emphasis mine). *One thing.* Paul understood the power that comes in concentrating on just one thing. *One thing* occurs in various places in the Bible:

- When the rich young ruler came to Jesus and asked him how to receive eternal life, Jesus said, "One thing you lack."
- When Martha complained to Jesus that Mary wasn't helping with meal preparations, Jesus said to Martha, "Only one thing is needed."
- David said, "One thing I have desired of the LORD, that I will seek" (Psalm 27:4 NKJV).

What was the one thing Paul was seeking? "I press on toward the goal for the prize of the upward call of God in Christ Jesus" (Philippians 2:14). Paul said the key to living a productive life is to focus. It's okay to have a one-track mind as long as your mind is on the right track.

Many Christ-followers are ineffective in their Christian life and many churches are ineffective in their mission because they are involved in too many things. I can't tell you the number of times people come to me and say, "I would like to serve in our church and go on a mission trip and share my story and be more active, but I've got too many irons in the fire." Sometimes I feel like shouting, "Either pull out some of your irons or put out the fire!"

Concentration is the secret of power. A river that flows in one direction and one direction only can become a tremendous source of electric energy. If you can take light and concentrate it and its power, you can make a laser that can cut through steel.

The key, then, is to make sure that you set at least one goal that is right. Take a few minutes to think about your goal. What's your *one thing* that will make you productive and pleasing to God and the world?

Fulfill What Is Ahead of You

You might think your *one thing* is too daunting a task. Maybe your *one thing* is to read through the Bible, host a neighborhood barbecue, say yes to a new volunteer role, or rid yourself of an old habit. Be determined just like Paul. Two times, once in verse 12 and once in verse 14, Paul says, "I press on." Say to yourself, "Today if I don't do anything else, this one thing I will do."

Some of us have the mindset that success should be easy. We might not understand determination, perseverance, and endurance. When our boss gets unreasonable, we quit. When the subject gets too difficult, we drop out of class. When our marriage gets unbearable, we get a divorce.

Jesus Christ's sacrifice made it possible for us to get right with God. Our faith in him as Savior makes it a reality. But more awaits us. Let's forge our ambition, foster a vision, forget our past, focus our goals, and fulfill the plans God has for us.

Prayer for This Week: *Father, show me the plans you have for me. Merge my life with your purpose that I might be pleasing to you.*

Question for This Week: What do you need to forget so that you can renew your efforts toward your goals? How are your goals advancing your character to be more like that of Christ?

42

Rest in Peace

Scriptures for This Week

- John 14:25-27
- Philippians 4:4-7
- Isaiah 41:8-10
- 1 Peter 5:6-11
- Isaiah 32:16-18

The Recipe for Peace

Dave Berry, the successful American author and humorist, said, "My therapist told me the way to achieve true inner peace is to finish what I start. So far I've finished two bags of M&Ms and a chocolate cake. I feel better already." I wish the way to peace was that easy and tasty.

The peace I'm talking about is the calmness of spirit that you can have even when you are in the middle of a raging storm. The happiest times of my life have always been when I was at peace. Within my heart, I had no worries, anxieties, concerns, or crushing burdens—just peace and quiet.

You would think that once you give your life to the Creator of this universe that the one thing you would have 24/7 is peace, but there are too many peace robbers—pressures, problems, and people—you can never get away from. They fill you with anxiety and worry, and your peace goes to the bottom and your blood pressure goes to the top.

Worry is my Achilles' heel. Maybe you don't worry about anything or maybe you worry about everything.

How can you bear the fruit of peace with all the pressures that you deal with? With all the problems that you must solve? With all the people you have to put up with? The apostle Paul had inexplicable, invincible peace in the most difficult of circumstances. If he's going to tell us what peace is and where peace is found, we should hear what he has to say.

Rejoice

Paul did not write the book of Philippians while lying on a beach soaking up the sun. He was a prisoner in Rome convinced that each day might be his last. He was in the middle of unbelievable pressure, and yet he experienced peace.

"Rejoice in the Lord always. I will say it again: Rejoice!" (Philippians 4:4 NIV). Paul knew we'd think he was crazy to say this, so he tells us *twice* to rejoice, as if we wouldn't believe him the first time. Rejoicing is difficult when pressures are great, problems are big, and people are mean. Paul knows it more than anyone, but he has learned the deep value in rejoicing.

We need to stop focusing on the pressures, problems, and people and focus on the Lord. Jesus came to die to forgive us of our sins and also give us joy. He gives us reason to rejoice, and so to have this joy, you've got to have Jesus. You can't rejoice in the Lord unless you know that Lord. If you are always with Jesus, then you can rejoice always. People try everything in the world to get some peace, from pills to possessions to pleasure, but without Jesus, our attempts take us to dead ends. Augustine was right when he said, "The heart is restless until it finds its rest in God."

You aren't going to find a lot of joy in big pressures, tough problems, and difficult people, but you can always rejoice *in the Lord.* You can always rejoice in the greatness, grace, and goodness of God. The first step to having peace in your heart is to rejoice.

Relax

You ought to learn four words to say to yourself every time the thief of anxiety tries to steal your peace. These four words are, "The Lord is near." Paul reassures us of this in Philippians 4:5 (NIV): "Let your gentleness be evident to all. The Lord is near."

Wouldn't it make a difference if every day you could know that God was right there beside you? If you knew that no matter what pressures came, what problems arose, what people would threaten you, that God would be close to you to help and defend you? He is not only right beside you, but he lives within you.

What robs our peace is when we focus on the problems and forget about God. When you focus on God, then your gentleness will be evident to everybody. You won't be anxious. You won't be nervous. You will be relaxed because you know that God is with you and is in control. Isaiah 26:3 says,

> You will keep in perfect peace
> those whose minds are steadfast,
> because they trust in you.
> (Isaiah 26:3 NIV)

The world thinks peace is the absence of conflict or when everything is going our way. But the Bible says peace is not the absence of difficulties; peace is the presence of God.

Release

How many times, in the midst of your most anxious moments, has someone who meant well said, "Don't worry!" How many times has that helped you? Paul does that, but he doesn't leave us wondering what to do instead. He says, "Do not be anxious about anything, but in every situation, by prayer and petition, with thanksgiving, present your requests to God" (Philippians 4:6 NIV). Paul says don't worry, pray. Turn your cares into prayers because prayer is the pathway to peace.

We aren't supposed to pretend that we don't have reasons to worry because we naturally do. But every time something bursts into our life that raises our anxiety level, that is God's engraved invitation to come to him in prayer and give the cause of our worry to him. He can handle it. We can't.

If you believe that God loves you and cares about you, that he is powerful enough to handle all your problems and wants to grow you through your problems, then release everything that is robbing you of peace to him—and do it "with thanksgiving."

What are you to be thankful for? That God loves you enough to care about your problems, he's powerful enough to handle your problems, and he's going to grow you through your problems.

We tend to thank God when things are good—when we get a paycheck, a raise, a favorable test result. How often do we thank God just because *he* is good? When you can look into the face of your heavenly Father and say, "I thank you for these pressures, these problems, and these people. I am releasing them to you and trusting you to grow me through my circumstances that are for my good," then you have released everything to God.

Rest

Paul goes on to tell us what peace provides for us: "And the peace of God, which transcends all understanding, will guard your hearts and your minds in Christ Jesus" (Philippians 4:7 NIV). God's peace, the peace that only God can give, will guard you and protect you from worry and anxiety. It is a peace that passes all understanding because God is the source.

The peace the Bible talks about is not the temporary peace you get through money or drugs or alcohol or sex, because that peace never lasts. This peace transcends understanding. It is so real and so strong that people will look at you and say, "How do you have such peace in the middle of what you are going through?"

You don't have to die to rest in peace. You can rest in peace even when life is at its most difficult. Jesus died not just so we could be forgiven of our sins but so we could have peace in this life. Not just any peace but peace with God. As Paul says, "Therefore, since we have been justified through faith, we have peace with God through our Lord Jesus Christ" (Romans 5:1 NIV).

When you have peace with God, then you can have the peace of God. No matter what comes your way, you can rejoice, release, and rest in peace.

Prayer for This Week: *Heavenly Father, thank you for being bold enough, strong enough, and compassionate enough to carry my burdens. Help me focus on you and to let the gentleness of your peace define my life.*

Question for This Week: If you find it hard to release worry, do you think it's because you don't pray and then listen for God's response or because you don't hand over your cares to him?

43

More Bang for the Buck

Scriptures for This Week

- Psalm 36:5-9
- 1 Timothy 6:17-19
- Psalm 25:20-22
- 2 Corinthians 9:6-11
- Matthew 6:19-21

Be Cheerful for God's Gifts to You

Have you ever gone to sleep thinking about how great it would be to wake up rich? A couple in California went out to walk their dog on their property. They noticed an old can sticking out of the ground on a trail they had walked almost daily for many years. They pulled it up and discovered the can was filled with gold coins. The coins dated from 1847 to 1894, were the biggest horde of gold coins ever unearthed in the US, and were worth ten million dollars.[57]

It's likely that instant riches are never far from any of our dreams. We can hope that we'll wake up and find such a treasure, or we can wake up and take hold of the treasure we already have. You are already rich, though most of us rarely consider ourselves to be. Being rich is relative. Almost every one reading this book is rich compared to the rest of the world. If you own your home, have two cars, and any retirement plan, you are in the top 2 percent of the world's richest people.

We have learned how to get rich, but we haven't learned how to be rich. Because we are blessed with resources, it's important to fight against our greed. A young pastor named Timothy oversaw the church in Ephesus, which at the time was one of the wealthiest cities in the world. Like today, the people in his church knew how to get rich, but they didn't know how to be rich. In Paul's first letter to Timothy, he communicates that true living is found in generous giving.

Be Grateful to God Who Blesses You

Greed affects everybody. If we don't think we have enough, we want more. Even if we do have enough, we still want more. All we need are food, clothing, and shelter. If we have more than what we need, we are rich.

Consider all you own. Are you the *owner* or the *manager*? An owner has rights while a manager has responsibilities. The way you answered that question will tell you whether you have financial amnesia. Financial amnesia has been around for a long time.

In Deuteronomy 8, God was preparing the people of Israel to enter into the Promised Land, and he gave them a warning. He told them that once they settled in and had eaten their fill, built beautiful houses, and stocked their bank accounts, they would need to be careful. In verse 14 God says, "Then your heart be lifted up, and you forget the LORD your God..." What is it about God they would forget? That God is "he who gives you power to get wealth" (8:18).

God owns everything and gave us what we have. We get financial amnesia when we believe we are the owner. We are just the manager and we need to manage his resources wisely. There's little room for pride. In Paul's words to Timothy, "As for the rich in this present age, charge them not to be haughty" (1 Timothy 6:17).

Be careful with what you do with money and be even more careful with what it can do to you. Look at everything you have, everything you think you own, and remember who owns it. Be grateful to God and do not forget his generosity toward you.

Be Hopeful in God Who Provides for You

Paul goes on to say to the rich, "nor to set their hopes on the uncertainty of riches, but on God, who richly provides us with everything to enjoy" (6:17). Notice that God doesn't condemn the rich for being rich. Using some of your excess money on yourself is not wrong. Living in a nice home, driving a nice car, or wearing nice clothes aren't evil. God doesn't put a penalty on prosperity and he doesn't put a premium on poverty.

What he does say is don't put your hope in your stuff. Long-lasting wealth is not certain for any of us. You can invest in the stock market, but you had better not put your hopes in it. Between 1948 and 2001, the United States endured ten recessions. Those recessions lasted an average of ten months and resulted in the loss of billions of dollars. We saw in the last decade two trillion dollars of American wealth wiped out almost overnight. While we all dream of waking up rich, it's far more common to go to bed rich and wake up poor.

If you've ever had the rug pulled out from under you, maybe you were standing on the wrong rug. If you put your hope in the stock market, when the stock market falls your hope is gone. If a farmer puts all his hopes in his crops and the crops fail, his hope is gone. If you put your hope in God, your hope will be gone only if God fails and God never does. Don't put your hope in what you have; put your hope in the One who has provided what you have.

Be Bountiful with What God Gives You

You might say, "I don't have much to give." What you are saying is you don't feel like you have enough left over. The richest people in the world are those who use what God has given them to bless others. Most people measure wealth by what they have, but God measures wealth by what you give. Nothing will rob you of joy quicker than greed and selfishness. Nothing will bless you more than being gracious and generous. Generosity is the only antidote to greed.

Paul says that generosity is how people who are rich get rich, live rich, die rich, and stay rich. "They are to do good, to be rich in good works, to be generous and ready to share" (1 Timothy 6:18). If you want to be rich, then look for people and causes that need you to help them and need you to give to them. Paul calls it being "ready to share." Always be ready to pull the trigger on serving and giving with joyful generosity. Real wealth is not found in what you get for yourself but in what you give to others.

Schindler's List is a film based on the true story of Oskar Schindler, the director of a munitions factory in Nazi Germany, who decided to save the lives of as many Jews as he could. By putting them to work in his factory, he was able to keep them from the gas chambers. He didn't have the money to pay them, and little by little he had to sell everything he had in order to keep the business and employ them.

Even with all his efforts, when Schindler looked at the books after the war, he made the sorrowful realization that he could have saved more lives. He looked at all the goods that he still had that could have been sold and said that if only he had known when the war was going to end, he would have done more.

Oskar Schindler was credited with saving more lives in World War II than any other single person. He died not thinking about what he had done but about how he could have done more.

Be Mindful of God Who Rewards You

Paul says that people who practice joyful generosity are "storing up treasure for themselves as a good foundation for the future, so that they may take hold of that which is truly life" (1 Timothy 6:19). When you give your earthly treasure for God's pleasure, he gives you eternal treasure with greater pleasure.

Earthly riches are either going to leave you or you are going to leave them, but eternal riches you keep forever. When you invest in your church, orphanages, missions, clean water, or food and clothing for the poor, you are taking hold of what Paul calls "truly life." True living is found in generous giving.

This is the cycle of generosity: God blesses you today, so you can bless others tomorrow, so he can bless you forever. If you stop the cycle at the beginning, the biggest loser is you because blessings boomerang in the kingdom of God. No matter what you give, how much you give, and how far you give it, God says in eternity it will come back to you many times over.

We all have the opportunity to be generous for the work of the kingdom of God because we know that God's generosity is reflected in our own. "For you know the grace of our Lord Jesus Christ, that though he was rich, yet for your sake he became poor, so that you by his poverty might become rich" (2 Corinthians 8:9). We have eternal riches because Jesus was joyfully generous with us. How can we not with our earthly riches be joyfully generous for him?

Prayer for This Week: *Almighty God, thank you for every gift you've presented to me. Let me not be a container that collects but a conduit that contributes to the generosity that begins with your own.*

Question for This Week: Generosity isn't an obligation but a posture you adopt toward money, possessions, and people. What are some practical expressions of generosity or the willingness to share that you can practice?

44

The Final Word

Scriptures for This Week

- Psalm 119:97-104
- 2 Timothy 3:14-17
- Psalm 119:65-72
- Hebrews 4:12-13
- 2 Corinthians 5:1-5

Lost Without a Guide

What one item would you want to have with you if you were stranded alone on a deserted island? To help you make this decision, let me eliminate some obvious choices. You will have fresh water to drink, plenty of food to eat, and you will have shelter from the elements. You can't carry anything that would help people find you. You will get to bring only one thing. What would it be?

I would bring a Bible. Because God has given his final word in this book, if I'm going to be alone, his presence will come through its pages. If I'm going to die, his comfort will speak to me in his word. If I'm to be rescued, his word will conform my character. The Bible would be a serious help to me.

Yet, people who take God seriously so often don't take the Bible seriously. The only way you and I can know anything meaningful about God is if he reveals it to us, and his special revelation is what the Bible is for us.

There are questions that only God can answer, and he has communicated them in a way that I can hear and understand. Through the Bible he answers questions such as, "What is his name?" "Can I have a personal relationship with him and if so how?" "Does he have a plan and purpose for my life?" "Is there life beyond death?" "What is right and wrong in his sight?"

The Bible addresses these concerns in a trustworthy way that assures me it is God's final word. We have reason to treasure the Bible as one of the greatest gifts we could ever have received.

Trusting the Guide

Either the Bible is just another book or it is unlike any other book that has ever been written. One of Paul's letters to Timothy asserts the latter: "And how from infancy you have known the Holy Scriptures, which are able to make you wise for salvation through faith in Christ. All Scripture is God-breathed and is useful for teaching, rebuking, correcting and training in righteousness, so that the servant of God may be thoroughly equipped for every good work" (2 Timothy 3:15-17 NIV).

God exhaled the word of God ("All Scripture is God-breathed") so that on every page you have the breath of God. It is God's word whether you read it or it sits on the shelf, whether you like it or you don't, whether you obey its teachings or ignore them.

Maybe you've heard the objection that men wrote the Bible. This is true, but God authored it. Because of this, we can conclude that it's not riddled with errors because God cannot lie. As Peter affirms, "Above all, you must understand that no prophecy of Scripture came about by the prophet's own interpretation of things. For prophecy never had its origin in the human will, but prophets, though human, spoke from God as they were carried along by the Holy Spirit" (2 Peter 1:20-21 NIV).

So what we have in the Bible is a book that originated in the mind of God, was communicated from the mouth of God, and was then articulated by the messenger of God. Therefore, it is the final word of God.

The Bible Guides Us in Our Spiritual Beliefs

The Library of Congress is the library to trump all libraries. It has twenty-nine million books printed in 460 different languages. Of all those books, all but one are just the words of man. Only one is the final word of God and that is the Bible.

If this is God's final word to the human race, then all that you ever need to believe spiritually is found here and nowhere else. That is why I call it God's final word not God's "best word" because it is God's only word. You don't need a Book of Mormon or a Koran or any other spiritual teaching. Genesis is the beginning of God's word. Revelation is the ending of God's word, and all of it is complete and final.

Since God is the author of all spiritual truth, every spiritual truth you need to know and to believe comes from his word. That means that everything you need to believe about God, life, salvation, sin, righteousness, and a thousand other things are all found only in this book. You don't have to wonder or worry about what you should believe. The guesswork is eliminated.

The Bible Guides Us to Our Moral Behavior

God's word is the most valuable book because it affects us in four life-altering ways: "All Scripture is God-breathed and is useful for teaching, rebuking, correcting and training in righteousness" (2 Timothy 3:16 NIV).

In order to do what is right, you've got to know what is right. This is *teaching*. The Bible records what God has to say on every important issue in life whether it is money, sex, power, ambition, greed, heaven, or hell. We can know how to live in a way that pleases God by ascribing to the Bible's teaching.

On the flipside, we need to know what is *not* right, and the Bible is useful in this *rebuking* way as well. When you read the Bible, God will speak to your heart to show you any faults or failures. Like a spiritual CAT scan, reading the Bible with an open mind and an open heart will reveal those wrong thoughts, attitudes, and habits.

The Bible doesn't just condemn us when we're wrong and praise us when we're right. It will also show us what God says we need to do in order to move from wrong to right. It is useful for *correcting*, for putting us in our proper condition. When you read it and obey it, it restores you to the spiritual condition of being right with God.

The Bible is God's final word to tell you not only what is right and what is not right and how to get right, but you will also hear in it how to stay right. It is profitable for *training in righteousness*.

Every action you take or reaction you experience will either be in line with the will of God or not. The Bible is the final word that helps us not just know the difference but to stay in the place where we can hear from and please and respond to God.

The Bible Guides Us to Our Eternal Blessing

Paul also tells Timothy, "you have known the Holy Scriptures, which are able to make you wise for salvation through faith in Christ Jesus" (3:15 NIV). This book is God's final word on how to make sure you spend eternity with him. If you believe in heaven and are interested in going there, this book is God's final word on how to get there.

The Bible is God's GPS. It can do things that not even satellites can do. It can tell you that you are lost even before you realize it, and it can tell you how to go from being lost to being where you need to be. It can guide you not only about life on this earth but also about life with God in heaven.

The Bible is a gift that leads us into life. Everything that God wants you to be and do comes from this book. You can know what to spiritually believe, how to morally behave, and where you eternally belong with the confidence that it is God's final word.

Prayer for This Week: *God, thank you for the gift of the Bible. Move me to open it daily, to read it expectantly, and to let it change my life.*

Question for This Week: What verses from the Bible have had the greatest impact on your life? List them and then consider just how much more transformation you can experience if you read God's word.

45

Amazing Grace

Scriptures for This Week

- John 1:14-18
- Titus 2:11-15
- Ephesians 2:4-10
- 2 Corinthians 12:6-10
- Romans 5:12-21

Relating by Grace

Everything about the American way of life teaches us that you get what you earn. You get what you work for. You get what you pay for. This is the American ethic. The problem comes when we begin to think that it is the Christian ethic, that the same way we relate to our paycheck or possessions is the same way we should relate to God. God does not relate to us on the basis of our goodness. He relates to us on the basis of his grace.

One of the sweetest words in the entire Bible is *grace*. Apart from grace you cannot know God, understand God, or relate to God. Without grace churches would close their doors because they would not have a ministry or a message.

Here are two definitions of grace:

- Grace is anything that I need but don't deserve and could never repay, but God gives to me anyway.
- Grace is the face that God puts on when he looks at my failures, my faults, and my flaws.

Most believers know what grace is, and untold numbers of unbelievers have sung about "Amazing Grace." Yet many don't understand what grace does. Fortunately, Paul tells us what we don't know.

Free Grace

How do you spell salvation? Many people spell salvation D-O. They think one has to do certain actions to be saved—join a church, give to the poor, read the Bible, and pray.

Some people want to spell salvation D-O-N-T. If you don't do certain things, like murder, rape, or steal, then you're saved. But God spells salvation D-O-N-E. No strings attached and no fine print. When you accept Jesus, God accepts you.

The apostle Paul says, "For the grace of God has appeared that offers salvation to all people" (Titus 2:11 NIV). Notice it is not the goodness or religious sincerity of people that brings salvation. It is the grace of God. Grace is an unconditional, unearned, unpurchased, no-strings-attached gift.

Salvation is not based on my performance. It is based on God's promise, not my merit. It is based on God's mercy, not my goodness. Salvation is based on grace. We have such a poor understanding of what grace is. I meet people daily who are striving, trying, yearning, and burning to earn the grace of God when all they must do is receive salvation as a gift.

Grace Saves Us from Sin's Penalty

You cannot understand what it means to have a relationship with God without understanding grace. Grace is the only way. Grace is only through Jesus. As Peter says in Acts 15:11 (NIV), "We believe it is through the grace of our Lord Jesus that we are saved."

Why can it come through Jesus Christ only? Why can't it come through Mohammad or Buddha? A pastor or a priest? Because Jesus is the only one who paid for it. Nobody else has ever died for your sins, nor has anyone else's payment been accepted for your sins. Grace is free but not cheap. Jesus paid for it himself. You can receive grace or you can reject it, but you cannot earn it because it has already been bought and paid for.

Grace Strengthens Us Against Sin's Power

We are told in Titus 2:12 that this grace that has appeared "teaches us." The moment you become a believer you are enrolled in Grace University.

The first day you go to school, you are taught that God loves you the way you are and that God loves you too much to let you stay that way.

We are taught some lessons over and over and over in Grace University. First, we can say no to doing wrong. Grace "teaches us to say 'No' to ungodliness and worldly passions" because grace changes us. It changes our heart, our head, and our habits. When grace comes into our life, it gives us not only a love for God but a hatred for sin. It does not give us the license to live like we want to, but it gives us the liberty to live like we ought to.

Our second lesson at Grace University is that grace teaches us to say yes to what is right. Verse 12 continues, "and to live self-controlled, upright, and godly lives in this present age." First, we are to live *self-controlled* in our soul or inward life. Through grace we allow God to control our thoughts and attitudes. Second, we are to live *upright*. That deals with our body or the outward life. The Christian is someone in whom Christ lives. When Christ comes to live within us, we will live out the Christ who lives in us. Finally, we are to live *godly*. This is the spiritual or upward life. We are to live like God would have us live. God not only gives us grace to live with him in heaven, he gives us grace so we can live for him and with him on earth.

Those three words take care of every part of our life as a body, a soul, and a spirit. When we give in to grace, every part of who we are can be "eager to do what is good" (Titus 2:14 NIV). Grace is stronger than the power of sin and will enliven us to be right and to do right.

Grace Will Separate Us from Sin's Presence

We are never going to get a better deal than the deal God has offered us. For your sin, God is willing to give you his salvation. For your failures, God is willing to give you his forgiveness. For your guilt, God is willing to give you his grace—all free.

Grace separates us from sin's presence. Paul says, "while we wait for the blessed hope—the appearing of the glory of our great God and Savior, Jesus Christ" (Titus 2:13 NIV). One day, by the grace of God, Jesus is going to come back and take us away from the presence of sin.

The older I get, the more I think about heaven. I consider how we won't need alarm systems for our homes or locks on our doors in heaven. There will be no police, no courts, and no jail because the crime rate is nil in heaven. Everything in heaven is all by the grace of God. And God can't wait.

Isaiah 30:18 (NIV) says, "The LORD longs to be gracious to you." The Lord longs to give us what we don't deserve and he can because his Son took what he didn't deserve. Jesus came the first time to take my sin away from me. He is coming the second time to take me away from all sin. When he comes back, not only is he going to take me *to* something, he's going to take me *from* something.

Prayer for This Week: *God, thank you for your grace that frees me from sin and opens me to experience and exude your love. Strengthen me against my sin today so that I might be self-controlled, upright, and godly.*

Question for This Week: How would you define grace? How does grace define you?

Section Seven

Curtain Call

The story of the Bible moves toward a curtain call for its hero, Jesus, as he returns for the final time to be acknowledged and acclaimed by the entire world. How should we live as we wait for the hero to return? The Bible has much to teach us about this. Read and be changed.

46

Breathing Your Last

Scriptures for This Week

- Hebrews 9:23-28
- Hebrews 10:26-31
- Romans 6:19-23
- John 3:10-21
- Philippians 3:7-11

Expirations and Exits

On a Saturday evening in 2009, a friend of mine, Lance Sperring, was killed in an automobile collision. The oncoming driver veered into his lane and Lance died at the scene. He was sixty-five years old. I'm sure Lance didn't believe he would die on the day he did. But God's death clock is ticking for every one of us, and we don't know when it will stop.

We all face death, but we don't have to fear it. Hebrews 2:15 (NLT) tells us that Jesus came to "set free all who have lived their lives as slaves to the fear of dying." One of these days, one of your breaths will be your last, and today may be the day you take it.

You Have an Appointment with Death You Must Keep

We read here in Hebrews 9:27 that "it is appointed for man to die once." The word *appointed* could be translated *reserved*. Every one of us has a reservation with death, a reservation we cannot cancel and an appointment we will keep. The world would call the death of my friend Lance an accident. But it was an appointment.

The certainty of death bothers us. We know we are going to die. Dustin Hoffman, the Academy Award-winning actor, was asked what epitaph he wanted on his tombstone. He smiled and said, "I want these words on my tombstone: 'I knew this was going to happen.'"

We know we are going to die, but we don't know when, where, or how. One of my favorite stories is an old legend of a merchant in Baghdad who one day sent his servant to the market. Before long the servant came running back to his master and said, "Master, I just bumped into a woman in the crowd, and when I turned around, I saw it was Death that bumped me. She looked at me with a threatening expression. Master, please lend me your horse for I have to get away from her. I will ride to Samarra and hide there so Death will not find me."

The merchant gave him his horse, and the servant galloped away in great haste. Later the merchant went down to the marketplace and saw Death standing in the crowd. He went over to her and said, "Why did you frighten my servant this morning? Why did you have such a threatening expression on your face?"

"That was not a threatening expression," Death said. "It was an expression of shock. I was surprised to see him in Baghdad, because I have an appointment with him tonight in Samarra." We all have that appointment with death, and we will keep it.

You Have an Appearance After Death You Must Make

I cannot tell you the number of times I've had someone ask me, "What happens after people die?" That is a deep question and it calls for a long answer, but I can say there will be a judgment.

Hebrews 9:27 says that "it is appointed for man to die once and after that comes judgment." There are three things that are linked together in life: sin, death, and judgment. The result of sin is death, but the result of death is judgment. Paul says, "Therefore, just as sin came into the world through one man, and death through sin, and so death spread to all men because all sinned" (Romans 5:12).

I read the other day that the number one cause of death in America is heart disease. The facts all back it up and medical doctors won't argue against it. But the number one cause of death in America and the world is actually sin.

Sometimes we think that people do get away with certain things. Here in America, if you burglarize somebody, your chance of being arrested is only 7 percent. If you are unlucky enough to be one of those

7 percent, only 87 percent of you will be prosecuted. If you are one of those 87 percent that are prosecuted, only 79 percent of you will be convicted. If you are one of those 79 percent that are convicted, only 25 percent of you will go to prison. When you multiply all of those probabilities, it means if you decide to become a burglar, you will have only a 1.2 percent chance of going to jail.[58]

The percentage of people who will stand before God and be judged is much higher—100 percent will face judgment. If you refuse to accept Jesus into your life, you will stand before God as your judge and give an account for your refusal. If you receive Jesus into your life you don't have to face that judgment, but you will be judged for what you did for Christ after you received him. The difference between the two judgments is that one determines punishment and the other determines rewards. How will you look when it's time for your appearance?

You Have an Appeal Before Death You Should Accept

Hebrews 9:27 tells us we have problems with sin, death, and judgment. Then verse 28 tells us that Jesus is the solution to every one of those problems. He died to save us from our sins, he was raised to deliver us from death, and he is coming again to spare us from the wrathful judgment of God. Verse 28 tells us, "so Christ, having been offered once to bear the sins of many, will appear a second time, not to deal with sin but to save those who are eagerly waiting for him." The little word *so* connects all the problems with the one faithful, knowable solution, which is Jesus Christ.

Jesus came to die for your sin problem. When he takes care of your sin problem, he takes care of your death problem. When he takes care of your death problem, he takes care of your judgment problem. When he comes again, if you have accepted his forgiveness, you will be spared any punishment, but if you haven't, you will be condemned by your own unbelief. If you refuse Jesus, you enter into the court of no appeal. You can't take a mulligan, there are no do overs, there are no mistrials, and there are no loopholes.

On a day of God's choosing, not your own, that clock will stop ticking. If you know Jesus, your last breath on earth will be your first breath in heaven. But if you don't know Jesus, your last breath on earth will be your first breath in hell, separated from the God who sent his Son to deliver us from the fear of death and judgment so we could spend eternity with him.

Ready to Die, Ready to Live

My friend Lance was a believer in Jesus. He lives, right now, in the presence of God where no one mourns or experiences pain. Hebrews 9:28 ends with some good news, that Jesus brings salvation to "those who are eagerly waiting for him." This is an assurance that we have as believers. Salvation will not fail. Jesus will bring it to completion, and once we have accepted his offer of grace, we wait for our final redemption.

Death is good news for those who believe. At last, we will enjoy the friendship of God, the end of the groaning of creation, a true resurrection life in the loving glory of our Lord, and the death of death once and for all. We will know Christ fully and be known. Breathing your last will mean wholeness, community, and grace.

Prayer for This Week: *God, I want to have a relationship with you for now and eternity. Show me the way to have life through Jesus now so that I may also have life with Jesus forever.*

Question for This Week: What do you want your life after death to look like? How will you be able to experience that?

47

Root Canal

Scriptures for This Week

- Deuteronomy 29:16-18
- 1 Kings 8:46-51
- Hebrews 12:14-17
- Matthew 15:1-20
- James 1:19-21

Understand the Hate of Your Bitterness

The root of bitterness ran deep in Ron Shanabarger's heart. When his father died, he called his girlfriend, Amy, with the news. But she was on an ocean cruise with her parents and had to refuse to come home early to attend the funeral. Ron never forgave her and instead determined to marry her, have a child with her, let her grow attached, and then kill the child. Less than three years later, on Father's Day, Ron jumped into the shower so that Amy would get up to wake their seven-month-old son, Tyler. Amy found him face down in his crib, stiff and cold. The doctors deemed it SIDS. They buried Tyler two days later.

Hours after the funeral, Amy sat in her living room sobbing. Racked with grief and guilt, wishing she'd checked on Tyler instead of falling into bed exhausted the night before, she listened to Ron's unbelievable confession. As that precious baby boy was playing in his crib the night before, Ron wrapped his head in plastic wrap, sat down to eat, brushed his teeth, and came back just in time to see his little boy take his last breath. He removed the wrap, turned the baby onto his stomach, switched off the light, and went to bed before Amy got home from work. With a look of horror and shock, she asked him, "Why?" He said, "Now we're even."

A dead seven-month-old boy, a broken marriage, a shattered wife and mother, and a forty-nine-year prison sentence for a husband and father was the result of bitterness.[59] Being overwhelmed with bitterness puts us at risk of hurting other people, but nobody is hurt more through bitterness than the person who is bitter. Someone said bitterness is like drinking poison and waiting for the other person to die.

Confront the Honesty of Your Bitterness

Those who are bitter want to be bitter and feel they have a right to be bitter. A study in the *Journal of Adult Development* found that 75 percent of those surveyed believed they have been forgiven by God for past mistakes and wrongdoings, but only 52 percent said they have forgiven others, and even fewer (43 percent) have sought forgiveness for harm they have done to others.[60]

Who are you bitter toward?

- God because of a tragedy that you blame him for.
- A boss who unjustly fired you.
- A spouse who left you for someone else.
- A business partner who took financial advantage of you.
- A relative or a friend who abused you.
- A parent who did not spend enough time with you.
- The church because of a bad experience.

We can define bitterness as harbored hurt hidden in the heart. Like an emotional suicide bomber, you want to hurt others, and you're not averse to hurting yourself in the process. The deception of bitterness is that it destroys its own container—you.

If you are bitter, I encourage you right now to take stock of what your bitterness is doing. I guarantee it is helping no one and hurting you.

Go to the Heart of Your Bitterness

Bitterness and roots have enough in common that the Bible uses them together: "See to it that no one fails to obtain the grace of God; that no 'root of bitterness' springs up and causes trouble, and by it many become defiled" (Hebrews 12:15).

A root, like bitterness, is beneath the surface. It is invisible to the eye but just as real as the plant it supports. A root stretches deep into the soil just as bitterness grows deep into the soil of your heart. Just like roots grow from a seed, so does bitterness. Bitterness is harbored hurt hidden in the heart, so the seed of bitterness is the hurt and the soil of bitterness is the heart.

Our hurt can be inflicted or it can be imagined, but either way the hurt is real. Most hurts are minor enough that we either deal with the hurt or just walk away from it. However, a bitter person doesn't do that. When a bitter person is hurt, he takes that seed of hurt and plants it in his heart. Then he fertilizes it, cultivates it, dwells on it, and then justifies it. All the while, the plant of his life becomes negative and critical of everything attached to his hurt.

Bitterness is a root that we cannot see, but it always bears fruit that we will see. Bitterness finds its root in our heart, but it will bear its fruit in our life. To get to the root of the problem, we must get to our heart.

Admit the Hurt of Your Bitterness

The author of Hebrews warns us that if a root of bitterness springs up, it "causes trouble." As the root of bitterness grows, it moves from our heart to our mind. Like a relentless cancer, it invades and kills a healthy thought life. When we harbor deep hurt, we carry a mental picture of our abuser around with us everywhere. We dream about how we can hurt them. We spend waking moments thinking of how we can get even with them. It consumes our mind and turns our happy thoughts into dark thoughts.

Emotionally, bitterness acts like a depressant. Have you ever met a happy bitter person? They might say they're not bitter, but they are critical, negative, faultfinding, ungrateful, and might even battle depression. They keep an emotional distance and struggle to connect with other people because they are so emotionally disconnected in their own heart.

Physically, our body deteriorates under the control of bitterness. It was not created to nourish and carry grudges. There are over fifty ailments ranging from ulcers to high blood pressure that can be caused by bitterness.

Doctors Frank Minirth and Paul Meier researched ten thousand patients who had either quit their job or just given up on life itself. They discovered that the number one cause of physical and emotional burnout is not stress or perfectionism but bitterness. The unwillingness to forgive and let go of a grudge was the dominant cause of burnout.[61]

Spiritually, you will not look to God, love God, or live for God as you should if you are bitter. The author of Hebrews says, "Strive for peace with everyone, and for the holiness without which no one will see the Lord. See to it that no one fails to obtain the grace of God" (Hebrews 12:14-15). A bitter person will not be at peace on the inside, he will not be holy on the upside, and he will not be gracious on the outside.

Seek the Healing of Your Bitterness

The only cure for bitterness is a "spiritual root canal." During a root canal, the dentist will remove the nerve and pulp from inside a tooth, discarding the decay and infection. She will then seal that tooth so the infection doesn't return. The only alternative is to lose the tooth.

Bitterness is an infection in the heart that, if not removed, will kill the heart. What can you do when you acknowledge bitterness in your heart and that it's already defiling you? God has provided a remedy to cleanse the heart of bitterness and restore it to emotional and spiritual health.

The first way to deal with bitterness is to *abandon it*. You must take whatever infected the root of bitterness in your heart and discard it. Ephesians 4:31 says, "Let all bitterness and wrath and anger and clamor and slander be put away from you, along with all malice." It is natural from time to time to remember the hurt and the heartache someone caused you, but then bathe that hurt in the soothing antiseptic of grace and toss it away.

The second way you deal with bitterness is to *absolve it*. The only cure for the disease of bitterness is the antidote of forgiveness. Someone defined forgiveness as "giving up my right to hurt you for hurting me."

To forgive, you go back to the cross of Christ and remember how the grace of God has forgiven you. You will never forgive someone for what they have done to you until you realize and experience how God has forgiven you for what you have done to him. This gives you the power to experience God's forgiveness, and grace gives you the power to express God's forgiveness to others.

It takes two to forgive: you and Jesus. The great pastor Charles Spurgeon said, "Go to the cross to learn how you have been forgiven and then stay awhile to learn how to forgive." You can be full of bitterness and empty of Jesus or you can be full of Jesus and empty of bitterness, but you cannot be both. Bitterness is no way to live but a sure way to die. By the grace of God, you can live forgiving and die forgiven.

Prayer for This Week: *Lord, thank you for the forgiveness that empowers me with abundant life. Examine my heart and point out any bitterness within me that I might abandon and absolve it in the shadow of your cross.*

Question for This Week: What will you do this week to uncover and release the bitterness in your heart toward one person? How will you release your bitterness toward God?

48

The Test of Your Life

Scriptures for This Week

- Romans 12:1-2
- James 1:2-12
- Job 23:8-12
- Matthew 5:27-30
- 1 Peter 4:12-19

Toil and Trouble

If you were listening to the radio or watching television anytime in the forty years after 1963, from time to time you would be interrupted by a test of the Emergency Broadcast System. Right in the middle of *MASH* or *Magnum P.I.* the screen would flash a color spectrum, sound an obnoxious, lengthy beep, and follow it with an announcement, "This is a test of the Emergency Broadcast System. If this had been an actual emergency…"

I wish in life there were warnings like that before difficulties and troubles T-bone us. However, tests aren't just warnings, they're trainings. Most significant advancements in life involve a significant test, such as the SAT or MCAT, which we must take before we can get where we want to go.

The book of James is all about tests, experiences that prove our faith. The book's fifty-four imperative verses instruct our conduct because real faith responds in recognizable ways. God knows whether a person's faith is real by looking on the inside, but the only way we can tell is by looking on the outside. What would your faith look like on the outside if it was real on the inside?

Anybody can believe or trust God when life brings sunshine, but it's how you handle trouble that reveals whether your faith is living or dead, genuine or counterfeit. If you have a profession of faith but not a possession of faith, the fires of trouble may burn it up. In times of trouble, faith needs to work.

Trouble Strengthens Our Trust

Did you get up this morning and say, "I think I will have a bad day today. I'll get myself in a scrape I can't fix"? We don't go looking for trouble; trouble comes looking for us. James 1:2 (NIV) says, "Consider it pure joy, my brothers and sisters, whenever you face trials of many kinds." It's not a matter of *if* we have trouble but *when* we have trouble. Trouble is unavoidable for all of us, whether we believe in God or not.

Then James says these troubles will be "of many kinds." Troubles come in all shapes, sizes, and colors—from bankruptcy to breakups, from cancer to cutbacks, from dismissals to debt. You will never understand a lot of things about the troubles that come into your life, but you can trust that "the testing of your faith produces perseverance" (James 1:3 NIV). The word for *test* could be used of a young bird testing its wings. It means to prove whether something is real and works. Trials and troubles test the toughness of our faith.

Every trial and every trouble is a test made up of two questions. God is asking you: (1) Do you trust me? (2) How much? When you decide to trust God in the most untrustable times, your faith is strengthened. It grows and develops the ability to persevere and not quit.

Trouble Perfects Our Faith

Another benefit to trouble is maturity. "Let perseverance finish its work so that you may be mature and complete, not lacking anything" (James 1:4 NIV). The goal of every parent is to raise children to maturity. That's our heavenly Father's goal for us as well. Every trial that comes into our life is a test, true, but it doesn't leave us in the same place we once were. It matures us. We change.

Faith is like a muscle—it grows through exercise and is perfected through stresses and stretches. So many times we want to avoid trials or escape trials when we need the trial.

Watching a butterfly struggle its way free from its chrysalis looks exhausting. What if you thought, *I'm going to do that butterfly a favor and cut a hole in the shell for it to climb out?* It would only fall to the ground, unable to fly. The struggle to escape has been designed to strengthen that butterfly's muscular system so that when it does come out, it can fly once its wings dry. It is when we struggle and fight through difficulty that our faith grows and matures. When troubles and trials and tribulations broadside us, we may stagger for a moment, but real faith says, "No matter what is happening to me, God is doing something in me." When your wings harden after the struggle, you will fly.

The first half of James 1:2 sounds crazy: "Consider it pure joy, my brothers and sisters, whenever you face trials of many kinds." "Consider it pure joy" is a cognitive act, not a feeling. When you keep the perspective that God is working through you, even though you may not feel joy, you can at least consider it a joyful opportunity for God to do a new work in your life.

If you value your comfort more than you do your character or your feelings more than your faith, then trials, troubles, and tribulations will drive you away from God. If you value your character, your faith, and your walk with God more than anything material or physical, then you will be able to count troubles as joy because you know it grows you and makes you new.

Trouble Changes Our Focus

Even though we know it's unanswerable and even though asking keeps us locked in uncertainty, the first question we always ask when trouble hits is, "Why?" This is why James moves into talking about wisdom. "If any of you lacks wisdom, you should ask God, who gives generously to all without finding fault, and it will be given to you" (1:5 NIV). You need wisdom to understand how God is using your trouble.

We're using wisdom when we seek to see difficult times from God's point of view. When we're using wisdom, we aren't just saying, "Rescue me!" but, "Reveal to me what you are doing." That's real faith.

Troubles have a way of changing our focus. Bad times drive us to God. They force us to come before him and say, "Lord, I can't handle this situation. I don't understand it and need wisdom to see this from your point of view so that my faith will be strong." That is how real faith operates when trouble comes.

Trouble Blesses Our Future

A test is not designed to make you look bad but to make you look good. If you are prepared for the test, then you receive the reward of a good grade, an advancement, or an invitation to enter something new.

A tremendous and almost indescribable blessing awaits at the end of a life that has remained faithful and steadfast in spite of trouble. No matter how deep and hard and heartbreaking the trouble might be, God says to each one of us that if we refuse to buckle and keep believing, trusting, obeying, and serving him, we will receive the crown of life. "Blessed is the one who perseveres under trial because, having stood the test, that person will receive the crown of life that the Lord has promised to those who love him" (James 1:12 NIV). I don't know what that crown represents, but no earthly reward can compare.

One of the most fascinating and valuable jewels is a pearl. But pearls are the product of pain. The shell of the oyster gets pierced and an alien substance (a grain of sand) slips inside. The sensitive body of that oyster goes to work releasing healing fluids that otherwise would have remained dormant. That irritant is covered and the wound is healed by a pearl. A pearl is a healed wound.

Your life is much the same—conceived through irritation, born in adversity, nursed by adjustments. When all that could be lost is lost and everything that could go wrong does, a person of real faith acts in trust, love, worship, and service, and experiences a future reward of the loving presence of God. Your circumstances right now may be a test, but this test is *for* you.

Prayer for This Week: *God, I fall before you in my weakness and my doubt. Show me your perspective in my pain that I might cling to you with faith that is real and pure and firm.*

Question for This Week: What will it take for you to stop saying, "Rescue me!" and instead say, "Reveal to me what you're doing"?

49

Faith Works

Scriptures for This Week

- Hebrews 11:5-6
- James 2:14-26
- Titus 1:10-16
- Matthew 7:15-20
- Hebrews 11:32-40

Real Faith Really Works

James wrote his letter to Jewish Christians, people who had grown up in a religious tradition that taught relationship with God was earned through good works and keeping the law. Now that these Jewish Christians had heard that God accepts them by faith and not works, they were swinging to the other extreme. They believed they could claim to believe in Jesus and then live anyway they wanted. Good works in their life were unnecessary and no evidence of faith existed.

If you say you have faith in Jesus, yet there has been no life change that results in your obeying God and doing good, then your faith is not real. When it comes to faith, declaration without demonstration equals deception.

Faith works, but knowing how it works is both fascinating and formational to who we are in Christ. Faith is the only thing that works to bring people into a relationship with God. We can't please God without it. And faith, according to the book of James, has always been a real problem.

Put Up or Shut Up

James chapter 2 gets practical in verses 15-17 by describing someone cold and hungry. If we claim to have faith and are made aware of this person's need, we will not say, "I see that you're cold and hungry. Please go and I hope you will get warm and fed." Faithless people will do that. People with faith will build a fire or offer food.

James is not arguing that we need anything more than faith to know God and to be accepted by God. He is not saying we must add good works to faith in order to know God. *Good works prove faith, they don't provide it.*

Next, James introduces us to someone who says, "James, some people have faith and some people have works. What's good for you may not be good for me" (2:18). But faith and works isn't about either-or. It's both-and. Faith produces works that demonstrate that faith. Works alone may not demonstrate faith at all.

Nine out of ten people in America say they believe that Jesus is God's Son, but only three in ten say they have accepted him as their Lord and Savior.[62] James says talk is cheap. Real faith is shown in your life. Real faith can be seen by others. Real faith is substantiated by good works. If your faith stops at words and doesn't go on to works, what good is it? That is why James goes on to say, "Show me your faith without deeds, and I will show you my faith by my deeds" (James 2:18 NIV). James then draws a line between genuine faith and the counterfeit kind.

Dead Faith Is Defective

Someone has said, "A person who won't read is no better off than a person who can't read." A person who says he loves God but doesn't act like it and doesn't show it is no better off than the person who says they don't love God at all.

James 2:14 says, "What good is it, my brothers and sisters, if someone claims to have faith but has no deeds? Can such faith save them?" The key word in this verse is *claims*. The person James is describing doesn't have faith. The presence of good works does not prove the presence of faith, but the absence of good works points to the absence of faith. How alive is a faith that does not move a person to do good things in the world? Our commitment to church, giving, fidelity, compassion, and hospitality prove what we profess. If we have a relationship with God, we will want to demonstrate obedience to him.

Demonic Faith Is Deceptive

James would almost fall over laughing at people who think that believing in God or some higher power is all that matters. Listen to this statement: "You believe that there is one God. Good! Even the demons believe that—and shudder" (James 2:19 NIV).

There are no atheists in hell, and even the demons believe in God. They tremble at the thought of him. They fear God more than others do. Though these beings believe in God, they rebel against God and refuse to obey his commands.

If someone were to look at your life, would they see indisputable evidence that you believe in God? You can have good works without faith, but you cannot have real faith without good works. If you believe in God, your life will show it. Living any other way is just deceiving yourself.

You cannot earn salvation by being good. However, if you are truly saved, you cannot hide it. James's brother Jesus said the same thing: "Neither do people light a lamp and put it under a bowl. Instead they put it on its stand, and it gives light to everyone in the house. In the same way, let your light shine before others, that they may see your good deeds and glorify your Father in heaven" (Matthew 5:15-16 NIV).

Dynamic Faith Is Decisive

James interestingly points to Rahab as a classic example of how faith works (2:25). Rahab grew up in a pagan environment and didn't know God until the day she met some Jewish spies who were scouting out the Promised Land prior to the invasion led by Joshua. When she showed kindness to them by hiding them, they in turn promised if she would hang a scarlet thread in her window, they would spare her and her family's lives. She believed, hung that cord in her window, and she and her family were spared. You don't have to wonder whether she had given up paganism or if her faith was real. You don't read Rahab's story and think, *She just said she believed to get out of something*. All you must do is look at that scarlet cord in the window.

Faith justifies the believer, but works justify the faith. God sees our faith on the inside, but we demonstrate our faith on the outside. Faith is the root of salvation, but works are the fruit of it. Therefore, James says, "As the body without the spirit is dead, so faith without deeds is dead" (2:26 NIV).

You are not saved by Jesus plus baptism. You are not saved by Jesus plus church membership. You are not saved by Jesus plus giving or Jesus plus good works. Jesus doesn't need to add anything and you don't need anything except Jesus in order to know God. Is your faith real? The only way to know it is to show it. If your faith works, you will show it, God will grow it, and others will know it.

Prayer for This Week: *Father, give me the faith to serve the world in ways that reflect your character and your plan of redemption. Let good works be an expression of my unquestionable salvation in you.*

Question for This Week What are some good works that you've been too timid or skeptical to do? What does that say about how dead or alive your faith may be?

50

Off-Ramp

Scriptures for This Week

- James 2:8-11
- 1 John 1:1-10
- Psalm 32
- John 9:35-41
- 1 John 3:4-6

Guilt Trip

If you're like me, your life is full and even overfilled. Emails need answering, phone calls need returning, teams need leading, people need meeting, and so much more. I juggle it all with writing, exercise, golf, and being a husband, father, grandfather, friend, and neighbor. We have too many obligations and not enough time.

How often have you felt like you just don't have enough life in order to give what life demands? You don't have enough time, money, energy, emotion, or brainpower to pull off what you need to pull off? Discouragement, hopelessness, anger, bitterness, and guilt all seem to box us into a room without an exit.

Guilt can be so overwhelming that it causes tears in the middle of a laugh, indigestion in the middle of a meal, and even suicide in the middle of a sprouting life. It becomes an emotional ball and chain that we drag with us everywhere we go—guilt over that failed marriage, the DUI, the one-night stand, the neglected child, the broken friendship. Guilt is a ghost that will haunt you, hinder you, and hurt you to the day that you die unless you take it to the cross and the empty tomb.

Sin City

Consider the Saturday night before Jesus's resurrection. The disciples abandoned Jesus, were targeted by the religious establishment, and felt anger and discouragement over the death of Jesus and the death of a dream. They were heavy with stress and guilt. Everything they'd invested in and believed in looked lost. Even worse, they had sinned against Jesus when he needed them most by denying him and abandoning him.

When we enter sin city, we check into the hotel of guilt. But we were never made to sleep in this hotel. Adam was not put on this earth to sin, so when he was created he did not have the ability to cope with guilt. When he disobeyed and experienced guilt and shame, he did what we all do when we're guilty—run and hide. Adam had to learn as do we that even though guilt is an inside job, we need outside help to get over it.

One of the disciples, John, an eyewitness to both the crucifixion and the resurrection, wrote a little book in the Bible (1 John) that directs us to the exit and tells us how to counter the three things we tend to do on our joyride with sin.

The Fact of Your Sin

Sin is disobeying God or breaking God's law. But when you kneel at the foot of the cross and accept the risen Lord, every sin you have ever committed or ever will commit is forgiven and forgotten by Jesus Christ. The only word found in your legal file is *forgiven*. Guilt will condemn us, but God will clear us. If you're looking for the off-ramp for your guilt trip, take the exit marked "forgiveness."

Some people *deny* their sin. We know that denial must have been a big problem even in John's day because he mentions it twice between 1 John 1:3 and 1 John 1:10. "If we say we have no sin, we deceive ourselves, and the truth is not in us" (verse 8). Then, in verse 10 he says, "If we say we have not sinned, we make him a liar, and his word is not in us." We live in a world where the word *sin* is seldom, if ever, used. We deny that it affects us and we even deny that it exists.

When a politician is caught having an affair or a banker is caught embezzling or an investment broker bilks thousands of people out of their retirement, they all say, "I made a mistake." A sin is more than a mistake. If I am a mistaker and not a sinner, I don't need a Savior. I just need to do better and learn from my mistakes. Mistakes need to be corrected. Sins need to be forgiven.

The Fault of Your Sin

The only way to forgiveness is confession. Confession is more than just admission. To confess sin, we call sin what God calls it and we admit to God that our sin is our fault. He will agree with us and hear our confession. "If we confess our sins, he is faithful and just to forgive us our sins and to cleanse us from all unrighteousness" (1 John 1:9). When we confess sin, we take the stand and testify against ourselves. We cannot plead the Fifth with God.

My sons will always be my sons no matter what they do. Growing up they would, at times, disobey me. This damaged our fellowship until they confessed their disobedience and made things right. We still had relationship in spite of our injured fellowship. Confession brings us back into fellowship with God. John says, "If we say we have fellowship with him while we walk in darkness, we lie and do not practice the truth" (1 John 1:6). If you are a follower of Christ and deny sin, it won't damage your relationship, that is permanent, but it will damage your fellowship with God.

Some people *dilute* their sin with statements like, "Well, I'm not the only one who does this" or "Things happen." Do you think your sin is no big deal or maybe even justified? Are you unwilling to call your disconnection from God's desires and designs sin? Diluting sin may make you feel better for a while, but it won't remove your guilt.

If you are not a follower of Christ, then until you confess your sin you remain in need of a Savior. God longs to reveal the great distance that separates you from him. He longs to turn on the light. John says, "If we walk in the light, as he is in the light, we have fellowship with one another, and the blood of Jesus his Son cleanses us from all sin" (1 John 1:7). If our sins are no big deal, then the purifying blood of Jesus was an extreme response. There's no way around it; Jesus's blood was a big deal that equals the enormity of our sinfulness.

The good news is that God's goal isn't to crush us under the weight of our sins but to deliver us from them. Jesus specializes in replacing guilt with grace, sin with salvation, and failure with forgiveness. Once we see the enormity of our sin, we can still get off the highway of guilt via the off-ramp of forgiveness.

The Forgiveness for Your Sin

Some people *defend* their sin: "I was young, naïve, desperate, trapped, broke..." When we defend our sin, we're trying to avoid the consequences and continue to practice it. We are never going to get past our past until we quit trying to pass off our past. We will never get clean until we abandon our dirt. We will never get free until we admit guilt. The best way to be free of guilt is not to deny sin, dilute sin, or defend sin, but to declare our sin and then abandon it.

Call sin what it is—broken communion with God. If you nail a two-by-four over a wall outlet, your plug can't connect to electricity. Sin is like that two-by-four that keeps you from connecting with God, and only God can remove it. Once you confess that you put that two-by-four there, God will take it away. Don't nail it back up.

The cross and the resurrection tell us that no guilt is so deep that Jesus's blood cannot remove it. The cross created the exit for that guilt trip. Our part is to ask God for forgiveness; his part is to remove sin and guilt in love. How do we know that he will? John says, "If we confess our sins, he is faithful and just to forgive us our sins and to cleanse us from all unrighteousness" (1 John 1:9). Forgiveness is 100 percent guaranteed because God is faithful and God is just.

When God forgives, he cancels the debt completely. Listen to the last part of verse 9: "to cleanse us from all unrighteousness." In God's court there is no record of any sin that he has forgiven. The slate is clean because "the blood of Jesus his Son cleanses us from all sin" (1:7).

If the root cause of guilt is sin, then you must deal with the sin before the guilt disappears. You must not only acknowledge your sin but admit the fault of your sin and abandon the practice of sin. You must call sin what God calls it, take ownership of it, and confess it. Then you can watch God steer you clear off that highway for good.

Prayer for This Week: *Holy Father, thank you for the promise of an eternal relationship with you. Bring to light any chasms of sin that exist between us and restore your fellowship to me.*

Question for This Week: How does John's teaching about sin challenge the way you view your own guilt?

51

Sure Thing

Scriptures for This Week

- Psalm 147:7-11
- 1 John 5:9-15
- Deuteronomy 10:12-13
- 1 John 3:7-15
- John 17:1-5

Playing the Odds

My late grandmother was deathly afraid of thunderstorms. She was always convinced a tornado was coming and would insist we go to the middle of the house away from all the windows while she paced the floor until the storm passed. We all have these little uncertainties, don't we? When the thirteenth of the month falls on a Friday, does it get into your head a little bit? If you go to the ocean, do you stay out of the water for fear of sharks? I love to take my grandson, Harper, into the woods behind our house to play a game called Look for Grandpa's Golf Balls. Every time I do, Teresa warns me, with a stern grandmotherly look, to look out for snakes.

The good news is that our imaginations are almost always worse than our realities. For example, the odds of being struck by lightning are 1-in-240,000; only about 100 people in the United States die each year from lightning. The odds of being bitten by a poisonous snake are 1-in-37,250. Poisonous snakes bite 9,000 Americans every year and only 12 people each year die from such a bite. You are far more likely to sustain an injury from a toilet seat than you are from a shark.

But what are your odds of having a relationship with God and going to heaven?

Knowing for Sure

Every religion, aside from Christianity, struggles with uncertainty. If you ask a Muslim, a Buddhist, a Hindu, or a Jew how certain they are about going to be with God after they die, they will tell you they don't have any at all.

Gandhi, the famous Hindu leader of India, was once asked why he persuaded people to his point of view in politics but not in religion. He responded, "In the realm of the political and social and economic, we can be sufficiently certain to convert; but in the realm of religion there is not sufficient certainty to convert anybody, and therefore, there can be no conversions in religions."[63]

Christianity is distinct from every other religion because God's word tells us we can be 100 percent sure that we have eternal life. One of the most comforting verses in all the Bible says, "I write these things to you who believe in the name of the Son of God so that you may know that you have eternal life" (1 John 5:13 NIV).

Some of you make no claim or pretense that you have a relationship with God. Others do have a relationship with God, but you are not certain about it. Finally, some of you don't have a relationship with God, but you think you do. This group is in the most dangerous position of all because it is hard to hear something you think you already know.

I Can Be Sure of My Relationship with God

It is possible to have a relationship with God and be certain of it. However, even for a child of God doubts creep in, otherwise John would not have written, "so that you may know that you have eternal life" (5:13 NIV). The presence of doubt doesn't necessarily mean the absence of faith. Doubt can be a helpful signal to our spirit the way pain is to our body. Pain indicates that something is missing or wrong. Pain and uncertainty will drive us to find a remedy. The remedy for our spiritual doubt is in God's word. It is faith based on fact.

John doesn't say we can think, feel, or hope that we have eternal life; he says *know*. Assurance begins and ends with faith. There are three verbs in verse 13 (*believe*, *know*, *have*), but everything flows from belief. And this verse is in the present tense. It doesn't say, "If you have at one time believed." It says, "If you *now* believe."

The Bible never says that we are right with God because of something we remember in the past, such as getting christened, catechized, or baptized. What matters is not what happened in the past as much as what is happening right now.

I do believe we ought to be able to point to some experience when we realized we were a sinner, that Jesus was the Savior, and we surrendered to him as our Lord. But we don't have to bank on knowing the exact day and time. The great preacher Charles Haddon Spurgeon once said, "A man can know he is alive even if he can't remember his birthday." Thank God that our salvation is not dependent upon a good memory or even a good story.

We are not saved by some past experience. We are saved by our present belief. Being born again is to be made to walk a brand-new life in Jesus. It's a present-tense life with a past-present-future-tense God.

I Will Show I Have a Relationship with God

What we believe is what we live. The rest is just talk. John says this over and over in this first letter. Not only should we sense that we are saved, but others should be able to see we are saved. John tells us that if true believers are born again, they should have birthmarks. If we know God, it should show.

1. It will show in my following.

> But if anyone obeys his word, love for God is truly made complete in them. This is how we know we are in him: Whoever claims to live in him must live as Jesus did (1 John 2:5-6 NIV).

John is plain spoken. He says in effect, "If I can't point to Jesus's characteristics coming out of you, then God's love isn't complete in you." Strive daily to obey God's word and ask to be forgiven when you don't.

2. It will show in my fellowship.

> We know that we have passed from death to life, because we love each other. Anyone who does not love remains in death.

> Anyone who hates a brother or sister is a murderer, and you know that no murderer has eternal life residing in him (1 John 3:14-15 NIV).

If you have been born into God's family, you have a love for and a desire to be with God's family because his family is now yours. A true family loves each other regardless of faults and failures. Seek to fellowship with other believers in and out of church.

3. It will show by my fruit.

> This is how we know who the children of God are and who the children of the devil are: Anyone who does not do what is right is not God's child, nor is anyone who does not love their brother and sister (1 John 3:10 NIV).

Just as an apple tree bears apples and an orange tree bears oranges, if I am born again and have God in my life, I will bear the fruit of a righteous life. People should see evidence that something is spiritually different about you.

Pastor Joel Beeke said, "We cannot persist in low levels of obedience and have high levels of assurance."[64] If you're a believer in Jesus Christ, you'll still sin, but John says you will not make sin a habit and you'll show your relationship with God.

I Should Settle My Relationship with God

We are near the end of our journey together through the Bible. If you are in one of those three groups that I mentioned above, would you this moment, now and forever settle your relationship with God? John says, "Whoever has the son has life; whoever does not have the Son of God does not have life" (1 John 5:12 NIV). You have eternal life only if you have faith in God's Son.

If you call yourself a Christian, but you don't have the assurance of eternal life, you need to nail it down. Unless you know that you have eternal life, everything you are doing for Christ is an attempt to earn eternal life on your own, and therefore your motives and actions are sinful.

If you have never had a relationship with Christ, repent and let God renew your thinking and your heart through faith in Jesus.

If you were sure of your relationship with Christ but shouldn't have been, receive him and trust him to be Lord.

If you have a relationship with Christ, rejoice that your life will show the evidence of following, fellowship, and fruit.

One of my most important documents is my birth certificate. It proves that I am who I say I am. I may one day get Alzheimer's or amnesia and doubt that I am who I am, but I've got a legal certificate that nails it down. The only assurance we have for our spiritual identity is God's word. It holds the testimony of a God who cannot lie and who says that if you believe, you will receive and know you have that relationship. He loves you and wants to invite you into his family today.

Prayer for This Week: *Dear Jesus, thank you that you have the words of eternal life. Renew my mind, open my heart, and let me show the world my great love for you.*

Question for This Week: How much evidence is there in your life that you have a relationship with Jesus?

52

The Warrior Returns

Scriptures for This Week

- Genesis 3:14-15
- Isaiah 11:1-5
- Revelation 19:11-21
- Revelation 20:7-10
- 2 Corinthians 1:18-22

Jesus Flabbergasts the World

A distinctive facial expression is consistent across cultures. Regardless of skin color or language, we all demonstrate "the surprise brow." Our eyebrows rise, our eyes widen, and our jaws drop. It's the body's way of trying to see, to take in more. When we are taken by surprise, everything comes to a halt, and our attention is focused, involuntarily, on what surprised us.

The first two chapters of the Bible introduce us to a utopia called the Garden of Eden. The first man and woman were placed in this pure environment without sickness, suffering, or sorrow—a world no one else has ever seen.

The serpent tempts this first couple to go against the will of God and to disobey the Creator of their perfect world. From that moment until now, the human race has been at war against an enemy it cannot defeat, fighting a battle we're destined to lose.

God's answer to this turmoil is another surprise. He promises to send a warrior. In chapter 32 we learned that this warrior was Jesus, whom God foretold in Genesis 3:15, who was born to a young peasant girl, and who shocked everyone when he died. Just when everyone thought the warrior was dead and the war was lost, there was another surprise—the warrior rises.

His followers took great comfort in the resurrection because the warrior would now finish the task and bring in his kingdom. Nope. Still another surprise. The warrior ascends into heaven, and for over two thousand years, the world is in the same place as before—watching and waiting for the warrior's return.

Jesus Finishes the Struggle

What I have just given you is a thumbnail sketch of the entire Bible. Beginning with Genesis 3, it goes something like this:

Satan → Sin → Sorrow → Suffering → Savior

Yes, the warrior came. Yes, the warrior died. Yes, the warrior rose, but the story has not ended. The battle still rages. Satan is still alive. Sin is still real, sorrow still stings, and suffering still abounds. Satan started this war but the warrior is going to end it. He will return to defeat sin and death once and for all in the greatest battle in history. Peace is going to replace war. Justice is going to replace inequity. Righteousness is going to replace wickedness, and this world is going to be restored to that perfect place where God and his people dwell as it was intended from the beginning. I call this "the moment we have all been waiting for."

Ronald Reagan said his theory on the Cold War with the Soviet Union was simple: "We win and they lose." That is the message God sent all the way back in the Garden of Eden when the warrior was first mentioned. That message was clarified two thousand years ago when the warrior rose from the grave. That message will be confirmed one day when the warrior returns. Because of Jesus Christ, we can win the war against sin, Satan, suffering, and sorrow.

If you are a follower of this warrior, you may not hear another message in your life that will bring you greater joy, peace, and comfort than the scenes we see in Revelation 19–20.

Jesus Fights the Last War

All of history is heading toward a time when the warrior will return. "I saw heaven standing open and there before me was a white horse, whose rider is called Faithful and True. With justice he judges and wages war" (Revelation 19:11 NIV). That little description "I saw heaven standing open" sounds alarms all over earth and hell. The kingdom of God will be visible and present and obvious to all.

John gives important details that assure us he isn't just dreaming. Faithful and True is riding a white horse because that's what victorious Roman generals rode. White is the picture of both purity and supremacy. Remember the old Westerns where the hero rode in on a white horse? It's an image right out of the Bible.

This rider is given the names Faithful and True. He is faithful to his promise and he is true to his person. Because Jesus is the yes answer to every promise God has made, including the one in Genesis 3:15, we know this rider is Jesus Christ. When God promised that he would bruise the head of this serpent and finish him off once and for all, he told the truth.

This warrior came the first time as the meek Lamb of God to make peace between the Creator and the creature, but when he returns, "With justice he judges and wages war." He wants that peace to endure forever. Once and for all eternity, God is going to triumph over Satan. Justice is going to triumph over inequity. Good is going to triumph over evil.

Jesus Faces the Last Enemy

We get a detailed description of this tremendous war between the greatest armies ever assembled, but the war is over before it starts. "And I saw an angel standing in the sun, who cried in a loud voice to all the birds flying in midair, 'Come, gather together for the great supper of God, so that you may eat the flesh of kings, generals, and the mighty, of horses and their riders, and the flesh of all people, free and slave, great and small'" (Revelation 19:17-18 NIV).

An angel is so sure of victory he calls all the predatory birds together and says, "Get out your knives and forks. You are about to go to the greatest feast of corpses in your life."

"Then I saw the beast and the kings of the earth and their armies gathered together to wage war against the rider on the horse and his army" (19:19 NIV). Satan's chief deputies on the earth are known as "the beast" and "the false prophet." They have deceived this world and have amassed every army on the planet to fight against the warrior. It is the largest, most powerful army that will ever be assembled. Everything that Satan can muster up against God is here for this climatic showdown.

We are going to have a front-row seat at what is going to be the greatest battle ever fought. In this war there will be no surrender. No quarter will be given. No prisoners will be taken. No holds will be barred. Mercy will be scarce as God extends his justice.

Jesus Forges the Last Victory

I hate to let those of you down who enjoy a good fight, but there isn't one. It is going to be the weirdest war ever won. All the world's armies will be gathered with everything they have in their arsenal, but the warrior is the only one who fights and his only weapon will be his word. The God who spoke this world into existence will speak it into its end.

Jesus and his army all ride white horses and are dressed in white. While his army stays white and clean, "He is dressed in a robe dipped in blood" (19:13 NIV). There is not one stain of blood on any soldier's robe, only on the warrior. He doesn't need anyone fighting his battles. Verse 15 says that the warrior *speaks* and the battle is won. This is the only battle ever fought where the General does all the fighting.

It shouldn't surprise you. Jesus spoke a word to a fig tree and it withered. Jesus spoke a word to waves and wind and they lay down at his feet like whipped puppies. Jesus spoke a word to a legion of demons and they fled like rats on a sinking ship. He is the hero of the Bible. "On his robe and on his thigh he has this name written: KING OF KINGS AND LORD OF LORDS" (19:16 NIV).

Before he can put up his sword, lay down his shield, and take his rightful place as the King of this universe, he finishes the enemy in stages. First, he captures the beast and the false prophet, and the two of them are thrown alive into the fiery lake of burning sulfur. The rest of them are killed with the sword that came out of the mouth of the rider on the horse, and the blood of the corpses flowed bridle-deep along that vast battlefield.

The final stage, a thousand years later, is described in Revelation 20:10

(NIV), "And the devil, who deceived them, was thrown into the lake of burning sulfur, where the beast and the false prophet had been thrown. They will be tormented day and night for ever and ever." After this, the warrior-general hangs up his sword, puts down his shield, and puts on the crown of a King and reigns.

So the story of the warrior comes to a magnificent close, but those of us who are a part of his army must prepare. We should live now knowing that the warrior is coming. He is coming to bring peace, so we should be peacemakers *now*. He is coming to rule, so we should surrender to him *now*. He is coming to end evil and sin, so we should fight evil *now*. He is coming to eradicate suffering and death, so we should tend to the physical and spiritual needs of others *now*.

The warrior is coming. Will he meet you as friend or foe? I hope as you end this journey you can declare, "Come, Lord Jesus!"

Prayer for This Week: *Holy God, you are the powerful Lord of creation. Thank you for fighting my battles and winning every single time. Let me give all the glory to you.*

Question for This Week: Considering all that God's story has revealed through the Bible, what will you take hope in today?

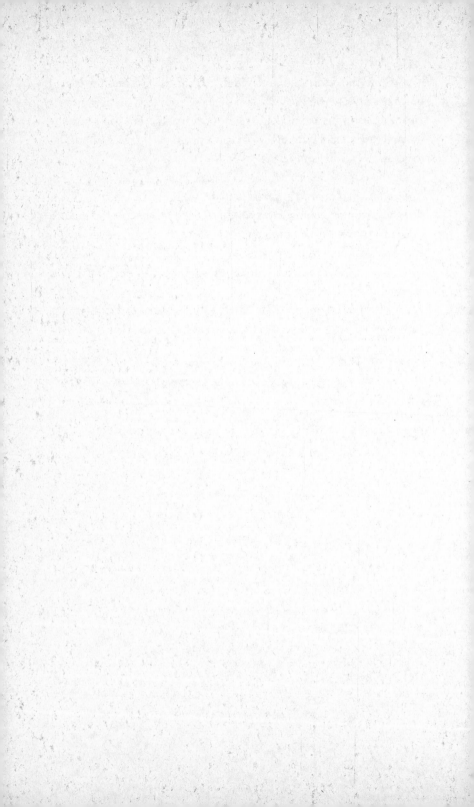

Notes

1. N.A. Woychuk, *The British Josiah Edward VI—The Most Godly King of England* (St. Louis, MO: SMF Press, 2001), 125.
2. www.forbes.com/billionaires/#version:static_page:2_country:United%20Kingdom. Accessed October 7, 2015.
3. Quoted in Lee Williams, *No Room for Doubt* (Nashville: Broadman Press, 1977), 36.
4. One need not believe in the Bible's divine inspiration to read it and be impacted by it, though the Bible itself teaches that only one committed to its true Author will truly understand its deepest truths. (See 1 Corinthians 2:14.)
5. Bart D. Ehrman, *Jesus, Interrupted: Revealing the Hidden Contradictions in the Bible (And Why We Don't Know About Them)* (San Francisco: Harper One, 2009), 225-26.
6. Caleb K. Bell, "Poll: Americans Love the Bible But Don't Read It Much," *Religion News Service*, April 4, 2013, www.religionnews.com/2013/04/04/poll-americans-love-the-bible-but-dont-read-it-much/.
7. *Your Church,* January/February 2004, 33.
8. The effort of many to attempt to use the Bible to justify slavery notwithstanding, both William Wilberforce, who is credited for being the catalyst for ending the worldwide practice of slavery, and Martin Luther King Jr., the leader of the American Civil Rights Movement, both publicly asserted the Bible as the basis for their leadership and beliefs in these movements. For Wilberforce see Jonathan Sarfati, "Anti-Slavery Activist William Wilberforce: Christian Hero," Creation.com, February 20, 2007, creation.com/anti-slavery-activist-william-wilberforce-Christian-hero; for King see David J. Lull, "Remembering Martin Luther King Jr.," National Council of Churches of Christ in the USA, www.ncccusa.org/newbtu/lullking.html.
9. https://books.google.com/books?id=Dd3FrYEQb4kC&pg=PA71&lpg=PA71&dq=Ann+landers+%22What%27s+wrong+with+me?%22&source=bl&ots=JB5d7G4s8G&sig=36fo38vf7IohgJsNegZdFKHXFrU&hl=en&sa=X&ved=0CB4Q6AEwAGoVChMIoMmv1KPYxgIVAlGIChlgBAsz#v=onepage&q=Ann%20landers%20%22What%27s%20wrong%20with%20me%3F%22&f=false.
10. Tim Keller, *The Reason for God* (New York: Dutton, 2011), 140.
11. Kent Crockett, *Making Today Count for Eternity* (Colorado Springs, CO: Multnomah, 2001), 30.
12. Jay Carty, *Coach Wooden One-on-One* (Ventura, CA: Regal, 2003), Day 41.
13. Eugene Peterson, *Reversed Thunder: The Revelation of John and Praying Imagination* (New York: Harper One, 1991), 169-70.
14. Max Lucado, *3:16: The Numbers of Hope* (Nashville: W Publishing, 2007), 107-8
15. www.goodreads.com/quotes/35183-earth-has-no-sorrow-that-heaven-cannot-heal.

16. Indeed, the rest of the Old Testament and the beginning of the New Testament with the birth of Jesus is truly the result of this yes.
17. You may ask, "How do you know this is talking about Jesus?" A Jewish rabbi by the name of Paul said, "And the Scripture, foreseeing that God would justify the Gentiles by faith, preached the gospel beforehand to Abraham, saying, 'In you shall all the nations be blessed'" (Galatians 3:8).
18. Jeremy Weber, "Sorry, John 3:16: The Top 10 Bible Verses YouVersion Shared Most in 2013," December 30, 2013, www.christianitytoday.com/gleanings/2013/december/sorry-john-316-you version-top-10-bible-verses-shared-most.html.
19. George MacDonald, "Self-Denial," *Unspoken Sermons* (New York: Cosimo Classics, 2007), 248.
20. Richard Capen, Jr., *Finish Strong: Living the Values that Take You the Distance* (San Francisco: HarperCollins, 1996), 15.
21. www.goodreads.com/quotes/8199-is-god-willing-to-prevent-evil-but-not-able-then.
22. John Blanchard, *Is God Past His Sell-By Date?* (Lancaster, PA: Evangelical Press, 2002), 179.
23. Ibid., 180.
24. H. Wayne House and Kenneth Durham, *Living Wisely in a Foolish World: A Contemporary Look at the Wisdom of Proverbs* (Nashville: Thomas Nelson Publishers, 1992), 12-13.
25. Eleanor Doan, *Speakers Source Book* (Grand Rapids, MI: Zondervan Publishing House, 1960), 284.
26. David C. Needham, *Close to His Majesty* (Portland, OR: Multnomah Press, 1987), 8.
27. David Jeremiah, *Searching for Heaven on Earth* (Nashville: Thomas Nelson Publishers, 2004), xv.
28. Ravi Zacharias, *Cries of the Heart* (Waco, TX: Word Books, 1998), 66-68.
29. Richard Taylor, *Ethics, Faith and Reason* (Englewood Cliffs, NJ: Prentice Hall, 1985), 90.
30. Richard Wurmbrand, *Tortured for Christ* (Bartlesville, OK: Living Sacrifice, 1990), 38.
31. Mark Batterson, *Circle Maker* (Grand Rapids, MI: Zondervan, 2011), 161-62.
32. "Diversity of Beliefs about Satan by the General Public," Religious Tolerance.org, www.religious tolerance.org/chr_sat4.htm.
33. Michael Useem, *The Leadership Moment* (New York: Times Business, 1998), 50.
34. Warren Wiersbe, *Be Resolute* (Colorado Springs, CO: Victor, 2000).
35. Useem, *Leadership Moment*, 51.
36. Timothy Keller, *Generous Justice* (New York: Penguin Books, 2012), 4.
37. Howard Peeskett, Vinoth Ramachandra, *The Message of Mission: The Glory of Christ in All Time and Space* (Downers Grove, IL: InterVarsity Press, 2003), 113.
38. "San Bernardino Suspect's Sister Breaks Her Silence," CBSNews.com, December 4, 2015, www .cbsnews.com/news/san-bernardino-shooting-syed-rizwan-farook-sister-saira-khan-speaks-out-disbelief/. Accessed December 5, 2015.
39. You might expect that there would be more material on Jesus than is in this book. I agree. I believe Jesus deserved his own book, which is why I wrote *52 Weeks with Jesus: Fall in Love with the One Who Changed Everything* (Eugene, OR: Harvest House Publishers, 2014).
40. See further, Mark D. Roberts, *Can We Trust the Gospels?* (Wheaton, IL: Crossway, 2007), Kindle edition.
41. Paul Barbagallo, "Howard Stern Renews Deal with SiriusXM for Another 5 Years,"

Bloomberg.com, December 15, 2015, www.bloomberg.com/news/articles/2015-12-15/howard-stern-renews-contract-with-siriusxm-for-another-5-years.

42. Wayne Grudem, *Systematic Theology* (Grand Rapids, MI: Zondervan, 1994), 412.

43. Rudolph Bultmann, *Kerygma and Myth* (London: S.P.C.K., 1953), 4-5.

44. Timothy Snyder, "Hitler vs. Stalin: Who Killed More?" NYBooks.com, March 10, 2011, www.nybooks.com/articles/2011/03/10/hitler-vs-stalin-who-killed-more/. Accessed December 31, 2015.

45. "U.S. Teens More Likely than Adults to Believe in God, Heaven and Angels," TheHarrisPoll.com, March 13, 2014, www.theharrispoll.com/health-and-life/U_S__Teens_More_Likely_than_Adults_to_Believe_in_God__Heaven_and_Angels.html. Accessed January 1, 2015.

46. Billy Graham, *Angels* (New York: Doubleday, 1975), 14-15.

47. Max Lucado, *Come Thirsty* (Waco, TX: Word Publishing, 2004), 98-99.

48. "The Truth About Angelic Beings," ChristianAnswers.net, www.Christiananswers.net/q-acb/acb-t005.html.

49. R.C. Sproul, *One Holy Passion* (Nashville: Thomas Nelson Publishers, 1987), 39.

50. www.youtube.com/watch?v=4HeLYQaZQW0.

51. Charles R. Swindoll, *So, You Want to Be Like Christ? Eight Essentials to Get You There* (Waco, TX: Word Publishing, 2005), 129.

52. Warren W. Wiersbe, *Be Dynamic* (Colorado Springs, CO: David C. Cook, 2009), 23.

53. John R.W. Stott, *The Spirit, the Church and the World* (Downers Grove, IL: InterVarsity Press, 1990), 42.

54. Ravi Zacharias, *Deliver Us from Evil* (Waco, TX: Word Publishing, 1996), 191-94.

55. Warren Wiersbe, *Why Us: When Bad Things Happen to Good People* (Grand Rapids, MI: Fleming H. Revell, 1984), 150.

56. Quoted in Charles Colson, *Loving God* (Grand Rapids, MI: Zondervan, 1983), 11.

57. Katherine Beard, "Buried Treasure Found in California Couple's Yard," *US News and World Report*, February 26, 2014, www.usnews.com/news/newsgram/articles/2014/02/26/buried-treasure-found-in-california-couples-yard.

58. Max Boot, *Out Of Order* (New York: Basic Books, 1999), 37-39.

59. Timothy Roche/Franklin, "A Cold Dose of Vengeance," *Time*, July 4, 1999, http://content.time.com/time/magazine/article/0,9171,27683,00.html.

60. *Journal of Adult Development*, reported in *Christian Century*, January 2-9, 2002, 15.

61. "How to Beat Burnout," *Focus on the Family*, cs315/1090, 1999.

62. George Barna, *Marketing the Church: What They Never Taught You About Church Growth* (Colorado Springs, CO: NavPress, 1988), 94.

63. Cited by Andy Stanley, *How Good Is Good Enough?* (Colorado Springs, CO: Multnomah, 2003), 14.

64. "Speaker Panel with Beeke, Miller, Chan, Rankin, and Piper," Desiring God 2011 Conference for Pastors, www.desiringgod.org/messages/speaker-panel-with-beeke-miller-chan-rankin-and-piper. Accessed January 27, 2016.

Acknowledgments

Obviously, to attempt to take anyone through the greatest book ever written in the history of the world, not to mention it being the word of God, is an admittedly impossible task. Yet this book was born out of a desire to at least give some "ESPN" highlights, if you will, to not only have a 30,000-foot view but to get a ground-level shot of just how inspiring and important this book is to everyone and every life.

The more I read the Bible, the more I fall in love with its author—God the Father; its subject—God the Son; and its producer—God the Holy Spirit. The more I get into the Bible, the more it gets into me, and the more the me becomes like Him. When I drill into the Bible, I am filled with divine truth and thrilled with what it does to my mind, heart, and soul. It is my prayer that this book will whet your appetite to get a shovel and dig into its eternal treasure for yourself, for this book is not meant to be nor could it be a substitute for reading the Bible itself.

I have so many to thank for this project.

Debra Anderson was a joy to work with as she took rough coal from my hands and somehow transformed it into diamonds of narrative that sparkle with fresh biblical truth.

As always, my son Jonathan was an invaluable resource and constant encouragement to get this book to the finish line with chest out and head held high. Man, I wish I could write and think like he does—but at least he looks like me!

So also is the team at Harvest House, a great bunch of folks led by a great friend and leader in Bob Hawkins. I proudly wear their uniform and am honored to work with them.

I am blessed to pastor Cross Pointe Church, and it is one of the greatest joys of my life to preach to people who love Jesus and his word.

My best friend and wife of four decades, Teresa, is the unseen driving force and support for all I do. I am more in love with her than ever, and if she ever leaves me, I am going with her!

Finally, as I said in my prior book *52 Weeks with Jesus*, "There is *nobody* like Jesus. Never has been and never will be." Likewise, there is *no book* like the Bible. Never has been and never will be.

When the poet and novelist Sir Walter Scott lay dying, he said to his son-in-law, Lockhart, "Son, please bring me the Book." The son-in-law was a bit uncertain because Walter Scott had a large library, so he replied, "Sir, which book? Which book?" The dying saint answered immediately, "My son, there is just one Book. Bring me the Book." He brought him his Bible. Yes there is only one book in the end that can bring eternal life—may my book move you to this one book now and forever.

About the Author

James Merritt is senior pastor of Cross Pointe Church in Duluth, Georgia, and the host of *Touching Lives,* a television show that broadcasts weekly in all 50 states and 122 countries. He formerly served as a two-term president of the Southern Baptist Convention, America's largest Protestant denomination. As a national voice on faith and leadership, he has been interviewed by *Time*, *Fox News*, *ABC World News*, *MSNBC*, and *60 Minutes*.

He is the author of nine books, including *How to Impact and Influence Others: 9 Keys to Successful Leadership*; *What God Wants Every Dad to Know*; and *8 Ways to Hold on When You Want to Give Up*.

Dr. Merritt holds a bachelor's degree from Stetson University and a master's and doctor of philosophy from Southern Baptist Theological Seminary. He and his wife, Teresa, reside outside of Atlanta near their three children and two grandchildren.

Follow him on Twitter at @DrJamesMerritt.

Other Harvest House Books
By James Merritt

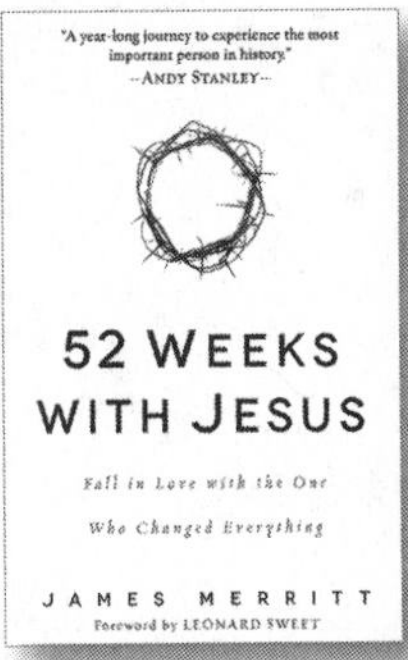

52 Weeks with Jesus

Jesus Christ is the most influential human to have ever walked on the earth. We've heard and seen so many depictions of Him that we think we know Him better than we actually do. If we took the time to really look at Him, we might be surprised at what we'd find. *In 52 Weeks with Jesus*, James Merritt leads you on a transformational journey that will allow you to know and encounter Jesus in new and surprising ways.

52 Weeks with Jesus Study Guide

Ideal for both individuals and groups, this guide will help you engage with all the main topics found in the book *52 Weeks with Jesus*. Each lesson will give you the opportunity to:

- Dig deeper into relevant Scripture passages with helpful discussion questions.
- Reflect on key quotations from each chapter with questions related to the main themes.
- Put into practice the truths you've learned—truths that are life-changing.

As you interact with this study guide, you'll come to know, appreciate, and love Jesus more than ever.

52 Weeks with Jesus Devotional

This year-long devotional (one entry per week) will reveal insights about Jesus and His ministry you may never have considered. You'll be inspired to embrace anew the Lord's invitation to "Come, follow Me."

52 Weeks with Jesus for Kids

Do you long for your kids to fall in love with Jesus? Do you desire for them to understand what it means to really live for Him? In an easy-to-read, kid-friendly style, James Merritt introduces kids (ages 9-12) to Jesus, explaining how much He loves them and demonstrating what it looks like to follow Him. Each devotion includes engaging stories, Scripture, a prayer, and a thought to consider.

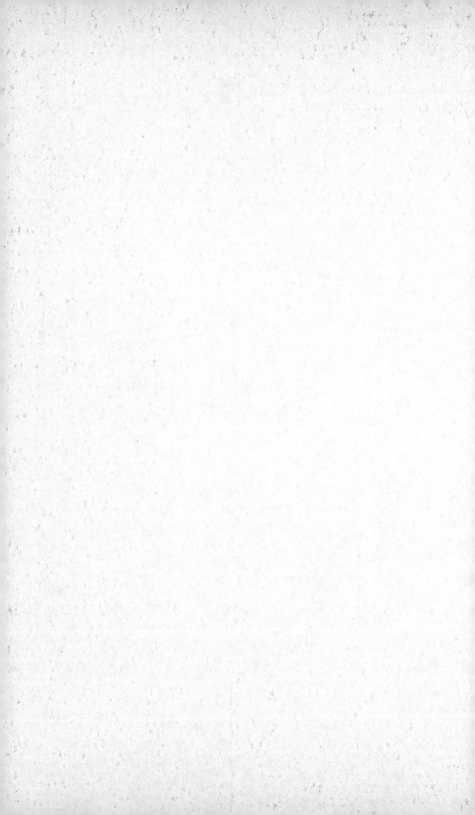